AF882694

Save YOUR Home From Probate

(Available in Most States)

First printing, 2022.

Front Page Publishing, LLC
5198 Arlington Ave., Suite 335
Riverside, CA 92504
www.frontpagepublishing.com

Disclaimer

This book is for EDUCATIONAL PURPOSES ONLY!

Seek the advice of an Attorney before using any aspects of this book.

Table of Contents

Introduction

SAVE YOUR HOME FROM PROBATE…is your personal guide to expedite a lengthy legal process while avoiding expensive attorney fees. Don't let a Judge decide who gets your home after you pass away!

Today, a simple process called; Transfer on Death Deed (TOD), also known as; Transfer Upon Death Deed, Beneficiary Deed or Lady Bird Deed, (now available to homeowners in 33 states) can protect your home from probate.

What is Probate? Upon death, probate is a court proceeding that determines who or whom will receive your home. This process can take years to complete and is avoidable if the necessary paperwork is completed prior to one's passing. You can avoid Probate by doing any one of the following;

1. File a Transfer on Death Deed/Beneficiary Deed/Lady Bird Deed
2. Place the property in a "Living Trust" (consult an Estate Planning Attorney).
3. Holding the property in "joint tenancy" or as "community property" with right of survivorship (consult an Estate Planning Attorney).

Why avoid Probate?

- Expensive Attorney fees and high Court costs.
- A Judge can decide who receives your property (even if you have a "Will").
- The property can be in court for an indeterminate amount of time.

Why TOD?

- Simple paperwork.
- Cost less than $50.
- It is more powerful than a "Will".
- No expensive Attorney Fees or high Court costs.
- You determine who receives your property.
- Can be revoked or changed at any time.
- Does not take effect until you die.

Each state has its own; forms, laws, fees, and deadlines that can only be obtained, and then processed by the county clerk's office or land management office. The TOD does not apply in all situations. Example forms are included in this book.

Questions regarding TOD's must be directed towards an Attorney. All information in this book is for EDUCATIONAL PURPOSES ONLY!

If you have found this book to be beneficial and you would like to give a testimony, send an email to: contact@frontpagepublishing.com.

All correspondence becomes the property of Front Page Publishing, LLC.

Front Page Publishing, LLC

5198 Arlington Ave., Suite 335

Riverside, CA 92504

Alaska

Table of Contents

What does the Transfer on Death (TOD) deed do?

When you die, this deed transfers the described real property, subject to any liens or mortgages (or other encumbrances) on the property at your death. Probate is not required. The TOD deed has no effect until you die. You can revoke it at any time. You are also free to transfer the property to someone else during your lifetime. If you do not own any interest in the property when you die, this deed will have no effect.

Do I have to file the TOD deed in court?

No. Before death, the property owner must record the TOD deed at the recorder's office in the recording district where the property is located. After the person's death. the property with the TOD deed does not need to go through probate in court because the title will automatically transfer to the person named in the TOD deed. However, if the person's estate had other real property or personal property that did not automatically transfer title upon death, that property may need to be probated in court.

How do I make a TOD deed?

Complete the Transfer on Death Deed form.

Sign the deed in front of a notary public or other individual authorized by law to take acknowledgments. Record the form in each recording district where any part of the property is located. The form has no effect unless it is acknowledged and recorded before your death.

Is the "legal description" of the property necessary?

Yes.

How do I find the "legal description" of the property?

This information may be on the deed you received when you became an owner of the property. This information may also be available in the office of the recorder in the recording district where the property is located. If you are not sure, consult a lawyer.

Can I change my mind before I record the TOD deed?

Yes. If you have not yet recorded the deed and want to change your mind, simply tear up or otherwise destroy the deed.

How do I "record" the TOD deed?

Take the completed and acknowledged form to the office of the recorder in the recording district where the property is located. Follow the instructions given by the recorder to make the form part of the official property records. If the property is in more than one recording district, you should record the deed in each recording district.

Can I later revoke the TOD deed if I change my mind?

Yes. You can revoke the TOD deed. Except for a court, no one, including the beneficiaries, can prevent you from revoking the deed.

How do I revoke the TOD deed after it is recorded?

There are three ways to revoke a recorded TOD deed:

- Complete and acknowledge a Revocation of Transfer on Death Deed form and record it in each recording district where the property is located.
- Complete and acknowledge a new Transfer on Death Deed form that disposes of the same property and record it in each recording district where the property is located.
- Transfer the property to someone else during your lifetime by a recorded deed that expressly revokes the TOD deed. You may not revoke the TOD deed by will.

I am being pressured to complete this form. What should I do?

Do not complete this form under pressure. Seek help from a trusted family member, friend, or talk to a lawyer.

Do I need to tell the beneficiaries about the TOD deed?

No, but it is recommended. Secrecy can cause later complications and might make it easier for others to commit fraud.

Does the estate have to go through probate if there is TOD deed?

If the real property had a TOD deed recorded before the person died, it will transfer to the beneficiaries named in the deed and is not included in the probate of the estate. However, other property owned by the person who died which does not pass automatically to a survivor must go through probate.

I have other questions about this form. What should I do?

This form is designed to fit some but not all situations. If you have other questions, should talk to a lawyer.

Forms

TRANSFER ON DEATH DEED

NOTICE TO OWNER: You should carefully read all information on this form. Transferring real property by using a Transfer on Death Deed may have important legal consequences in addition to designating who will receive the real property on the transferor's death. These consequences may include, but are not limited to: (1) affecting the beneficiary's eligibility for public assistance; and (2) affecting creditors' rights. **If you have any questions, you should consult an attorney.**

This form must be recorded before your death, or it will not be effective.

<u>OWNER INFORMATION</u>

[Please complete the following information for the owner(s) of the property.]

Owner

Full Name: ______________________________

Marital Status: ______________________________

Mailing Address: ____

Owner

Full Name: ______________________________

Marital Status: ______________________________

Mailing Address: ____

Property Description

Legal Description of Property: ______________________________________

Recording District Where Property is Located: ____________________________

[You must record the form in each recording district where any part of the property is located. Find the recording districts here: http://dnr.alaska.gov/ssd/recoff/distlist*.]*

<u>BENEFICIARY/BENEFICIARIES INFORMATION</u>

[Complete the following information for your beneficiary/beneficiaries. You may want to obtain legal advice before listing more than one primary beneficiary. There is more than one way to transfer property to several persons.]

Primary Beneficiary

I designate the following beneficiary if the beneficiary survives me:

Full Name: ______________________________

Marital Status: ______________________________

Mailing Address: ____

Alternative Beneficiary - Optional
If my primary beneficiary does not survive me, I designate the following alternate beneficiary if that beneficiary survives me:
Full Name: ______________________________
Marital Status: ___________________________
Mailing Address: ____

TRANSFER ON DEATH

At my death, I transfer my interest in the described property to the beneficiaries as designated above. Before my death, I have the right to revoke this deed.
NOTE: *You can revoke your Transfer on Death Deed in three ways: (1) Complete and acknowledge a Revocation of Transfer on Death Deed (form P-151) and record it in each recording district where the property is located; (2) Complete and acknowledge a new Transfer on Death Deed (form P-150) that disposes of the same property, and record it in each recording district where the property is located; and (3) Transfer the property to someone else during your lifetime by a recorded deed that expressly revokes the Transfer on Death deed. You may not revoke the Transfer on Death deed by will.*

AUTHORITY OF DESIGNATED AGENT TO REVOKE THIS DEED

I authorize the following designated agent to revoke this deed before my death:
Full Name: ______________________________
Mailing Address: ____

SIGNATURE OF OWNER(S) MAKING THIS DEED

______________________ ______________________ ____________
Full Name Signature Date

______________________ ______________________ ____________
Full Name Signature Date

ACKNOWLEDGMENT

This instrument was acknowledged before me at ______________________, Alaska on *(date)*:________________.

______________________________ ______________________________
Signature of Person Taking Acknowledgment Printed Name

______________________________ ______________________________
Title or Rank Serial Number, if any
My commission expires:________________

Return To: Name:______________________________
Mailing Address: ______________________________________

Page 2 of 2 AS 13.48.10-.190
P-150 (7/20)
TRANSFER ON DEATH DEED

REVOCATION OF TRANSFER ON DEATH DEED

NOTICE TO OWNER: This revocation must be recorded before you die or it will not be effective. This revocation is effective only as to the interests in the property of owners who sign this revocation.

OWNER INFORMATION

Owner

Full Name: ______________________________ Marital Status: ______________

Mailing Address: ____

Owner

Full Name: ______________________________ Marital Status: ______________

Mailing Address: ____

Property Description

Legal Description of Property: ________________________________

Recording District Where Property is Located: ____________________

REVOCATION

I revoke all my previous Transfer on Death deed(s). The following are the serial number(s) of previously recorded deed(s):

____

SIGNATURE OF OWNER(S) MAKING THIS DEED

Full Name	Signature	Date
Full Name	Signature	Date

ACKNOWLEDGMENT

This instrument was acknowledged before me at ______________________, Alaska on *(date)*:____________________.

Signature of Person Taking Acknowledgment	Printed Name
Title or Rank	Serial Number, if any

My commission expires:_______________

Return To: Name:______________________________

Mailing Address: ______________________________

P-151 (7/20)
REVOCATION OF TRANSFER ON DEATH DEED

AS 13.48.10-.190

Alaska Transfer on Death Deed Revocation Form

Recording requested by (name):

____

When recorded mail to
and mail tax statements to:

____

____

____

____

Recorder's Use Only

REVOCATION OF REVOCABLE TRANSFER ON DEATH DEED

This document is exempt from documentary transfer tax under Rev. & Tax. Code § 11930. This document is exempt from preliminary change of ownership report under Rev. & Tax. Code § 480.3.

Assessor's Parcel No.:

____

Declaration of Exemption From Gov't Code § 27388.1 Fee

☐ Transfer is exempt from fee per GC § 27388.1(a)(2):
- ☐ recorded concurrently "in connection with" transfer subject to Documentary Transfer Tax
- ☐ recorded concurrently "in connection with" a transfer of residential dwelling to an owner-occupier

☐ Transfer is exempt from fee per GC 27388.1(a)(1):
- ☐ Fee cap of $225.00 reached ☐ Not related to real property

IMPORTANT NOTICE: THIS FORM MUST BE RECORDED TO BE EFFECTIVE

This revocation form MUST be RECORDED before your death or it will not be effective. This revocation form only affects a transfer on death deed that YOU made. A transfer on death deed made by a co-owner of your property is not affected by this revocation form. A co-owner who wants to revoke a transfer on death deed that he/she made must complete and RECORD a SEPARATE revocation form.

PROPERTY DESCRIPTION

Print the legal description of the property affected by this revocation:

____

____

____

REVOCATION

I, ________________________, am the transferor under the Revocable TOD deed dated ____________ and recorded on ____________ as Instrument No. __________ in Book/Reel ______, Page/Image ______, of Official Records of ________________________ County, Alaska, which named as beneficiary(ies) ____.

I hereby revoke any TOD deed to transfer the described property that I executed before executing this form, including the TOD deed described above.

SIGNATURE AND DATE

Sign and print your name below (your name should exactly match the name shown on your title documents):

Date: __________________

____
(Signature of declarant)

____
(Typed or written name of declarant)

Notary Acknowledgment

State of ____________________

County of __________________

The foregoing was acknowledged before me this ____ day of ________________, by the undersigned, ________________, who is personally known to me or satisfactorily proven to me to be the person whose name is subscribed to the within instrument.

____
Printed Name of Notary Public

____
Signature of Notary Public

My commission expires: ___________________ (seal)

Arizona

Table of Contents

Transfer on Death Deed in Arizona

Planning for what happens to your home after your death can be difficult. Transfer on death deeds provide a simple, cheap way to make sure your home is passed on as you wish.

How It Works

A transfer on death deed names the person or people who will get your home after your death. During your lifetime, you keep ownership of your home and you may revoke the transfer on death deed. Upon your death, your home goes to any surviving person named in the transfer on death deed.

How We Transfer Property

Deeds usually convey property immediately in Arizona. So, if you sign a deed transferring your home to your son, he would take ownership immediately. Another way to pass on property is through your Will or a trust.

A transfer-on-death deed, otherwise known as a beneficiary deed, handles the property transfer in a completely different way. The process is still about the same: draft the deed, sign the deed, and record the deed. However, the transfer-on-death deed does just what the name implies: it transfers the property on the death of the grantor, the owner who is transferring the property.

Why We Use the Transfer-On-Death Deed

One great reason: avoiding probate. When you use a transfer-on-death deed to pass on your property, your heirs don't have to wait through probate to get the property. It passes to them automatically.

However, the property owner still owns and the property that's transferred in the deed. In our situation, Marvin could sell the property or mortgage it before his death. His heirs, however, can't sell, mortgage, or otherwise dispose of the property while Marvin is still alive.

The property owner has the right to revoke the beneficiary deed at any time. If Marvin changes his mind about giving the property to his son and daughter, he can either formally revoke the deed or file a new deed that takes the place of the first one.

For example, let's say Marvin signs a transfer-on-death deed for his home and the 12 acres of ground around it. He is the grantor. His son and daughter are the grantees. After signing the Will, Marvin lives another 15 years before passing away. He still owned the property at the time of his death, and the transfer-on-death deed has not been revoked, his son and daughter take the property.

Benefits of a Transfer on Death Deed

- Allows you to plan for what happens to your house during your lifetime.
- May be canceled at any time if you want to change what happens to your home.
- Your heirs may avoid probate.
- You keep ownership of your home, so you may still sell, mortgage, or transfer the home.
- You may also keep any tax benefits for senior homeowners.
- Unlike wills, there is no risk the deed is lost or destroyed

Creating a Transfer on Death Deed

A transfer on death deed requires the following information be filed with the Office of Recorder of Deeds in a notarized form:

- The names and addresses of all owners of the property.
- The legal description of the property to be transferred.
- The people receiving the property. You may name as many people as you wish.
- A statement that the property will transfer at the owner's death.
- The signature of the owner making the transfer and the date.

The Office of the Recorder of Deeds provides one example of what this form could look like online at http://otr.cfo.dc.gov/node/501452. You do not have to use this exact form, however, as long as what you file has all the information listed above. More information about filing with the Office of Recorder of Deeds also can be found online at http://otr.cfo.dc.gov/service/otr-recorder-deeds.

Downsides To the Transfer-On-Death Deed

The value of the property is still considered part of your estate when it comes time to calculate estate tax.

Unlike trusts, beneficiary deeds don't offer any form of asset protection for the **beneficiaries in Arizona.**

There can be problems if the beneficiary dies before the grantor. If Marvin's son passed away before Marvin, his estate will not receive the share of Marvin's property that passes through the beneficiary deed. It's difficult to build a successor beneficiary structure into the transfer-on-death deed. Another good reason to update your estate plans in Arizona!

This type of transfer may affect your ability to get Medicaid benefits to pay for long-term care. Also, unlike other estate planning tools, the transfer-on-death deed does not address incapacity.

Disadvantages of a Transfer on Death Deed (TODD) & Special Considerations

To be eligible for a TODD, your real property **deed** must show that you have an **ownership interest** in your home.

There are special considerations to take into account if you own the property as a **joint tenant**, as opposed to a tenant in common, with another individual. As a **joint tenant**, if you predecease your co-owner, the TODD will not have any effect because the property automatically would transfer upon your death to the surviving joint tenant.

If you name **two people** as the **primary beneficiaries** and one predeceases you, the survivor will receive the entire property (unless you revoke the TODD). For example, if two daughters are beneficiaries, and one daughter passes away before you, her interest will **not** pass on to your deceased daughter's children. Your surviving daughter will own the whole house.

If you are **married**, but your spouse is **not** on the deed, and you give your home to **someone other** than your spouse in a TODD, then your spouse may not have a legal claim to a spousal share of the home because a TODD is not part of your Last Will & Testament.

If you become incompetent, you **cannot** revoke a TODD, but your power of attorney with authority over real property can sell or transfer your home for your benefit in your lifetime.

Forms

Recording requested by:

When recorded mail to and mail tax statements to:

Space above this line for recorder's use

Arizona Transfer on Death Deed
(Beneficiary Deed)

I, ______________________, with a mailing address of ________________________ ______________________________________ (hereinafter referred to as the "Owner") being of competent mind and having the legal capacity to execute this document, as owner transfer on death to ______________________ with a mailing address of ______ ____ (hereinafter referred to as the "Primary Beneficiary") as grantee beneficiary, the following described interest in real estate:

____

____

____

____

____

____

____

Legal description of the property (including square, suffix, and lot number)

If the Primary Beneficiary does not survive me, I designate ____________________ with a mailing address of ____ _________ (hereinafter referred to as the "Alternate Beneficiary") as grantee beneficiary.

This Transfer on Death Deed is revocable. It does not transfer any ownership until the death of the owner. It revokes all prior beneficiary designations by this owner for this

interest in real estate. The grantor has the right to withdraw or rescind this deed at any time. Any beneficiaries named in this deed are hereby advised that this deed may be withdrawn or rescinded whether or not money or any other consideration was paid or given.

Owner's Name	Primary Beneficiary's Name	Alternate Beneficiary's Name
Owner's Signature	Primary Beneficiary's Signature	Alternate Beneficiary's Signature
Date	Date	Date

Notary Acknowledgment

State of ____________________

County of __________________

The foregoing was acknowledged before me this ____ day of ________________, by the undersigned, ________________, who is personally known to me or satisfactorily proven to me to be the person whose name is subscribed to the within instrument.

____
Printed Name of Notary Public

____
Signature of Notary Public

My commission expires: __________________ (seal)

Arizona Transfer on Death Deed Revocation Form

Recording requested by (name):

____

When recorded mail to
and mail tax statements to:

____

____

____

____

Recorder's Use Only

REVOCATION OF REVOCABLE TRANSFER ON DEATH DEED

This document is exempt from documentary transfer tax under Rev. & Tax. Code § 11930. This document is exempt from preliminary change of ownership report under Rev. & Tax. Code § 480.3.

Assessor's Parcel No.:

____

Declaration of Exemption From Gov't Code § 27388.1 Fee

☐ Transfer is exempt from fee per GC § 27388.1(a)(2):
- ☐ recorded concurrently "in connection with" transfer subject to Documentary Transfer Tax
- ☐ recorded concurrently "in connection with" a transfer of residential dwelling to an owner-occupier

☐ Transfer is exempt from fee per GC 27388.1(a)(1):
- ☐ Fee cap of $225.00 reached ☐ Not related to real property

IMPORTANT NOTICE: THIS FORM MUST BE RECORDED TO BE EFFECTIVE

This revocation form MUST be RECORDED before your death or it will not be effective. This revocation form only affects a transfer on death deed that YOU made. A transfer on death deed made by a co-owner of your property is not affected by this revocation form. A co-owner who wants to revoke a transfer on death deed that he/she made must complete and RECORD a SEPARATE revocation form.

PROPERTY DESCRIPTION

Print the legal description of the property affected by this revocation:

____

____

____

REVOCATION

I, ______________________________, am the transferor under the Revocable TOD deed dated ______________ and recorded on ______________ as Instrument No. ____________ in Book/Reel ________, Page/Image ________, of Official Records of ______________________________ County, Arizona, which named as beneficiary(ies) ____.

I hereby revoke any TOD deed to transfer the described property that I executed before executing this form, including the TOD deed described above.

SIGNATURE AND DATE

Sign and print your name below (your name should exactly match the name shown on your title documents):

Date: ____________________

____
(Signature of declarant)

____
(Typed or written name of declarant)

Notary Acknowledgment

State of ____________________

County of __________________

The foregoing was acknowledged before me this ____ day of ________________, by the undersigned, ________________, who is personally known to me or satisfactorily proven to me to be the person whose name is subscribed to the within instrument.

____
Printed Name of Notary Public

____
Signature of Notary Public

My commission expires: __________________ (seal)

Arkansas

Table of Contents

How Transfer on Death Deeds works in Arkansas?

As an Arkansas resident, you are able to take advantage of this tool. This can be an easy way to control who will receive your real estate property after your death.

To accomplish your property transfer goals, you will need to utilize a special deed. The transfer-on-death deed will contain special language that explains that the property will not be transferred until after your death.

You will list a beneficiary who will receive the property. This beneficiary will have no legal rights to the property until after your death. The beneficiary doesn't need to sign the deed or even know about it.

You're also able to name an alternate beneficiary who will inherit your property if your first choice isn't alive at your death or disclaims the property.

For the deed to be valid, you must record it with local county land records office before your death. Otherwise, it will be invalid.

After your death, the property is transferred to the beneficiary that you have named. It's important to note that the new owner will be responsible for any mortgage debt that comes along with the property.

This can be a beneficial way to avoid the process of probate. This can save on time, money, and stress.

You're always able to change your mind about the transfer-on-death beneficiary. You can do this by revoking the deed or creating a new one and naming a new beneficiary.

If you have any questions about transfer-on-death deeds, consult with a qualified estate planning attorney.

Benefits of a Transfer on Death Deed

- Allows you to plan for what happens to your house during your lifetime.
- May be canceled at any time if you want to change what happens to your home.
- Your heirs may avoid probate.
- You keep ownership of your home, so you may still sell, mortgage, or transfer the home.
- You may also keep any tax benefits for senior homeowners.
- Unlike wills, there is no risk the deed is lost or destroyed

Disadvantages of a Transfer on Death Deed (TODD) & Special Considerations

To be eligible for a TODD, your real property deed must show that you have an ownership interest in your home.

There are special considerations to take into account if you own the property as a joint tenant, as opposed to a tenant in common, with another individual. As a joint tenant, if you predecease your co-owner, the TODD will not have any effect because the property automatically would transfer upon your death to the surviving joint tenant.

- If you name two people as the primary beneficiaries and one predeceases you, the survivor will receive the entire property (unless you revoke the TODD). For example, if two daughters are beneficiaries, and one daughter passes away before you, her interest will not pass on to your deceased daughter's children. Your surviving daughter will own the whole house.
- If you are married, but your spouse is not on the deed, and you give your home to someone other than your spouse in a TODD, then your spouse may not have a legal claim to a spousal share of the home because a TODD is not part of your Last Will & Testament.

- If you become incompetent, you cannot revoke a TODD, but your power of attorney with authority over real property can sell or transfer your home for your benefit in your lifetime.

Creating a Transfer on Death Deed

A transfer on death deed requires the following information be filed with the Office of Recorder of Deeds in a notarized form:

- The names and addresses of all owners of the property.
- The legal description of the property to be transferred.
- The people receiving the property. You may name as many people as you wish.
- A statement that the property will transfer at the owner's death.
- The signature of the owner making the transfer and the date.

The Office of the Recorder of Deeds provides one example of what this form could look like online at http://otr.cfo.dc.gov/node/501452. You do not have to use this exact form, however, as long as what you file has all the information listed above. More information about filing with the Office of Recorder of Deeds also can be found online at http://otr.cfo.dc.gov/service/otrrecorder-deeds.

Forms

Recording requested by:

When recorded mail to and mail tax statements to:

Space above this line for recorder's use

Arkansas Transfer on Death Deed

(Beneficiary Deed)

I, ______________________, with a mailing address of ________________________ ______________________________________ (hereinafter referred to as the "Owner") being of competent mind and having the legal capacity to execute this document, as owner transfer on death to ______________________ with a mailing address of ______ ____ (hereinafter referred to as the "Primary Beneficiary") as grantee beneficiary, the following described interest in real estate:

____

____

____

____

____

____

____

Legal description of the property (including square, suffix, and lot number)

If the Primary Beneficiary does not survive me, I designate ______________________ with a mailing address of ____ _________ (hereinafter referred to as the "Alternate Beneficiary") as grantee beneficiary.

This Transfer on Death Deed is revocable. It does not transfer any ownership until the death of the owner. It revokes all prior beneficiary designations by this owner for this

interest in real estate. The grantor has the right to withdraw or rescind this deed at any time. Any beneficiaries named in this deed are hereby advised that this deed may be withdrawn or rescinded whether or not money or any other consideration was paid or given.

Owner's Name	Primary Beneficiary's Name	Alternate Beneficiary's Name
Owner's Signature	Primary Beneficiary's Signature	Alternate Beneficiary's Signature
Date	Date	Date

Notary Acknowledgment

State of ____________________

County of __________________

The foregoing was acknowledged before me this ____ day of ________________, by the undersigned, ________________, who is personally known to me or satisfactorily proven to me to be the person whose name is subscribed to the within instrument.

____

Printed Name of Notary Public

____

Signature of Notary Public

My commission expires: __________________ (seal)

Arkansas Transfer on Death Deed Revocation Form

Recording requested by (name): ______________________

When recorded mail to
and mail tax statements to: ______________________

____

____

____

Recorder's Use Only

REVOCATION OF REVOCABLE TRANSFER ON DEATH DEED

This document is exempt from documentary transfer tax under Rev. & Tax. Code § 11930. This document is exempt from preliminary change of ownership report under Rev. & Tax. Code § 480.3.

Assessor's Parcel No.: ______________________

Declaration of Exemption From Gov't Code § 27388.1 Fee

- ☐ Transfer is exempt from fee per GC § 27388.1(a)(2):
  - ☐ recorded concurrently "in connection with" transfer subject to Documentary Transfer Tax
  - ☐ recorded concurrently "in connection with" a transfer of residential dwelling to an owner-occupier
- ☐ Transfer is exempt from fee per GC 27388.1(a)(1):
  - ☐ Fee cap of $225.00 reached ☐ Not related to real property

IMPORTANT NOTICE: THIS FORM MUST BE RECORDED TO BE EFFECTIVE

This revocation form MUST be RECORDED before your death or it will not be effective. This revocation form only affects a transfer on death deed that YOU made. A transfer on death deed made by a co-owner of your property is not affected by this revocation form. A co-owner who wants to revoke a transfer on death deed that he/she made must complete and RECORD a SEPARATE revocation form.

PROPERTY DESCRIPTION

Print the legal description of the property affected by this revocation:

____

____

____

REVOCATION

I, ______________________, am the transferor under the Revocable TOD deed dated ____________ and recorded on ____________ as Instrument No. ____________ in Book/Reel ________, Page/Image ________, of Official Records of ______________________ County, Arkansas, which named as beneficiary(ies) ______________________

____.

I hereby revoke any TOD deed to transfer the described property that I executed before executing this form, including the TOD deed described above.

SIGNATURE AND DATE

Sign and print your name below (your name should exactly match the name shown on your title documents):

Date: ____________________

____
(Signature of declarant)

____
(Typed or written name of declarant)

Notary Acknowledgment

State of ____________________

County of __________________

The foregoing was acknowledged before me this ____ day of ________________, by the undersigned, ________________, who is personally known to me or satisfactorily proven to me to be the person whose name is subscribed to the within instrument.

____

Printed Name of Notary Public

____

Signature of Notary Public

My commission expires: __________________ (seal)

California

Table of Contents

Means of Transferring Real Property Upon Death

The Most Common Means of Transferring Real Property upon Death

The most common means of transferring real property upon death of the owner are three well-known methods: (1) holding property in joint tenancy or as community property with right of survivorship, (2) a living trust, or (3) a will. However, in 2016, a lesser-known alternative to keep a decedent's home out of probate became available to Californians: the revocable transfer on death or "TOD" deed, a simple and inexpensive way to transfer real property to a beneficiary in California.

Including California, TOD deeds are now permitted in 31 states and the District of Columbia. The TOD deed allows a person to leave his or her real property to a designated person or persons such as a family member, friend, life-long partner or other loved one without having to set up a living trust. The TOD deed is considered a nonprobate transfer under Division 5 of the California Probate Code.

Limiting Criteria for Transfer on Death Deed (TOD Deed)

While a TOD deed is attractive because of its simplicity and inexpensiveness, there are specific limiting criteria and procedural requirements for TOD deeds. First and foremost, there are limitations on the type of property that can be transferred through this deed. Only the following are covered:

1. A single-family home or condominium unit,
2. A single-family residence on agricultural property of 40 acres or less, or
3. A residence with no more than four residential dwelling units.

Other requirements are that a revocable TOD deed must be signed and dated before a notary public to be effective and valid; a TOD deed must be recorded within 60 days or less from the date it is signed; and, as its name indicates, the revocable TOD deed can be revoked by the transferor at any time. Upon death of the transferor, the beneficiary must file a Change in

Ownership Statement with the county assessor within 150 days of date of death in accord with Revenue and Taxation Code section 480(b).

It is important to note that the TOD deed must be substantially in the form provided at Probate Code Section 5642, a copy of which follows this article.

Revoking a Transfer on Death Deed

The transferor or owner can revoke a TOD deed in any of three ways: (1) the owner can record a formal notice of revocation; (2) a new TOD deed may be recorded; or (3) the real property can be transferred to someone else prior to the transferor's death.

Effect of Recording a TOD Deed

Although the transfer on death deed must be recorded within 60 days or less from the date it is it signed and before the owner's death, the interest in the real estate only transfers when the owner dies. Accordingly, the beneficiary identified on the TOD deed does not have any rights to the real property when the owner is alive. Furthermore, creditors of a named beneficiary cannot place any liens on the property. Of course, while the owner is living, the owner has the right to sell or encumber the property and it is also subject to involuntary liens that may be recorded by creditors of the owner which would transfer with the property to the beneficiary upon the owner's death.

TOD Deeds, Joint Tenancy, and Community Property

A TOD deed may not be ideal for use with property held in joint tenancy or owned as community property. Pursuant to Probate Code section 5664, if title is held in joint tenancy or community property with right of survivorship, then at the time of the transferor's death, the TOD deed is void if the other spouse, registered domestic partner, or joint tenant is still alive. Under those circumstances, executing a TOD deed has no effect. However, if the transferor decedent is the last joint tenant or spouse to die, the TOD deed takes effect and controls the ownership of the property upon date of death.

TOD deeds and Creditors' Claims

Real property subject to a TOD deed remains subject to the claims of the transferor's creditors. The beneficiary of a TOD deed is personally liable to the transferor's estate and the transferor's creditors. The personal representative of the transferor's estate may demand restitution from a TOD deed beneficiary. This demand may occur as late as three years after the decedent's death.

Pros & Cons of a Transfer on Death Deed

As with any method of estate planning, there are advantages and disadvantages with TOD deeds. Whether these will balance out in any particular circumstance will differ from person to person and from property to property. Summarized below are some of the more important pros and cons that will affect the decision of whether a TOD deed would be appropriate.

Pros

1. Filing and recording the transfer on death deed is fast, simple, and very inexpensive (especially compared to the living trust and last will options).
2. The TOD deed protects the property from probate as long as the beneficiary does not predecease the grantor.
3. The TOD deed is fully revocable during the real property owner's lifetime.
4. The TOD permits the grantor to retain full ownership of the property during his or her lifetime, instead of adding the beneficiary as a joint tenant and making him or her an immediate legal owner.
5. The recording of a TOD deed is not a taxable event. By contrast, adding a joint tenant is considered a gift by the IRS and requires the filing of a gift tax return, not to mention possible higher taxes in the future.

Cons

1. The property will be subject to probate if the beneficiary predeceases the grantor and there is no alternate estate plan.
2. If property is co-owned in joint tenancy, the surviving joint tenant becomes the sole owner upon the other's death and has full control of the property despite the TOD deed,

unless the co-tenant has also filed a TOD deed separately naming the same beneficiary or beneficiaries.

3. If the beneficiary is a minor upon the death of the property owner, a court-appointed custodian will be granted control and management of the property until the child reaches legal age, and only then will the child own the property outright. This process may incur legal and court fees.
4. If the owner becomes incapacitated through stoke, dementia, or other event, there may be no one to revoke the deed, which may be necessary due to a change in family circumstances or the need to qualify the person for Medicaid assistance.
5. Should the real property owner pass away, the named beneficiary will be held personally liable for all unsecured debts (mortgages and taxes) of the deceased property owner, up to the value of the property that passes to the named beneficiary.
6. The property may still be subject to Medi-Cal estate recovery if the property owner was a recipient of Medi-Cal benefits.

Sunset Date

As stated above, the use of TOD deeds is relatively new, and they are not allowed in all states. In California, we have undertaken a five-year trial period for TOD deeds. According to the California legislation, the use of TOD deeds needs to be re-authorized by the California legislature or approval of the use of TOD deeds will expire on December 31, 2020. In that event, after January 1, 2021, any revocable TOD deed that is properly executed during the five-year period will remain valid until the property owner dies or revokes the deed.

Preparation Of the Transfer on Death Deed

How Do I Prepare the Transfer on Death Deed?

Fortunately, the process of filing and recording the transfer on death deed to leave real estate for a beneficiary is quite simple. The copy of the deed you prepare must meet state requirements and contain the correct language and formatting. This simple, one-page document can be found for free at your county clerk's office or website. Los Angeles County offers the form for free here. These are the simple steps to making sure your transfer on death deed is prepared correctly:

1. Fill out all general required information about your identity and address. Make sure the "Assessor's Parcel Number" and "Property Description" directly matches the description from your property's current deed, or your deed may be invalid if it isn't titled correctly.
2. Name your beneficiary or beneficiaries. Be specific and do not use categories such as "my children" or "my brother." The state will likely not recognize these types of titles even if your identity is clear. It is safest to list the full legal name of each beneficiary you wish to name.
    a. If you name more than one beneficiary, be sure to indicate how they will take title to your property upon your death. Will they be titled "as joint tenants" who will own the property in equal shares?
3. Sign and date the transfer on death deed before a notary public. If you're not the sole owner of your property, then the transfer on death deed is useless if you predecease your co-tenant, who will own the property outright. Your co-tenant (such as a spouse or sibling) would have to file a separate transfer on death deed naming the same beneficiaries in order to ensure the transfer of property in the event of both property owners' deaths.
4. Have the notarized deed recorded with your county clerk's office. Remember that the law requires you to record the deed within 60 days of notarization, otherwise it will be null. This can be done by mailing or bringing your deed to your local recorder/county clerk's office. Be prepared to any filing and recording fees.

How Do I Revoke a Transfer on Death Deed?

The transfer on death deed is fully revocable before the death of the real property owner. There are 3 effective ways to revoke this deed:

1. File and record a Revocation of Revocable Transfer on Death Deed form.
2. Record a new transfer on death deed naming a different beneficiary. The newest recorded deed will automatically revoke any and all previous deeds of the same type.

3. Sell or transfer the real property to someone else prior to the real property owner's death.

Potential Risks and Uncertainties of the Transfer on Death Deed

Since the transfer on death deed was only recently introduced as a legal way to transfer property upon a property owner's death, there are several legal implications that have not been fully studied and understood yet.

There are possible unforeseen or unintended consequences of having the transfer on death deed as a new option for real property transfer:

1. Opponents of the transfer on death deed have cited concerns relating to issues of undue influence, fraud, or incompetence when it comes to preparing these deeds. For example, scammers or predators may persuade or pressure an elderly person to prepare this type of deed to transfer a home to them upon death. Elder abuse and other types of undue influence or fraud are a main concern. The current safeguard for this is a law that prohibits a beneficiary from selling a home within 120 days of the grantor's death.
2. Claims of undue influence, fraud, or incompetence may invite litigation by family members and friends upon the death of a property owner who prepared a transfer on death deed.
3. Any mortgage or debt that is attached to the property is transferred along with the property to the beneficiary upon the property owner's death.
4. Any liens placed upon a property by the homeowner's creditors are transferred to the beneficiary upon the homeowner's death.

What if I'm a Co-Owner of a Property?

There are several ways to own a property jointly, with one or more people such as a spouse, family member, or friends. There is joint tenancy with right of survivorship, community property (with or without right of survivorship), or tenancy in common. Joint tenancy is the main form of co-ownership that may affect the use of a transfer on death deed.

If you co-own a property under joint tenancy, things can get tricky if you want to leave property to a beneficiary with a transfer on death deed. Legally, your joint tenant(s) has the right of survivorship and would inherit your share of the property upon your death. This means that even if you had a transfer on death deed prepared, it becomes useless since your joint tenant now owns the property in full. There are only two ways to avoid your transfer on death deed from becoming null:

1. You outlive the other joint tenant(s).
2. Your joint tenant(s) shares your interests and prepares a separate transfer on death deed naming the same beneficiary. However, since this deed is fully revocable, your joint tenant may choose to revoke the deed upon your death, making your joint tenant the sole owner of the property.

The Transfer on Death Deed In A Nutshell

The transfer on death deed, like any other method of estate planning, has its benefits and drawbacks. These pros and cons all depend on the status of your finances, the amount of assets you possess, the urgency of your situation, and much more. Any type of estate planning is a step in the right direction if you have your loved ones' futures in mind. However, it is always safest to consult with a trusted estate planning attorney if you are ever unsure about your options.

Conclusion

Because of the disadvantages outlined above, particularly concerns regarding joint tenancy, community property, transfers to minors, and capacity to revoke, some estate planners believe that transfer on death deeds should only be used as a last resort if there is insufficient time to prepare proper estate documents. Additionally, this type of deed is not particularly necessary for married couples who can avoid probate by simply owning their home under joint tenancy or community property where, if one spouse dies, the surviving spouse would fully inherit the other's share. But despite these limitations, a revocable transfer upon death deed may be an ideal option for a single person whose only asset is the home in which he or she lives.

Forms

SIMPLE REVOCABLE TRANSFER ON DEATH (TOD) DEED
(California Probate Code Section 5642)

Recording Requested By:

When Recorded Mail This Deed To

Name:

Address:

Assessor's Parcel Number:Space Above For Recorder's Use

This document is exempt from documentary transfer tax under Rev. & Tax. Code § 11930. This document is exempt from preliminary change of ownership report under Rev. & Tax. Code § 480.3.

IMPORTANT NOTICE: THIS DEED MUST BE RECORDED ON OR BEFORE 60 DAYS AFTER THE DATE IT IS SIGNED AND NOTARIZED

Use this deed to transfer the residential property described below directly to your named beneficiaries when you die. YOU SHOULD CAREFULLY READ ALL OF THE INFORMATION ON THE OTHER PAGES OF THIS FORM. You may wish to consult an attorney before using this deed. It may have results that you do not want. Provide only the information asked for in the form. DO NOT INSERT ANY OTHER INFORMATION OR INSTRUCTIONS. This form MUST be RECORDED on or before 60 days after the date it is signed and notarized or it will not be effective.

PROPERTY DESCRIPTION

Print the legal description of the residential property affected by this deed:

BENEFICIARY(IES)

Print the FULL NAME(S) of the person(s) who will receive the property on your death (DO NOT use general terms like ' my children") and state the RELATIONSHIP that each named person has to you (spouse, son, daughter, friend, etc.):

TRANSFER ON DEATH

I transfer all of my interest in the described property to the named beneficiary(ies) on my death. I may revoke this deed. When recorded, this deed revokes any TOD deed that I made before signing this deed. Sign and print your name below (your name should exactly match the name shown on your title documents):

Date

NOTE: This deed only transfers MY ownership share of the property. The deed does NOT transfer the share of any co-owner of the property. Any co-owner who wants to name a TOD beneficiary must execute and RECORD a SEPARATE deed.

WITNESSES

To be valid, this deed must be signed by two persons, both present at the same time, who witness your signing of the deed or your acknowledgment that it is your deed. The signatures of the witnesses do not need to be acknowledged by a notary public.

Witness #1 Print and sign your name:	Witness #2 Print and sign your name:
------------------------------------	------------------------------------

ACKNOWLEDGMENT OF NOTARY

A notary public or other officer completing this certificate verifies only the identity of the individual who signed the document to which this certificate is attached, and not the truthfulness, accuracy, or validity of that document.

State of California)

County of)

On ___________________________ before me, (here insert name and title of the officer), personally appeared ___________________________, who proved to me on the basis of satisfactory evidence to be the person(s) whose name(s) is/are subscribed to the within instrument and acknowledged to me that he/she/they executed the same in his/her/their authorized capacity(ies), and that by his/her/their signature(s) on the instrument the person(s), or the entity upon behalf of which the person(s) acted, executed the instrument.

I certify under PENALTY OF PERJURY under the laws of the State of California that the foregoing paragraph is true and correct.

WITNESS my hand and official seal.

Signature ___________________________ (Seal)

(b) Subsequent pages of a form executed under this section shall be in substantially the following form.

COMMON QUESTIONS ABOUT THE USE OF THIS FORM

WHAT DOES THE TOD DEED DO? When you die, the identified property will transfer to your named beneficiary without probate. The TOD deed has no effect until you die. You can revoke it at any time.

CAN I USE THIS DEED TO TRANSFER BUSINESS PROPERTY? This deed can only be used to transfer (1) a parcel of property that contains one to four residential dwelling units, (2) a condominium unit, or (3) a parcel of agricultural land of 40 acres or less, which contains a single-family residence.

HOW DO I USE THE TOD DEED? Complete this form. Have it notarized. RECORD the form in the county where the property is located. The form MUST be recorded on or before 60 days after the date you sign it or the deed has no effect.

IS THE "LEGAL DESCRIPTION" OF THE PROPERTY NECESSARY? Yes.

HOW DO I FIND THE "LEGAL DESCRIPTION" OF THE PROPERTY? This information may be on the deed you received when you became an owner of the property. This information may also be available in the office of the county recorder for the county where the property is located. If you are not absolutely sure, consult an attorney.

HOW DO I "RECORD" THE FORM? Take the completed and notarized form to the county recorder for the county in which the property is located. Follow the instructions given by the county recorder to make the form part of the official property records.

WHAT IF I SHARE OWNERSHIP OF THE PROPERTY? This form only transfers YOUR share of the property. If a co-owner also wants to name a TOD beneficiary, that co-owner must complete and RECORD a separate form.

CAN I REVOKE THE TOD DEED IF I CHANGE MY MIND? Yes. You may revoke the TOD deed at any time. No one, including your beneficiary, can prevent you from revoking the deed.

HOW DO I REVOKE THE TOD DEED? There are three ways to revoke a recorded TOD deed: (1) Complete, have notarized, and RECORD a revocation form. (2) Create, have notarized, and RECORD a new TOD deed. (3) Sell or give away the property, or transfer it to a trust, before your death and RECORD the deed. A TOD deed can only affect property that you own when you die. A TOD deed cannot be revoked by will.

CAN I REVOKE A TOD DEED BY CREATING A NEW DOCUMENT THAT DISPOSES OF THE PROPERTY (FOR EXAMPLE, BY CREATING A NEW TOD DEED OR BY ASSIGNING THE PROPERTY TO A TRUST)? Yes, but only if the new document is RECORDED. To avoid any doubt, you may wish to RECORD a TOD deed revocation form before creating the new instrument. A TOD deed cannot be revoked by will, or by purporting to leave the subject property to anyone via will.

IF I SELL OR GIVE AWAY THE PROPERTY DESCRIBED IN A TOD DEED, WHAT HAPPENS WHEN I DIE? If the deed or other document used to transfer your property is RECORDED before your death, the TOD deed will have no effect. If the transfer document is not RECORDED before your death, the TOD deed will take effect.

I AM BEING PRESSURED TO COMPLETE THIS FORM. WHAT SHOULD I DO? Do NOT complete this form unless you freely choose to do so. If you are being pressured to dispose of your property in a way that you do not want, you may want to alert a family member, friend, the district attorney, or a senior service agency.

DO I NEED TO TELL MY BENEFICIARY ABOUT THE TOD DEED? No. But secrecy can cause later complications and might make it easier for others to commit fraud.

WHAT DOES MY BENEFICIARY NEED TO DO WHEN I DIE? Your beneficiary must RECORD evidence of your death (Prob. Code § 210), and file a change in ownership notice (Rev. & Tax. Code § 480). If you received Medi-Cal benefits, your beneficiary must notify the State Department of Health Care Services of your death and provide a copy of your death certificate (Prob. Code § 215).

WHAT IF I NAME MORE THAN ONE BENEFICIARY? Your beneficiaries will become co-owners in equal shares as tenants in common. If you want a different result, you should not use this form.

HOW DO I NAME BENEFICIARIES? You MUST name your beneficiaries individually, using each beneficiary's FULL name. You MAY NOT use general terms to describe beneficiaries, such as "my children." For each beneficiary that you name, you should briefly state that person's relationship to you (for example, my spouse, my son, my daughter, my friend, etc.).

WHAT IF A BENEFICIARY DIES BEFORE I DO? If all beneficiaries die before you, the TOD deed has no effect. If a beneficiary dies before you, but other beneficiaries survive you, the share of the deceased beneficiary will be divided equally between the surviving beneficiaries. If that is not the result you want, you should not use the TOD deed.

WHAT IS THE EFFECT OF A TOD DEED ON PROPERTY THAT I OWN AS JOINT TENANCY OR COMMUNITY PROPERTY WITH RIGHT OF SURVIVORSHIP? If you are the first joint tenant or spouse to die, the deed is VOID and has no effect. The property transfers to your joint tenant or surviving spouse and not according to this deed. If you are the last joint tenant or spouse to die, the deed takes effect and controls the ownership of your property when you die. If you do not want these results, do not use this form. The deed does NOT transfer the share of a co-owner of the property. Any co-owner who wants to name a TOD beneficiary must complete and RECORD a SEPARATE deed.

CAN I ADD OTHER CONDITIONS ON THE FORM? No. If you do, your beneficiary may need to go to court to clear title.

IS PROPERTY TRANSFERRED BY THE TOD DEED SUBJECT TO MY DEBTS? Yes.

DOES THE TOD DEED HELP ME TO AVOID GIFT AND ESTATE TAXES? No.

HOW DOES THE TOD DEED AFFECT PROPERTY TAXES? The TOD deed has no effect on your property taxes until your death. At that time, property tax law applies as it would to any other change of ownership.

DOES THE TOD DEED AFFECT MY ELIGIBILITY FOR MEDI-CAL? No.

AFTER MY DEATH, WILL MY HOME BE LIABLE FOR REIMBURSEMENT OF THE STATE FOR MEDI-CAL EXPENDITURES? Your home may be liable for reimbursement. If you have questions, you should consult an attorney.

5644.

A transferor may revoke a revocable transfer on death deed by an instrument in substantially the following form:

Revocation of
Revocable Transfer on Death (TOD) Deed

(California Probate Code Section 5600)

Recording Requested By:

When Recorded Mail This Deed To

Name:

Address:

Assessor's Parcel Number:Space Above For Recorder's Use

This deed revocation is exempt from documentary transfer tax under Rev. & Tax. Code §11930. This deed revocation is exempt from preliminary change of ownership report under Rev. & Tax. Code § 480.3.

IMPORTANT NOTICE: THIS FORM MUST BE RECORDED TO BE EFFECTIVE

This revocation form MUST be RECORDED before your death or it will not be effective. This revocation form only affects a transfer on death deed that YOU made. A transfer on death deed made by a co-owner of your property is not affected by this revocation form. A co-owner who wants to revoke a transfer on death deed that he/she made must complete and RECORD a SEPARATE revocation form.

PROPERTY DESCRIPTION

Print the legal description of the property affected by this revocation:

REVOCATION

I revoke any TOD deed to transfer the described property that I executed before executing this form.

SIGNATURE AND DATE

Sign and print your name below (your name should exactly match the name shown on your title documents):

_______________________________ Date

To be valid, this deed must be signed by two persons, both present at the same time, who witness your signing of the deed or your acknowledgment that it is your deed. The signatures of the witnesses do not need to be acknowledged by a notary public.

Witness #1
Print and sign your name:

Witness #2
Print and sign your name:

____

____

ACKNOWLEDGMENT OF NOTARY

A notary public or other officer completing this certificate verifies only the identity of the individual who signed the document to which this certificate is attached, and not the truthfulness, accuracy, or validity of that document.

State of California)

County of)

On ___________________________ before me, (here insert name and title of the officer), personally appeared ___________________________, who proved to me on the basis of satisfactory evidence to be the person(s) whose name(s) is/are subscribed to the within instrument and acknowledged to me that he/she/they executed the same in his/her/their authorized capacity(ies), and that by his/her/their signature(s) on the instrument the person(s), or the entity upon behalf of which the person(s) acted, executed the instrument.

I certify under PENALTY OF PERJURY under the laws of the State of California that the foregoing paragraph is true and correct.

WITNESS my hand and official seal.

Signature ___________________________ (Seal)

California Transfer on Death Deed Revocation Form

Recording requested by (name):
____

When recorded mail to
and mail tax statements to:
____

____

____

____

Recorder's Use Only

REVOCATION OF REVOCABLE TRANSFER ON DEATH DEED

(California Probate Code Section 5600)

This document is exempt from documentary transfer tax under Rev. & Tax. Code § 11930. This document is exempt from preliminary change of ownership report under Rev. & Tax. Code § 480.3.

Assessor's Parcel No.:
____

Declaration of Exemption From Gov't Code § 27388.1 Fee

- ☐ Transfer is exempt from fee per GC § 27388.1(a)(2):
  - ☐ recorded concurrently "in connection with" transfer subject to Documentary Transfer Tax
  - ☐ recorded concurrently "in connection with" a transfer of residential dwelling to an owner-occupier
- ☐ Transfer is exempt from fee per GC 27388.1(a)(1):
  - ☐ Fee cap of $225.00 reached ☐ Not related to real property

IMPORTANT NOTICE: THIS FORM MUST BE RECORDED TO BE EFFECTIVE

This revocation form MUST be RECORDED before your death or it will not be effective. This revocation form only affects a transfer on death deed that YOU made. A transfer on death deed made by a co-owner of your property is not affected by this revocation form. A co-owner who wants to revoke a transfer on death deed that he/she made must complete and RECORD a SEPARATE revocation form.

PROPERTY DESCRIPTION

Print the legal description of the property affected by this revocation:

____

____

____

REVOCATION

I, ________________________________, am the transferor under the Revocable TOD deed dated ________________ and recorded on ________________ as Instrument No. ______________ in Book/Reel ________, Page/Image ________, of Official Records of ______________________________________ County, California, which named as beneficiary(ies) ____.

I hereby revoke any TOD deed to transfer the described property that I executed before executing this form, including the TOD deed described above.

SIGNATURE AND DATE

Sign and print your name below (your name should exactly match the name shown on your title documents):

Date: ____________________

____
(Signature of declarant)

____
(Typed or written name of declarant)

ACKNOWLEDGMENT

A Notary Public or other officer completing this certificate verifies only the identity of the individual who signed the document to which this certificate is attached, and not the truthfulness, accuracy, or validity of that document.

State of California)
County of ______________________)

On __________________________ before me, ______________________________________
(insert name and title of the officer)

personally appeared ____
who proved to me on the basis of satisfactory evidence to be the person(s) whose name(s) is/are subscribed to the within instrument and acknowledged to me that he/she/they executed the same in his/her/their authorized capacity(ies), and that by his/her/their signature(s) on the instrument the person(s), or the entity upon behalf of which the person(s) acted, executed the instrument.

I certify under PENALTY OF PERJURY under the laws of the State of California that the foregoing paragraph is true and correct.

WITNESS my hand and official seal. **(Seal)**

Signature ____________________________________

Colorado

Table of Contents

Transfer on Death Deed

A transfer on death deed (known as a beneficiary deed in Colorado) is a document that allows you to pass ownership of property to an individual or entity without the necessity of probate. In Colorado, this document is defined as "a deed, subject to revocation by the owner, which conveys an interest in real property and which contains language that the conveyance is to be effective upon the death of the owner..."

How Do I Obtain a Beneficiary Deed?

The state of Colorado provides a substantive example of the form in Colorado Revised Statutes § 15-15-404. The form needs to be filled out in its entirety and signed before a public notary. You will then need to record the deed at the clerk and recorder's office in the county where the property is located.

Should An Attorney Draft my Transfer on Death Deed?

It is highly recommended that you seek the help of an experienced attorney to assist with this process. Form outlines provided by the state often lack the nuance necessary to be applied to every individual's situation. An experienced attorney will ensure that all necessary language is included and correctly expressed for your unique circumstance. Also, there are often many considerations to explore alongside the process of filing a beneficiary deed. An attorney who has been active with this type of law will know what questions to ask to help navigate setting up end-of-life arrangements most effectively.

Can a Beneficiary Deed be Revoked in Colorado?

Yes. Any beneficiary deed already filed with the clerk and recorder's office can be revoked by the owner. Obviously, this revocation must occur by the owner before the time of death and must also be recorded prior to death. In many cases, a revocation may not be the best option. It is often the case that another beneficiary be named instead. Be sure you understand all of the considerations you should make before moving forward with executing or revoking a beneficiary deed.

Is it Better to Use a Transfer on Death Deed?

This depends on your unique situation, and we would encourage you to speak to an attorney if you're unsure. For example, leaving a house to all of your children through a beneficiary deed will give them all equal rights to the property. This could result in the family being unable to come to a consensus on what to do with the property. However, if you use a will to leave the house to your children, an executor will be assigned. The executor will have the authority to make decisions in a timely manner.

A tax benefit of Colorado transfer-on-death deeds

For many couples in retirement, their main asset is their home. Frequently the property is jointly owned, and the property smoothly transfers to a wife at the death of her husband or vice versa.

But what is the best way to transfer the property to the next generation? In many cases, especially in smaller estates a beneficiary (transfer on death) deed can solve many problems. In a previous post, we explained how these deeds work. Here, we will discuss how the manner of transfer can affect taxes.

Stepped-up basis

First, it is important to note that a beneficiary deed is not a completed gift. The owner continues to have the ability to do what he or she wants with the property and has the power to revoke the deed.

When a transfer occurs at death through the beneficiary deed, the heir takes the property with a stepped-up basis. This is the fair market value of the property at the death.

An example is helpful. Assume a couple purchased a property in the 80s for $125,000. They enjoy the neighborhood and made improvements over the years. The husband, now a widower, would like to give the home to his only daughter. The current value of the property is about

$400,000. A beneficiary deed would allow his daughter to inherit the property with the higher basis. Deeding it to her during his lifetime would mean she receives the property with the lower basis and a later sale could incur capital gains tax

Forms

Recording requested by:

When recorded mail to and mail tax statements to:

Space above this line for recorder's use

Colorado Transfer on Death Deed

(Beneficiary Deed)

I, ______________________, with a mailing address of ______________________ ______________________________________ (hereinafter referred to as the "Owner") being of competent mind and having the legal capacity tc execute this document, as owner transfer on death to ______________________ with a mailing address of______ ____ (hereinafter referred to as the "Primary Beneficiary") as grantee beneficiary, the following described interest in real estate:

____

____

____

____

____

____

____

Legal description of the property (including square, suffix, and lot number)

If the Primary Beneficiary does not survive me, I designate ______________________ with a mailing address of ____ _________ (hereinafter referred to as the "Alternate Beneficiary") as grantee beneficiary.

This Transfer on Death Deed is revocable. It does not transfer any ownership until the death of the owner. It revokes all prior beneficiary designations by this owner for this

interest in real estate. The grantor has the right to withdraw or rescind this deed at any time. Any beneficiaries named in this deed are hereby advised that this deed may be withdrawn or rescinded whether or not money or any other consideration was paid or given.

____________________	____________________	____________________
Owner's Name	Primary Beneficiary's Name	Alternate Beneficiary's Name
____________________	____________________	____________________
Owner's Signature	Primary Beneficiary's Signature	Alternate Beneficiary's Signature
____________________	____________________	____________________
Date	Date	Date

Notary Acknowledgment

State of ____________________

County of __________________

The foregoing was acknowledged before me this ____ day of ________________, by the undersigned, ________________, who is personally known to me or satisfactorily proven to me to be the person whose name is subscribed to the within instrument.

____
Printed Name of Notary Public

____
Signature of Notary Public

My commission expires: __________________ (seal)

Colorado Transfer on Death Deed Revocation Form

Recording requested by (name):

____

When recorded mail to
and mail tax statements to:

____

____

____

____

Recorder's Use Only

REVOCATION OF REVOCABLE TRANSFER ON DEATH DEED

This document is exempt from documentary transfer tax under Rev. & Tax. Code § 11930. This document is exempt from preliminary change of ownership report under Rev. & Tax. Code § 480.3.

Assessor's Parcel No.:

____

Declaration of Exemption From Gov't Code § 27388.1 Fee

☐ Transfer is exempt from fee per GC § 27388.1(a)(2):
- ☐ recorded concurrently "in connection with" transfer subject to Documentary Transfer Tax
- ☐ recorded concurrently "in connection with" a transfer of residential dwelling to an owner-occupier

☐ Transfer is exempt from fee per GC 27388.1(a)(1):
- ☐ Fee cap of $225.00 reached ☐ Not related to real property

IMPORTANT NOTICE: THIS FORM MUST BE RECORDED TO BE EFFECTIVE

This revocation form MUST be RECORDED before your death or it will not be effective. This revocation form only affects a transfer on death deed that YOU made. A transfer on death deed made by a co-owner of your property is not affected by this revocation form. A co-owner who wants to revoke a transfer on death deed that he/she made must complete and RECORD a SEPARATE revocation form.

PROPERTY DESCRIPTION

Print the legal description of the property affected by this revocation:

____

____

____

REVOCATION

I, ______________________________, am the transferor under the Revocable TOD deed dated ______________ and recorded on ______________ as Instrument No. ____________ in Book/Reel ________, Page/Image ________, of Official Records of ______________________________ County, Colorado, which named as beneficiary(ies) ______________________________

______________________________.

I hereby revoke any TOD deed to transfer the described property that I executed before executing this form, including the TOD deed described above.

SIGNATURE AND DATE

Sign and print your name below (your name should exactly match the name shown on your title documents):

Date: ____________________

____
(Signature of declarant)

____
(Typed or written name of declarant)

Notary Acknowledgment

State of ____________________

County of __________________

The foregoing was acknowledged before me this ____ day of ________________, by the undersigned, ________________, who is personally known to me or satisfactorily proven to me to be the person whose name is subscribed to the within instrument.

____
Printed Name of Notary Public

____
Signature of Notary Public

My commission expires: __________________ (seal)

District of Columbia

Table of Contents

District of Columbia Transfer on Death Deed

Owners of real property in the District of Columbia now have access to a useful estate planning tool: the transfer on death deed (TODD). Modeled after the Uniform Real Property Transfer on Death Act and located at D.C. Code 19-604.01 et seq (2013), this statute governs the use of transfer on death deeds in the District of Columbia.

Transfer on death deeds are no testamentary (not using a will) instruments that allow transferors/owners to retain absolute ownership of and control over their land during their lives (19-604.07). Because they deal with after-death assets, however, their execution requires the same level of competency as a will (19-604.08). The owners may sell, mortgage, rent, or otherwise use the real estate however they choose, with no penalty for waste or obligation to notify the beneficiaries (19-604.12).

By recording the executed TODD, property owners may also take advantage of one of the most unique aspects of these instruments: revocability (19-604.06). Revocability is possible for two primary reasons: there is no obligation to notify the beneficiaries about the potential future interest they stand to gain when the owner dies; and these conveyances generally do not involve consideration (something of value given in exchange for the property) (19-604.10).

The statutes provide several methods for revoking a TODD. The owner may execute and record a new TODD, cancelling the prior deed and designating a different beneficiary. The owner may also sell the real estate to someone else using a standard inter vivos conveyance such as a warranty deed or a quitclaim deed that contains a comment revoking the TODD. A third option uses a revocation form, which, after recording, cancels all previously recorded TODDs (19-604.11).

In much the same way that owners may wish to change or revoke a beneficiary designation, sometimes beneficiaries are unable or unwilling to accept the property after the owner dies. To address this need, beneficiaries may disclaim all or part of the interest in land (19-604.14).

TRANSFER ON DEATH DEEDS AND ASSOCIATED REVOCATIONS MUST BE RECORDED WHILE THE OWNER IS ALIVE OR THEY HAVE NO EFFECT.

Overall, TODDs offer a useful, flexible estate planning tool to owners of real property in Washington, DC. Before committing to a TODD, consider the effect it will have on taxes, access, and eligibility for income-and/or-asset-based benefits. Each situation is unique, so for complex circumstances or additional questions, contact a local attorney.

The District of Columbia enacts the Uniform Real Property Transfer on Death Act, authorizing a property owner to transfer interest in the property to a beneficiary upon the death of the owner through a Transfer on Death Deed that must be notarized and filed in the local land records.

Is a transfer on death deed a good idea?

If you'd like to avoid having your property going through the probate process, it's a good idea to look into a transfer on death deed. A transfer on death deed allows you to select a beneficiary who will receive your property, but only when you've passed.

What does a transfer on death deed do?

A Transfer on Death Deed lets you keep all ownership rights to the property during your lifetime, so you can sell it or use is as collateral on a loan. When you die, your property interest passes to the person you named in the Transfer on Death Deed (the "beneficiary") without any probate action.

Because probate court proceedings to transfer decedents' assets to heirs can be so long, costly, and burdensome, the District of Columbia (D.C.) Government has established specific methods for avoiding probate in Washington D.C.:

Living Trusts. In D.C., living trusts avoid probate for real estate, bank accounts, vehicles, virtually any asset. A trust document similar to a will names the asset owner as the trustee and someone to administer an owner's assets as successor trustee after the owner's death. Control of the asset is dictated under the terms of the trust. At the owner's death, the successor trustee can transfer the asset to a beneficiary without probate court proceedings. Joint Ownership. If the ownership includes the "right of survivorship," when an owner dies the property transfers automatically to the surviving owner(s). No probate is necessary to transfer ownership.

Joint Tenancy. When an owner dies, property in joint tenancy passes to the surviving owner(s) automatically. No probate is necessary. In D.C., each joint tenant must own an equal share.

Tenancy by the Entirety. This form of joint ownership is like joint tenancy but for married couples.

Do you pay taxes on transfer on death?

The amount that's in a TOD account at the time of your death is not taxable under federal law to the person who receives the account, although it may be taxable to your estate. If your beneficiary or the account are in a state with an inheritance tax, he may have to pay that.

Revocation by instrument authorized; revocation by act not permitted.

(a) Subject to subsection (b) of this section, an instrument is effective to revoke a recorded transfer on death deed, or any part of it, only if the instrument:

(1) Is one of the following:

(A) A transfer on death deed that revokes the deed or part of the deed expressly or by inconsistency;

(B) An instrument of revocation that expressly revokes the deed or part of the deed; or

(C) An inter vivos deed that expressly revokes the transfer on death deed or part of the deed; and

(2) Is acknowledged by the transferor after the acknowledgment of the deed being revoked and recorded before the transferor's death in the public records in the Office of the Recorder of Deeds.

(b) If a transfer on death deed is made by more than one transferor:

(1) Revocation by a transferor does not affect the deed as to the interest of another transferor; and

(2) A deed of joint owners is revoked only if it is revoked by all of the living joint owners.

(c) After a transfer on death deed is recorded, it may not be revoked by a revocatory act on the deed.

(d) This section does not limit the effect of an inter vivos transfer of the property.

(Mar. 19, 2013, D.C. Law 19-230, § 2(b), 59 DCR 13606.)

Forms

★★★
[logo]nment of the
District of Columbia
Office of Tax
and Revenue
Recorder of Deeds
1101 4th Street, SW
Washington, DC 20024
Phone (202) 727-5374

REVOCABLE TRANSFER-ON-DEATH DEED

NOTICE TO OWNER

You should carefully read all information on this form. You May Want to Consult a Lawyer Before Using This Form. This form must be recorded before your death, or it will not be effective.

IDENTIFYING INFORMATION

Owner or Owners Making This Deed:

____________________ ____________________
Printed name Mailing address

____________________ ____________________
Printed name Mailing address

Legal description of the property, including square, suffix and lot number:

PRIMARY BENEFICIARY

I designate the following beneficiary if the beneficiary survives me.

____________________ ____________________
Printed name Mailing address, if available

Upon recording return to:

ALTERNATE BENEFICIARY – Optional

If my primary beneficiary does not survive me, I designate the following alternate beneficiary if that beneficiary survives me.

____________________ ____________________
Printed name Mailing address, if available

ROD 39 revised 05/2013

TRANSFER ON DEATH

At my death, I transfer my interest in the described property to the beneficiaries as designated above.

Before my death, I have the right to revoke this deed.

SIGNATURE OF OWNER OR OWNERS MAKING THIS DEED

______________________________ [(SEAL)]________________
Signature Date

______________________________ [(SEAL)]________________
Signature Date

ACKNOWLEDGMENT

DISTRICT OF COLUMBIA

CITY OF WASHINGTON

STATE OF: ______________________)

COUNTY OF: ____________________) ss:

I, the undersigned, a Notary Public in and for the jurisdiction aforesaid, do hereby certify that ______________ and ____________________ personally appeared before me and being known to me as the person(s) whose name(s) is/are subscribed to the within instrument and did acknowledge that s/he/they executed the same for the purposes therein contained this ____ day of _____, 20____.

(SEAL)

____

Notary Public

My Commission Expires: __________

Government of the
District of Columbia
Office of Tax
and Revenue
Recorder of Deeds
1101 4th Street, SW
Washington, DC 20024
Phone (202) 727-5374

REVOCATION OF TRANSFER-ON-DEATH DEED

NOTICE TO OWNER

This revocation must be recorded before you die or it will not be effective. This revocation is effective only as to the interests in the property of owners who sign this revocation.

IDENTIFYING INFORMATION

Owner or Owners of Property Making This Revocation:

__________________________ ______________________________
Printed name Mailing address

__________________________ ______________________________
Printed name Mailing address

Legal description of the property, including square, suffix and lot number:

____

REVOCATION

I revoke all my previous transfers of this property by transfer on death deed.

SIGNATURE OF OWNER OR OWNERS MAKING THIS REVOCATION

______________________________ [(SEAL)] ________________
Signature Date

______________________________ [(SEAL)] ________________
Signature Date

Upon recording return to:

ACKNOWLEDGMENT

DISTRICT OF COLUMBIA

CITY OF WASHINGTON

STATE OF: ________________________)

COUNTY OF: _______________________) ss:

ROD 40 revised 05/2013

I, the undersigned, a Notary Public in and for the jurisdiction aforesaid, do h ereby certify that ______________ and ____________________ personally appeared before me and being known to me as the person(s) whose name(s) is/are subscribed to the within instrument and did acknowledge that s/he/they executed the same for the purposes therein contained this ____ day of _____, 20____.

(SEAL)

____

Notary Public

My Commission Expires: __________

District of Columbia Transfer on Death Deed Revocation Form

Recording requested by (name): ______________________ When recorded mail to and mail tax statements to: ______________________ ______________________ ______________________ ______________________	Recorder's Use Only

REVOCATION OF REVOCABLE TRANSFER ON DEATH DEED

This document is exempt from documentary transfer tax under Rev. & Tax. Code § 11930. This document is exempt from preliminary change of ownership report under Rev. & Tax. Code § 480.3.

Assessor's Parcel No.: ______________________

Declaration of Exemption From Gov't Code § 27388.1 Fee

- ☐ Transfer is exempt from fee per GC § 27388 1(a)(2):
  - ☐ recorded concurrently "in connection with" transfer subject to Documentary Transfer Tax
  - ☐ recorded concurrently "in connection with" a transfer of residential dwelling to an owner-occupier
- ☐ Transfer is exempt from fee per GC 27388.1(a)(1):
  - ☐ Fee cap of $225.00 reached ☐ Not related to real property

IMPORTANT NOTICE: THIS FORM MUST BE RECORDED TO BE EFFECTIVE

This revocation form MUST be RECORDED before your death or it will not be effective. This revocation form only affects a transfer on death deed that YOU made. A transfer on death deed made by a co-owner of your property is not affected by this revocation form. A co-owner who wants to revoke a transfer on death deed that he/she made must complete and RECORD a SEPARATE revocation form.

PROPERTY DESCRIPTION

Print the legal description of the property affected by this revocation:

____

____

____

REVOCATION

I, ______________________, am the transferor under the Revocable TOD deed dated ______________ and recorded on ______________ as Instrument No. ____________ in Book/Reel ________, Page/Image ________, of Official Records of ______________________ County, District of Columbia, which named as beneficiary(ies)

____

____.

I hereby revoke any TOD deed to transfer the described property that I executed before executing this form, including the TOD deed described above.

SIGNATURE AND DATE

Sign and print your name below (your name should exactly match the name shown on your title documents):

Date: ______________

____
(Signature of declarant)

____
(Typed or written name of declarant)

Notary Acknowledgment

State of ____________________

County of __________________

The foregoing was acknowledged before me this ____ day of ________________, by the undersigned, ________________, who is personally known to me or satisfactorily proven to me to be the person whose name is subscribed to the within instrument.

____
Printed Name of Notary Public

____
Signature of Notary Public

My commission expires: __________________ (seal)

Florida

Table of Contents

A life enhanced estate deed, more commonly called a "Lady Bird Deed," is one of the best kept secrets for estate planning purposes. The lady bird deed in Florida allows you to avoid probate court, reserve powers to yourself, maintain Medicaid eligibility, and qualify for the Florida Homestead exemption. I will go over some of the features, benefits, and disadvantages of lady bird deeds to give you a better understanding of why and when they should be used.

What is a Florida Lady Bird Deed?

With the Florida lady bird deed, you give yourself a life estate interest in your property. A life estate is a right to live in the property until your death. When you pass away, the real property passes to your beneficiaries designated in the lady bird deed, called the remaindermen.

The lady bird deed works similarly to a pay-on-death provision on a bank account. With a pay-on-death account you can spend the funds in the account during your lifetime and change the beneficiaries at any time, and the beneficiary is only entitled to what is left on the account when you die.

What makes Florida lady bird deeds so valuable is that you are able to retain certain interests in the real property even being the life tenant. I will go over those rights in the next section.

Some terms used in this article are as follows:

- Grantor*: the person(s) that transfer the property right into the Lady Bird Deed.*
- Remainder Beneficiary: *the person listed under the Lady Bird Deed to inherit the property once you have passed away.*

Reserved Rights of the Life Tenant with a Lady Bird Deed Florida

You as the life tenant reserve yourself the right to sell, encumber, and otherwise consume the real property during your lifetime without and knowledge or consent of the beneficiaries. You may also change the beneficiaries/remaindermen at any point in time or even revert the whole interest back to yourself.

An example of the retained rights in a Florida lady bird deed is as follows:

> *The Grantor reserves to herself, as Life Tenant, an enhanced life estate in the Property, being the exclusive possession, use and enjoyment of the Property and its rents and profits, without liability for waste, and specifically reserves to herself the following rights, exercisable without the joinder of the remainder beneficiary and with or without consideration: to sell, lease, encumber, or pledge the Property; to manage or dispose of all or part of the Property or to grant any interest in the Property, all by gift, sale, or otherwise; to retain any and all proceeds generated by a sale, lease, or encumbrance, as the Life Tenant in her sole discretion decides; to terminate the interest of the Grantee by the exercise of any right retained in this deed, including the right to cancel this deed by further conveyance to herself or to anyone else.*

Differences Between Lady Bird Deed and Ordinary Life Estate Deed in Florida

Compared to an ordinary life estate deed, the lady bird deeds allows you to retain all the rights of fee simple ownership in a real estate property as outlined above.

The second major difference between a lady bird deed and an ordinary life estate deed is that your beneficiaries have no vested interest during your lifetime. In an ordinary life estate deed, the beneficiaries/remaindermen have a vested interest and they are expected beneficiaries of the real property. With an ordinary life estate, the beneficiaries' interest cannot be given away or sold without their consent. However, with a lady bird deed you can free change the beneficiaries/remaindermen at any point in time.

The third major difference is that with a Florida lady bird deed, you do not have a duty to preserve and maintain the real property for the benefit of the beneficiaries. You may free consume the real property, sell the property without the beneficiaries' knowledge or consent, and will not have any liability to the beneficiaries.

Benefits of a Lady Bird Deed Florida

There are four (4) major benefits of a lady bird deed in Florida: 1) probate avoidance; 2) preserve homestead benefits; 3) preserve Medicaid eligibility; and 4) step-up in basis at your death. I will go over each benefit in more extent below.

1. A Florida Lady Bird Deed Allows You to Avoid Probate Court

The first major benefit of a lady bird deed is that it allows you to avoid Florida probate court for the real property being deeded. In Florida, only assets that are titled individually under your name and without a beneficiary designation or a survivorship provision pass through probate court. In the case of lady bird deed, when you pass away you interest extinguishes and the beneficiaries you listed under the deed will inherit the property outside of probate code.

The only thing that your beneficiaries/remaindermen will need to do is to take your death certificate to the appropriate county clerk where the real property is located to show proof of death.

2. A Florida Lady Bird Deed Allows You to Preserve Homestead Rights

The second major benefit of the lady bird deed is that it allows you to preserve your Florida homestead benefits. This means that you will not lose your homestead exemption in your real property for tax purposes and your property taxes will not increase due to the change of ownership in the deed. Florida Department of Revenue is not pursuing any Doc Stamp Tax in Florida and at the time of recording only minimum taxes are required (approximately $20-30 dollars).

In addition, you will also be able to maintain your homestead protection against forced sale for your interest in the Homestead. Meaning that a creditor will not be able to force sale your property, the creditor will only be able to place a lien on your property. See below for a possible disadvantage of the Florida Lady Bird Deed regarding protection against the creditors of the remainder beneficiary.

3. A Florida Lady Bird Deed Allows You Preserve Medicaid Eligibility

In Florida, Medicaid considers your assets for the purpose of Medicaid eligibility. However, your Homestead is typically not counted as an asset for Medicaid eligibility purpose to a certain extent. If you create a Florida lady bird deed, to the extent it is your homestead, it should not affect your Medicaid eligibility. The reason for this is as I explained above, because you reserve most of the rights which are an indicia of ownership, the transfer is not treated as a completed gift.

In this area is important to consult with an estate planning attorney that has knowledge of the Medicaid rules. I will strongly advise you against doing lady bird deeds on your own.

4. A Florida Lady Bird Deed Allows You to Get a Step-Up in Basis Upon Your Death

For tax purposes, the lady bird deed is not seeing as a completed gift. It is not a completed gift because you have the right to revert the ownership back to you and you reserve a lot of the rights in the real property. Section 1014 of the IRS Code, allows a step-up in basis at your death. The benefit of a step-up in basis is that your beneficiaries can turn around and sell the real property without incurring any federal income tax liability.

Let me give you an example. If you buy a property today for $100,000, that will be your basis (cost) for tax purposes. If the real property increases in value to $200,000, then you have a gain of $100,000 if you sell the real property, subject to some exceptions under IRC 121. However, if you pass away when the real property is worth $200,000, in the hands of your beneficiaries the basis of the property will step-up to fair market value, thus not paying any income tax on the sale.

Disadvantage of a Lady Bird Deed in Florida

1. **Homestead Limitations on Devise**

The first disadvantage of a Lady Bird Deed in Florida is the Florida Homestead restrictions on devise. You may not use the Lady Bird Deed to circumvent the devise rules of the Florida homestead law. Florida Homestead Law states that if you are surviving by minor children, you many not devise (transfer) your Homestead in a Will or a Trust to anyone. However, if you have no minor children, then you may devise your Homestead only to your spouse, if any.

If you are not married and have no minor children, then you may devise your homestead to whoever you want, but if it is not someone listed under the Florida Intestacy Statute then the protection of the forced sale will not inure to your beneficiary.

This means that if you are married and have minor children you have to be careful of not running afoul of the Homestead restrictions on devise. In most situations the Lady Bird Deed is best suited for single and/or widowed individuals that want to avoid Probate court or are looking to qualify for Medicaid benefits.

2. **Homestead Protection Against Forced Sale for the Remainder Beneficiary**

The second disadvantage of a Lady Bird Deed in Florida is the lack of statutory and case law regarding the rights of judgment creditors to attack the interest of the remainder beneficiary while you are alive.

There are two sides of the argument. The first side is that a judgment creditor of the remainder beneficiary does not have a right to the Homestead because the transfer is not a completed gift and the remainder beneficiary can be divested at any point by you. The other side is that the remainder beneficiary has a vested interest and the judgment creditor can attack his or her interest in the Homestead and pursue a lien or levy in the property. Unfortunately, this issue is still unsettled as there is a lack of guidance from the statutes and the courts.

Therefore, if you feel that the remainder beneficiary might be involved in a Bankruptcy or has any lawsuits or creditors in the horizon, the Lady Bird Deed might not be the best option in that circumstance. Remember, that the Florida Homestead protection against forced sale protects you against your creditors, not the creditors of third persons.

3. Multiple Beneficiaries

The Lady Bird Deed should be used with caution when there are multiple remainder beneficiaries. The Lady Bird Deed could be a disadvantage if the remainder beneficiary do not get along or if one of them were to pass away during your lifetime. If one of the beneficiaries passes away and you don't get to correcting the deed, then Florida probate will be needed for that beneficiaries interest, unless you designated a right of survivorship as between the remainder beneficiaries.

Forms

Lady Bird Deed

This Deed is made on this day of ___________, 20__, between the

Grantor __________________________

Of address _______________________________ and the

Grantee Beneficiary ____________________________

Of address ____.

For good and valuable consideration paid by the Grantee Beneficiary, the receipt of which is hereby acknowledged, the Grantor does transfer and convey the following described property to the Grantee Beneficiary effective on the Grantor's death:

Property Address: ____

Legal Description: ____

____

____

The Grantor reserves a life estate for himself/herself during the Grantor's lifetime Coupled with an unrestricted power to convey during the Grantor's lifetime, which includes the power to sell, gift, mortgage, lease and otherwise dispose of the property, and to retain the proceeds from the conveyance.

Executed this day of _________________, 20__.

Grantor Name: _______________________

Grantor Signature: ___________________

STATE OF _____________________

COUNTY OF ___________________

On this day, personally appeared before me, _____________________, to me known to be the person(s) described in and who executed the within instrument and acknowledged that he/she signed the same as his/her voluntary act and deed, for the uses and purposes therein mentioned.

Witness my hand and official hereto affixed on this day of _________________, 20__.

Notary's Public Signature: ____________________________________

Florida Transfer on Death Deed Revocation Form

Recording requested by (name):

____

When recorded mail to
and mail tax statements to:

____

____

____

____

Recorder's Use Only

REVOCATION OF REVOCABLE TRANSFER ON DEATH DEED

This document is exempt from documentary transfer tax under Rev. & Tax. Code § 11930. This document is exempt from preliminary change of ownership report under Rev. & Tax. Code § 480.3.

Assessor's Parcel No.:

____

Declaration of Exemption From Gov't Code § 27388.1 Fee

☐ Transfer is exempt from fee per GC § 27388.1(a)(2):
- ☐ recorded concurrently "in connection with" transfer subject to Documentary Transfer Tax
- ☐ recorded concurrently "in connection with" a transfer of residential dwelling to an owner-occupier

☐ Transfer is exempt from fee per GC 27388.1(a)(1):
- ☐ Fee cap of $225.00 reached ☐ Not related to real property

IMPORTANT NOTICE: THIS FORM MUST BE RECORDED TO BE EFFECTIVE

This revocation form MUST be RECORDED before your death or it will not be effective. This revocation form only affects a transfer on death deed that YOU made. A transfer on death deed made by a co-owner of your property is not affected by this revocation form. A co-owner who wants to revoke a transfer on death deed that he/she made must complete and RECORD a SEPARATE revocation form.

PROPERTY DESCRIPTION

Print the legal description of the property affected by this revocation:

____

____

____

REVOCATION

I, ________________________________, am the transferor under the Revocable TOD deed dated _______________ and recorded on _______________ as Instrument No. ______________ in Book/Reel ________, Page/Image ________, of Official Records of ______________________________ County, Florida, which named as beneficiary(ies) ____ ____.

I hereby revoke any TOD deed to transfer the described property that I executed before executing this form, including the TOD deed described above.

SIGNATURE AND DATE

Sign and print your name below (your name should exactly match the name shown on your title documents):

Date: ____________________

____
(Signature of declarant)

____
(Typed or written name of declarant)

ACKNOWLEDGMENT

> A Notary Public or other officer completing this certificate verifies only the identity of the individual who signed the document to which this certificate is attached, and not the truthfulness, accuracy, or validity of that document.

State of Florida)
County of ____________________)

On ________________________ before me, ____
(insert name and title of the officer)

Personally appeared ____
who proved to me on the basis of satisfactory evidence to be the person(s) whose name(s) is/are subscribed to the within instrument and acknowledged to me that she/he/ they executed the same in his/her/their authorized capacity(ies), and by his/her/their signature(s) on the instrument the person(s), or the entity upon behalf of which the person(s) acted, executed the instrument.

I certify under PENALTY OF PERJURY under the laws of the State of Florida that the foregoing paragraph is true and correct.

Witness me hand and official seal. **(Seal)**

Signature ____

Hawaii

Table of Contents

How should you hold title to your property in Hawaii?

So you've found your own piece of paradise in Hawaii or maybe you've owned property here for years, how should you hold title to this property on the deed? In very simplified terms, here are your options for how to hold title to real estate in Hawaii:

Joint tenants (with rights of survivorship)

When multiple people own EQUAL interest in one property. When one joint owner dies, their ownership interest automatically goes to the surviving joint owners (no matter what the deceased owner's will or trust says)

Tenants by the entirety

Only an option for SPOUSES. Just like Joint Tenants with Rights of Survivorship but also has CREDITOR PROTECTION from creditors that only have a claim against one spouse.

How do you avoid going through probate after a property owner dies?

Probate has a bad reputation for being a slow, cumbersome, and expensive process to go through, when you're already dealing with the loss of a loved one, so most people try to avoid it. Simply put, probate is a judicial process, on the State-level, that attempts to ensure that a deceased person's property ends up in the right hands. Real property is one of the assets that triggers probate (even if the person who passed away has a will).

There are three common ways to hold property jointly between two people in the State of Hawaii: joint tenants (with rights of survivorship), tenants by the entirety, or tenants in common. If a property is held jointly between two people, either joint tenants (with rights of survivorship) or tenants by the entirety, if one owner dies, the surviving owner becomes the 100% owner by rights of survivorship. On the other hand, if the property is held tenants in common, between two joint owners, if one owner dies, their interest does not automatically go to the surviving joint owner, it triggers probate.

Other ways to avoid probate is transferring a property to a new owner with a transfer on death deed or holding it in a trust.

What is a transfer on death deed?

As of June 27, 2011 Hawaii passed the Uniform Real Property Transfers on Death Act which allows real estate to go to a beneficiary when the owner dies, without having to go to court for probate. A revocable transfer on death deed is kind of like a designated beneficiary provision for your property. Do you remember that form you filled out for your retirement account or life insurance policy saying who you want to get your account remainder when you pass away? That was your designated beneficiary provision. In the case of a retirement account, when someone passes away, the beneficiary just needs to provide the death certificate to the financial institution who holds the account and they will be paid, bypassing any estate administration or probate. Likewise, with a transfer on death deed, the beneficiary just needs to provide the death certificate to the Bureau of Conveyances and they will become the new owner of that property, bypassing any estate administration or probate.

Transfer on Death Deeds in Hawaii

In 2011, Hawaii enacted its version of the Uniform Real Property Transfer on Death Act (URPTODA), found at Chapter 527 of the Hawaii Revised Statutes.

Along with Hawaii, a growing number of states are choosing to adopt the provisions of the URPTODA. The new law allows landowners to direct the distribution of what is often their most significant asset, their real estate, with a correctly executed and recorded transfer on death deed.

Transfer on death deeds are no testamentary, which means ownership of the property passes to the beneficiary without instructions in a will or the need for probate (5277). Unnecessary conflicts are likely to add confusion and expense, however, so property owners should take care to ensure that their wills and TODDs contain the same instructions.

Hawaii's version of the URPTODA sets out the specific requirements for lawful transfer on death deeds:

- The capacity required to make or revoke a transfer on death deed is the same as the capacity required to make a will (5278, 560:2-501).
- It must contain the essential elements and formalities of a properly recordable inter vivos deed, such as warranty or quitclaim deed (5279(1))
- It must state that the transfer to the designated beneficiary is to occur at the transferor's death (5279 (2))

Most importantly, it must be recorded before the transferor's death in the office of the clerk of the county commission in the county where the property is located (5279 (3)).

The named beneficiary gains no present rights to the property, only a potential future interest. Instead, the transferors retain absolute control during their lives. This includes the freedom to sell or transfer it to someone else, and to modify or revoke the intended transfer on death (52712). These details, along with the fact that TODDs only convey the property rights remaining, if any, at the owner's death, explain why they do not require notice or consideration (52710).

According to 52713(a), the beneficiary gains equitable interest in the property ONLY when the owner dies. Note, however, that the beneficiary must be alive at the time of the transferor's death or the interest returns to the estate. To prevent this from happening, the owner may identify one or more contingent beneficiaries. All beneficiaries take title subject to any obligations (contracts, easements, etc.) associated with the property when the transferor dies (52713(b)).

With the new transfer on death deeds, real property owners in Hawaii have access to a convenient, flexible tool for managing one aspect of a comprehensive estate plan. Even so, a

TODD may not be appropriate for everyone. Since each situation is unique, contact an attorney with specific questions or for complex circumstances.

2018 Hawaii Revised Statutes

TITLE 28. PROPERTY

527. Uniform Real Property Transfer on Death Act

527-13 Effect of transfer on death deed at transferor's death.

Universal Citation: HI Rev Stat § 527-13 (2018)

[§527-13] Effect of transfer on death deed at transferor's death. (a) Except as otherwise provided in the transfer on death deed, this section, or sections 560:2-202, 560:2-603, 560:2-702, 560:2-706, 560:2-707, 560:2-803, and 560:2-804, on the death of the transferor, the following shall apply to the subject property owned by the transferor at death:

(1) Subject to paragraph (2), the interest in the subject property shall be transferred to the designated beneficiary in accordance with the deed; provided that, for property of which any portion is registered in the land court pursuant to chapter 501, a petition noting the death of the transferor and requesting that a new certificate of title be issued in the name of the designated beneficiary shall be filed and processed with the land court before the interest in the subject property is transferred;

(2) The interest of a designated beneficiary is contingent on the designated beneficiary surviving the transferor and the interest of a designated beneficiary that fails to survive the transferor shall lapse;

(3) Subject to paragraph (4), concurrent interests are transferred to the beneficiaries in equal and undivided shares with no right of survivorship; and

4) If the transferor has identified two or more designated beneficiaries to receive concurrent interests in the subject property, any share that lapses or fails for any reason shall be transferred to the other beneficiaries in proportion to the interest of each in the remaining concurrently-held subject property.

(b) Pursuant to the filing requirements of chapter 501 or the recording provisions of [chapter] 502, as applicable, a beneficiary shall take the subject property subject to all conveyances, encumbrances, assignments, contracts, mortgages, liens, and other interests to which the subject property is subject at the transferor's death. For purposes of this subsection and the filing provisions of chapter 501 or the recording provisions of chapter 502, the filing or recording of the transfer on death deed is deemed to have occurred at the transferor's death.

(c) If a transferor is a joint owner and is survived by one or more other joint owners, the subject property shall belong to the surviving joint owner or owners with the right of survivorship and the transfer on death deed shall have no effect. If a transferor is a joint owner and is the last surviving joint owner, the transfer on death deed shall be effective.

(d) A transfer on death deed transfers the subject property without covenant or warranty of title even if the transfer on death deed contains a contrary provision. [L 2011, c 173, pt of §1]

Law Journals and Reviews

The Hawai`i Uniform Real Property Transfer on Death Act--Another Tool in the Estate Planner's Arsenal. 15 HBJ, no. 13, at 43 (2013).

Forms

Recording requested by:

When recorded mail to and mail tax statements to:

Space above this line for recorder's use

Hawaii Transfer on Death Deed

(Beneficiary Deed)

I, ______________________, with a mailing address of ________________________ ______________________________________ (hereinafter referred to as the "Owner") being of competent mind and having the legal capacity to execute this document, as owner transfer on death to ______________________ with a mailing address of ______ ____ (hereinafter referred to as the "Primary Beneficiary") as grantee beneficiary, the following described interest in real estate:

____

____

____

____

____

____

____

Legal description of the property (including square, suffix, and lot number)

If the Primary Beneficiary does not survive me, I designate ______________________ with a mailing address of ____ _________ (hereinafter referred to as the "Alternate Beneficiary") as grantee beneficiary.

This Transfer on Death Deed is revocable. It does not transfer any ownership until the death of the owner. It revokes all prior beneficiary designations by this owner for this

interest in real estate. The grantor has the right to withdraw or rescind this deed at any time. Any beneficiaries named in this deed are hereby advised that this deed may be withdrawn or rescinded whether or not money or any other consideration was paid or given.

______________________	______________________	______________________
Owner's Name	Primary Beneficiary's Name	Alternate Beneficiary's Name
______________________	______________________	______________________
Owner's Signature	Primary Beneficiary's Signature	Alternate Beneficiary's Signature
______________________	______________________	______________________
Date	Date	Date

Notary Acknowledgment

State of ____________________

County of __________________

The foregoing was acknowledged before me this ____ day of ________________, by the undersigned, ________________, who is personally known to me or satisfactorily proven to me to be the person whose name is subscribed to the within instrument.

____

Printed Name of Notary Public

____

Signature of Notary Public

My commission expires: __________________ (seal)

Hawaii Transfer on Death Deed Revocation Form

Recording requested by (name):

____

When recorded mail to
and mail tax statements to:

____

____

____

____

Recorder's Use Only

REVOCATION OF REVOCABLE TRANSFER ON DEATH DEED

This document is exempt from documentary transfer tax under Rev. & Tax. Code § 11930. This document is exempt from preliminary change of ownership report under Rev. & Tax. Code § 480.3.

Assessor's Parcel No.:

____

Declaration of Exemption From Gov't Code § 27388.1 Fee

☐ Transfer is exempt from fee per GC § 27388.1(a)(2):
- ☐ recorded concurrently "in connection with" transfer subject to Documentary Transfer Tax
- ☐ recorded concurrently "in connection with" a transfer of residential dwelling to an owner-occupier

☐ Transfer is exempt from fee per GC 27388.1(a)(1):
- ☐ Fee cap of $225.00 reached ☐ Not related to real property

IMPORTANT NOTICE: THIS FORM MUST BE RECORDED TO BE EFFECTIVE

This revocation form MUST be RECORDED before your death or it will not be effective. This revocation form only affects a transfer on death deed that YOU made. A transfer on death deed made by a co-owner of your property is not affected by this revocation form. A co-owner who wants to revoke a transfer on death deed that he/she made must complete and RECORD a SEPARATE revocation form.

PROPERTY DESCRIPTION

Print the legal description of the property affected by this revocation:

____

____

____

REVOCATION

I, ______________________________, am the transferor under the Revocable TOD deed dated ______________ and recorded on ______________ as Instrument No. ______________ in Book/Reel ________, Page/Image ________, of Official Records of ______________________________ County, Hawaii, which named as beneficiary(ies) ______________________________
______________________________.

I hereby revoke any TOD deed to transfer the described property that I executed before executing this form, including the TOD deed described above.

SIGNATURE AND DATE

Sign and print your name below (your name should exactly match the name shown on your title documents):

Date: ____________________

____
(Signature of declarant)

____
(Typed or written name of declarant)

Notary Acknowledgment

State of ____________________

County of __________________

The foregoing was acknowledged before me this ____ day of ________________, by the undersigned, ________________, who is personally known to me or satisfactorily proven to me to be the person whose name is subscribed to the within instrument.

____
Printed Name of Notary Public

____
Signature of Notary Public

My commission expires: __________________ (seal)

Illinois

Table of Contents

Illinois Transfer on Death Deed

The Illinois TOD deed form allows property to be automatically transferred to a new owner when the current owner dies, without the need to go through probate. It also gives the current owner retained control over the property, including the right to change his or her mind about the transfer.

Is a transfer on death deed a good idea?

If you'd like to avoid having your property going through the probate process, it's a good idea to look into a transfer on death deed. A transfer on death deed allows you to select a beneficiary who will receive your property, but only when you've passed away

What does a transfer on death deed do?

The transfer-on-death deed allows a homeowner to transfer title to their property upon their death without a will or without having to endure the probate process.

Does a transfer on death deed supersede a will?

A TOD designation supersedes a will. For bank accounts, you can set up a similar account known as payable-on-death, sometimes referred to as a Totten trust. Your beneficiaries can't touch the account while you're alive, and you're free to change beneficiaries or close the accounts at any time

Transfer on Death Instrument: Advantages and Disadvantages

The newly enacted Illinois Residential Real Property Transfer on Death Instrument Act authorizes another way to transfer real property, starting on January 1, 2012. PA 97-0555, HB 1153. The transfer on death instrument is a revocable instrument that allows an owner to transfer residential real estate to one or more beneficiaries on the owner's death. The transfer on death instrument gives Illinois residents another choice when trying to avoid probate while transferring ownership of residential real property. Other options for bypassing probate include living trusts, joint tenancies and life estates. This article will examine the advantages and disadvantages of the transfer on death instrument in comparison to living trusts, joint tenancies and life estates. The analysis will offer guidance on which option, based on the needs and circumstances of the owner of real property, will lead to the most beneficial outcome.

Transfer on Death Instrument

The Illinois transfer on death instrument allows an owner of residential real property to designate one or more beneficiaries who will receive interest in the property on the owner's death, bypassing probate. The definition of "residential real property" is defined as "real property improved with not less than one nor more than four residential dwelling units ... or condominium units ... or a single tract of agriculture real estate consisting of 40 acres or less which is improved with a single family residence."

When making or revoking a transfer on death instrument, the owner must have the same capacity required to make a will. Any person who is 18 years or older and is of "sound mind and memory" has the capacity to make a will. 755 ILCS 5/4-1. The requirements for making a transfer on death instrument are as follows:

- The document must contain the "essential elements and formalities of a properly recordable inter vivos deed," although a transfer on death instrument does not require notice, delivery, or consideration to be effective. That means that there must be a grantor, a grantee, a description of the property to be conveyed, language of conveyance, and a signature by the grantor.
- The document must be signed by two witnesses.
- The document must be notarized.
- The document must state that the transfer to the designated beneficiary occur at the owner's death.
- The document must be recorded before the owner's death.
- The beneficiary has a right to either accept or disclaim the transfer on death instrument. If the beneficiary chooses to accept the transfer on death instrument, the beneficiary must sign and file a "notice of death affidavit and acceptance" after the owner's death.

If a notice of death affidavit and acceptance is not filed within two years after the owner's death, then the transfer on death instrument is void and ineffective and the residential real estate will pass to the owner's estate. The act specifies the information needed in the notice of death affidavit and acceptance and provides a sample form.

While the transfer on death instrument must be recorded before the owner's death, the interest in the real estate only transfers on the owner's death. This means that the beneficiary does not have any rights to the real estate while the owner is alive and the beneficiary's creditors cannot place a lien on title to the property. On the other hand, during the owner's life, the owner retains the right to sell or encumber the residential real estate and the owner's creditors can claim an interest in the property, which would transfer to the beneficiary on the owner's death.

Joint owners may also execute a transfer on death instrument and it would not sever a joint tenancy or tenancy by the entirety. If all of the joint owners execute the transfer on death instrument, then it can only be revoked by all of the living joint owners and the last surviving joint owner may revoke the instrument. If less than all of the joint owners execute the transfer on death instrument, then the last surviving joint owner governs the validity of the instrument. If the last joint owner to die did not execute a transfer on death instrument, then any prior joint owner's designation of a beneficiary is ineffective.

The transfer on death instrument is revocable. There are two ways an owner can revoke a transfer on death instrument: with another transfer on death instrument that expressly or by inconsistency revokes the original document; and/or with an instrument of revocation that expressly revokes the original transfer on death instrument.

Similar to the requirements for making the transfer on death instrument, the revocation must be witnessed, notarized and recorded before the owner's death in the public records.

Advantages and Disadvantages of a Transfer on Death Instrument

A transfer on death instrument is less complex and less costly to draft than a living trust. It is also revocable, which gives the owner flexibility to change his or her mind regarding who he or she wants to designate as the beneficiary. Another benefit of the transfer on death instrument is that it allows the owner to retain a present interest in the residential real estate during the owner's life. The beneficiary's creditors cannot burden the property while the owner is alive because interest only transfers on the owner's death.

Alternatively, while the owner is alive, the owner retains the right to sell or encumber the residential real estate. The owner's creditors can claim an interest in the property and liens attached to the property transfer to the beneficiary on the owner's death. Additionally, joint owners can complicate the transfer of real property if not all of the joint owners execute the transfer on death instrument. Generally, the last surviving joint owner dictates whether there will be a beneficiary and who is designated as the beneficiary.

Another disadvantage is that a transfer on death instrument likely cannot avoid estate taxes. Because the instrument is still new in Illinois, no rulings or statements has been made by courts or the legislation. However, states with a similar transfer on death law have announced that a transfer on death of residential real property cannot avoid estate taxes. See below for a discussion of estate taxes and life estates, which may also apply to transfer on death property.

While the transfer on death instrument is intended as a means to bypass probate when transferring an owner's residential real estate, there are obstacles to a probate-free transfer if the designated beneficiary dies before the owner. If the sole designated beneficiary does not survive the owner and is a descendant of the owner, then the residential real estate passes per stirpes to the designated beneficiary's living descendants at the time of the owner's death. However, probate cannot be avoided if the sole designated beneficiary does not survive the owner and is not a descendant of the owner; in this case, the residential real estate passes via the owner's estate. Furthermore, the owner can name more than one beneficiary. If one of the designated beneficiaries does not survive the owner, then the living beneficiaries can take the shares of the deceased beneficiary. If the deceased designated beneficiary is a descendant of the owner, then the deceased beneficiary's living descendants can take the deceased beneficiary's shares per stirpes.

The transfer on death instrument would be most beneficial for small estates, particularly situations where there is one owner and one beneficiary, or between committed partners who are not married or do not have a civil union, or those who do not need the tax benefits of a living trust. For example, a widow might create a transfer on death instrument to transfer her sole asset, a house, to her only child as the beneficiary. This would ensure that the widow retains rights in her house during her lifetime. On her death, the house would transfer to her child while avoiding the delay of probate. A transfer on death instrument can avoid the complexity and expenses of a living trust and the disadvantages of forming a joint tenancy or life estate. These disadvantages will be discussed in the sections below.

Living Trusts

Living trusts are a flexible, private way to manage a person's assets during his life and provides for orderly distribution of the assets after death, while avoiding probate. Living trusts are most beneficial for large estates with many different types of assets to be distributed to multiple beneficiaries. The provisions in a living trust can be adjusted to meet the needs of each specific property owner. The flexibility of the living trust instrument gives the owner great control over the distribution of his property. The living trust document can specify when the beneficiary receives property. For example, the living trust can state that property will be held in trust for the beneficiary until the beneficiary reaches age 25. This condition is effective regardless of whether the owner is alive or dead. On the other hand, a transfer on death instrument only passes residential real estate to the beneficiary on the owner's death.

Another advantage is that the living trust can ensure management of the owner's property during the owner's life as well as after death. If the owner becomes incompetent or disabled, the trustee of the living trust will manage the trust estate on the owner's behalf. On the other hand, a transfer on death instrument does not provide for management of the owner's residential real estate if the owner is alive but unable to manage the estate for himself. If the owner does not have a property power of attorney, the estate will likely be managed by a court-appointed guardian.

A living trust can be structured to avoid estate taxes and prevent creditors of the beneficiary from reaching the assets of the trust. As noted previously, a transfer on death instrument likely cannot avoid estate taxes. Additionally with a transfer on death instrument, after the residential real estate has transferred to the beneficiary on the owner's death, the beneficiary's creditors can reach that residential real estate.

Finally, living trusts can completely bypass probate, even if the beneficiary predeceases the owner. On the other hand, a transfer on death instrument may have to go through the probate process if the sole designated beneficiary predeceases the owner and that deceased beneficiary is not a descendant of the owner.

However, the main disadvantages of a living trust are its complexity and high costs. Because the living trust can be structured to meet the specific needs of a property owner, there are a myriad of ways to prepare the living trust instrument, which could lead to a greater likelihood for ambiguities or mistakes. A lawyer's expertise is is generally necessary to minimize the ambiguities and mistakes that may arise. The process requires careful consideration and analysis, hence the high cost.

Joint Tenancy

A joint tenancy can be created by stating in the deed instrument that the property is held not as tenants in common but with right of survivorship. 765 ILCS 1005/1b. Joint tenancy allows two or more people to share equal ownership of property and have an equal, undivided interest in the property. The right of survivorship provides that if a joint tenant dies, the remainder of the property is transferred to the survivors. This survivorship right is similar to the effect of a transfer on death instrument when the owner dies.

While joint tenancy can avoid probate through right of survivorship, there are many drawbacks to consider. The main disadvantage of a joint tenancy is that one tenant can burden the property independently of the other joint tenants. Because each joint tenant has a present interest and ownership right in the real estate, any creditor of a joint tenant may place a lien on the property. Conversely, a transfer on death instrument does not convey an immediate interest in the beneficiary. Thus, a designated beneficiary's creditors cannot reach the residential real estate until the owner's death.

Decisions regarding joint tenancy property must be made jointly by all of the tenants. This can harm the joint tenants if there is a disagreement regarding how to manage the property. Additionally, a joint tenant can force a partition by conveying or selling his interest in the property to a new owner. This act would break the joint tenancy and the parties would own the property as tenants in common. A distinctive feature of a tenancy in common is that there is no right of survivorship. This would defeat the purpose of a property owner creating a joint tenancy in order to transfer title while avoiding probate.

Note on Tenancy by the Entirety

Tenancy by the entirety is a form of joint tenancy that is only available to a married couple or parties in a civil union. See 765 ILCS 1005/1c. A key advantage of tenancy by the entirety is that one tenant cannot burden the property independently. That is, unlike joint tenancy, creditors of only one tenant cannot place a lien on property held in tenancy by the entirety. Creditors of both tenants can however take the property to satisfy debts owed by both tenants. While tenancy by the entirety can avoid probate, it is inapplicable for owners wishing to transfer property to a beneficiary who is not a spouse or civil union partner.

Life Estates

A life estate gives a person the right to use and enjoy property during that person's life. The owner of the present interest in the life estate property is known as a life tenant. After the life tenant's death, the property reverts to the remainder man, who may be the grantor of the life estate or someone else designated by the grantor. Life estates can be used to avoid probate and ensure that the intended beneficiary receives title to real property. An owner of real estate can transfer title to the property to the intended beneficiary while the owner retains a life estate in the home. The owner then has a present interest in the real estate and the intended beneficiary has a future interest or vested fee simple remainder. When the owner dies, the beneficiary automatically has a fee simple title to the real estate without going through probate. The life estate is easy and inexpensive to create. It requires a deed that creates the life estate and documents to transfer title.

The life tenant has rights to use and enjoy the property as well as the responsibility for the costs of maintenance and taxes on the life estate. A life tenant cannot give a greater interest in the estate than what he owns. Thus, a life tenant cannot give complete and definite ownership to another person because the life tenant's ownership in the property ends at the life tenant's death. Additionally, the life tenant cannot sell the full title to the property without permission of the remainder man. Therefore, the life tenant's limited rights to convey and encumber the life estate means that claims against the life tenant are not liens on the full title to the property. This is distinguished from the transfer on death instrument, where the owner retains all rights to the property and can convey or encumber it during the owner's life, thus affecting the beneficiary's rights without the beneficiary's signature.

Unlike the transfer on death instrument, the life estate is irrevocable. The owner cannot recover the property conveyed to the remainder man unless the remainder man is willing to give it back. Another disadvantage of the life estate is that though the property is conveyed to a remainder man, the property remains in the life tenant's estate for state and federal estate tax purposes. 26 USC § 2036; 20 CFR § 20.2036-1. Thus, neither the life estate nor transfer on death instrument avoids estate taxes. Creation of a life estate may also result in gift tax liability. While a life estate is easy to create and avoids probate, it may be prudent to hire a lawyer to avoid tax liability.

Additionally, it is important to consider the consequences of creating a future interest in a remainder man who may not be alive when the life tenant dies. Complications could arise in determining whose interested has vested. Therefore, a life estate is most beneficial for elderly parents wanting to transfer a house to their child while continuing to live in their home before death. Life estates are also beneficial if the parties involved want to ensure that the property remains in the family by naming remainder men that are closely related to the owner. However, a life tenant has less ability to convey or mortgage the title, which makes the new transfer on death instrument a more attractive option for accomplishing most of the same goals. Of course, the transfer on death instrument is only available for title to residential land whereas a life estate can be used for title to any type of land.

Conclusion

The Illinois transfer on death instrument is a straightforward and inexpensive means to transfer title to residential real estate directly to a beneficiary without going through the probate process. There are other ways to bypass the probate process, such as living trusts, joint tenancies or life estates. Each form of transferring property, while avoiding probate, offers unique advantages and disadvantages. Deciding which form to use will depend on the specific circumstances and needs of the owner of

Forms

Recording requested by:

When recorded mail to and mail tax statements to:

Space above this line for recorder's use

Illinois Transfer on Death Deed

(Beneficiary Deed)

I, ______________________, with a mailing address of ______________________ ______________________________________ (hereinafter referred to as the "Owner") being of competent mind and having the legal capacity to execute this document, as owner transfer on death to ____________________ with a mailing address of ______ ____ (hereinafter referred to as the "Primary Beneficiary") as grantee beneficiary, the following described interest in real estate:

____

____

____

____

____

____

____

Legal description of the property (including square, suffix, and lot number)

If the Primary Beneficiary does not survive me, I designate ______________________ with a mailing address of ____ _________ (hereinafter referred to as the "Alternate Beneficiary") as grantee beneficiary.

This Transfer on Death Deed is revocable. It does not transfer any ownership until the death of the owner. It revokes all prior beneficiary designations by this owner for this

interest in real estate. The grantor has the right to withdraw or rescind this deed at any time. Any beneficiaries named in this deed are hereby advised that this deed may be withdrawn or rescinded whether or not money or any other consideration was paid or given.

______________________	______________________	______________________
Owner's Name	Primary Beneficiary's Name	Alternate Beneficiary's Name
______________________	______________________	______________________
Owner's Signature	Primary Beneficiary's Signature	Alternate Beneficiary's Signature
______________________	______________________	______________________
Date	Date	Date

Notary Acknowledgment

State of ____________________

County of __________________

The foregoing was acknowledged before me this ____ day of ________________, by the undersigned, ________________, who is personally known to me or satisfactorily proven to me to be the person whose name is subscribed to the within instrument.

____
Printed Name of Notary Public

____
Signature of Notary Public

My commission expires: __________________ (seal)

Illinois Transfer on Death Deed Revocation Form

Recording requested by (name): ______________________

When recorded mail to
and mail tax statements to:

____

____

____

____

Recorder's Use Only

REVOCATION OF REVOCABLE TRANSFER ON DEATH DEED

This document is exempt from documentary transfer tax under Rev. & Tax. Code § 11930. This document is exempt from preliminary change of ownership report under Rev. & Tax. Code § 480.3.

Assessor's Parcel No.: ______________________

Declaration of Exemption From Gov't Code § 27388.1 Fee

☐ Transfer is exempt from fee per GC § 27388.1(a)(2):
- ☐ recorded concurrently "in connection with" transfer subject to Documentary Transfer Tax
- ☐ recorded concurrently "in connection with" a transfer of residential dwelling to an owner-occupier

☐ Transfer is exempt from fee per GC 27388.1(a)(1):
- ☐ Fee cap of $225.00 reached ☐ Not related to real property

IMPORTANT NOTICE: THIS FORM MUST BE RECORDED TO BE EFFECTIVE

This revocation form MUST be RECORDED before your death or it will not be effective. This revocation form only affects a transfer on death deed that YOU made. A transfer on death deed made by a co-owner of your property is not affected by this revocation form. A co-owner who wants to revoke a transfer on death deed that he/she made must complete and RECORD a SEPARATE revocation form.

PROPERTY DESCRIPTION

Print the legal description of the property affected by this revocation:

____

____

____

REVOCATION

I, ______________________, am the transferor under the Revocable TOD deed dated ______________ and recorded on ______________ as Instrument No. ______________ in Book/Reel ________, Page/Image ________, of Official Records of ______________________ County, Illinois, which named as beneficiary(ies) ______________________

______________________.

I hereby revoke any TOD deed to transfer the described property that I executed before executing this form, including the TOD deed described above.

SIGNATURE AND DATE

Sign and print your name below (your name should exactly match the name shown on your title documents):

Date: ______________

____
(Signature of declarant)

____
(Typed or written name of declarant)

Notary Acknowledgment

State of ____________________

County of ___________________

The foregoing was acknowledged before me this ____ day of ________________, by the undersigned, ________________, who is personally known to me or satisfactorily proven to me to be the person whose name is subscribed to the within instrument.

____

Printed Name of Notary Public

____

Signature of Notary Public

My commission expires: ___________________ (seal)

Indiana

Table of Contents

Transfer on Death Deed Indiana

The Transfer on Death Property Act, codified at Indiana Code 32-17-14 et. seq., creates a means to plan for the transfer of real property upon death that allows the grantor to transfer their interest in real property without probate.

A transfer on death deed can be a very helpful planning tool when designing an estate plan. Indiana is one of many states that allows the transfer of real property by a transfer on death deed.

The Basics: Transfer on Death Deed

The Transfer on Death Property Act, codified at Indiana Code 32-17-14 et. seq., creates a means to plan for the transfer of real property upon death that allows the grantor to transfer their interest in real property without probate.

Prior to the real property owner's death, the transfer on death deed must: (1) be executed by the owner of the real property, or their legal representative, and (2) be recorded in the county where the real property is located. Indiana Code Section 32-17-14-11. The transfer on death deed does not need to be supported by consideration or delivered to the beneficiary. Upon the owner's death, a properly-executed transfer on death deed will convey the real property to the beneficiary designated in the deed without probate administration. To learn more about what happens when a property owner or loved one dies without a will, please read this blog post.

Beneficiary Responsibility

The transfer on death deed designates a beneficiary, but does not actually complete the transfer of the real property to that beneficiary until the time of the owner's death. The owner of the real property retains full control over the property during their lifetime, meaning the owner can still sell or encumber the property as usual. The owner also has the option to change or revoke the transfer on death deed at any time prior to their death. Additionally, the beneficiary has no responsibility for the property until after the owner's death when the property is conveyed to that beneficiary. The beneficiary will receive an additional benefit of a step-up in basis, in addition to the grant of the real property. The basis for the beneficiary will be the fair market value of the real property upon the date of the owner's death. To finalize the transfer, upon the death of the real property owner, the beneficiary of the transfer on death deed will need to record a simple Affidavit of Survivorship with the county recorder to complete the transfer of title of the property from the owner to the beneficiary.

Securing a Transfer of Death Deed

The use of a transfer of death deed can be useful if the goal is to keep a home out of the probate process, and can work in conjunction with a will or trust. Additionally, a transfer on death deed may be used to transfer an owner's real property to a revocable or irrevocable trust upon the death of the owner. Both options can be very beneficial in the estate planning process. The Estate Planning Group at CCHA offers comprehensive estate planning services. Please consult with one of our experienced estate planning lawyers today.

Indiana TOD Deed Form – Summary

The Indiana TOD deed form allows property to be automatically transferred to a new owner when the current owner dies, without the need to go through probate. It also gives the current owner retained control over the property, including the right to change his or her mind about the transfer.

Special language is required to ensure that the deed qualifies as a TOD deed. This language is automatically included by our deed preparation service and valid in all Indiana counties.

An Indiana TOD deed form allows Indiana property owners to achieve two goals.

It allows the owner to avoid probate at death. Upon the owner's death, the property passes automatically to the beneficiaries named in the deed, without the need for Indiana probate.

It allows the owner to retain control during life. If the owner wants to name new beneficiaries, transfer or lease the property to someone else, or even revoke the deed, he or she may do so freely and without involving the beneficiaries.

These features make a TOD form a popular estate planning tool in Indiana. Since Indiana first authorized TOD deeds on July 1, 2009, TOD deeds have become a popular alternative to living trusts due to the cost savings and simplicity they offer.

Like other Indiana deed forms, a TOD deed transfers Indiana real estate. But unlike most other types of deeds, the TOD does not become effective until the owner's death. Until the owner dies, he or she keeps complete control over the property. At death, the TOD deed becomes effective to transfer the property to the designated beneficiaries.

Unlike some other Indiana deed forms, a TOD deed does not require consideration and need not be delivered or even reported to the beneficiary. The deed may leave property to a trust, allowing the property to ultimately end up in a living trust if that is the owner's intent.

Benefits of Transfer-on-Death Deeds

Indiana TOD deeds offer several important benefits that contribute to their popularity as an estate planning tool. These benefits include:

Probate Avoidance – A TOD deed allows the property to pass to the beneficiaries named in the deed without going through Indiana probate. Indiana law has a $50,000 limit on nonprobate transfers using the small estate procedure. The TOD deed can be used even if the value exceeds $50,000. Depending on the circumstances, it can lower the remaining estate value to under $50,000, allowing the entire estate to pass outside of probate.

Retained Control – A person who makes a TOD deed keeps complete control over the property. He or she can revoke the deed, change the beneficiaries, or sell, mortgage, or lease the property. The beneficiary does not have to consent and need not know that the TOD deed even exists.

Continuity of Ownership – A TOD deed does not change the character of the property in the hands of the owner. The property continues to qualify for any state and federal tax benefits, including homestead exemption, the capital gains exclusion for sale of a principal residence, and the federal gift tax exemption.

Savings in Legal Fees and Costs – As mentioned above, a living trust can also provide many of the same benefits as a TOD deed. But living trusts can be expensive to set up and complicated to administer after death. A TOD deed is a low-cost, low-hassle alternative to a living trust. We make it easy to create your own Indiana Transfer-on-Death Deed. Just complete our user-friendly interview and our software will create a custom, ready-to-file Indiana transfer-on-death deed that includes the right language based on choices you make in the interview. We also include customized, step-by-step instructions for completing the real estate transfer. Documents are delivered instantly.

Other Names for Indiana Transfer-on-Death Deeds

Although the legal name under Indiana law is transfer-on-death deed, these deeds may also be called TOD deeds or simply TODDs. In other states, a similar deed form may be called a beneficiary deed (in Arizona, for example), deed upon death (in Nevada, for example), or transfer-on-death instrument (in Illinois). Each of these names refers to the same type of statutorily created deed that transfers property at an owner's death without requiring probate.

An Indiana life estate deed form may also transfer Indiana real estate at death without going through probate. But life estate deeds have their own drawbacks, the most notable of which is loss of control. A person who creates a life estate deed loses the ability to sell, mortgage, lease, or otherwise deal with the property without involving the remainder beneficiaries. Indiana TOD deed forms avoid this drawback by allowing the owner to retain complete control over the property.

Some states—including Florida, Texas, and Michigan—recognize an enhanced form of life estate deed called a lady bird deed. Although lady bird deeds serve some of the same purposes as TOD deeds, there are differences that have important legal consequences. Lady bird deeds are not used in Indiana.

Relationship of Transfer-on-Death Deed Form to Warranty of Title

Key Term: Warranty of Title. Title issues can be caused by many things, including errors in the public record, unknown liens against the property, undisclosed prior conveyances, forged deeds, missing heirs or unprobated wills, or disputes about boundary lines or surveys. Title issues often require legal action to fix and can decrease the value of real estate. If the property has no title issues, it is said to have clear title. A warranty of title is a legal guarantee from the transferor to the transferee that there are no title issues. If a deed makes a warranty of title, the transferee can sue the transferor over any title issues.

In many states, TOD deeds cannot include a warranty of title. Indiana law is different. Section 32-17-14-11(f) of the Indiana Transfer on Death Property Act allows an Indiana TOD deed to contain a warranty of title.

TOD Deeds with Multiple Owners or Multiple Beneficiaries

An Indiana TOD deed can be from multiple owners. It can also be to multiple new owners (beneficiaries). Indiana law has special rules for multiple owner and multiple beneficiaries.

If the TOD deed is from multiple owners, then the consequences of the deed depend on the form of co-ownership:

- If the owners hold title as tenants in common, then each owner may freely dispose of his or her interest. Any owner that makes a TOD deed may pass his or her interest to the beneficiaries named in the TOD deed.
- If the owners hold title as joint tenants with right of survivorship and only one owner signs the TOD deed, then the signing of that deed severs the joint tenancy. The owners no longer have a joint tenancy with right of survivorship. Instead, the owners will hold title as tenants in common under the rule described above.
- If the owners hold title as joint tenants with right of survivorship and all owners sign the TOD deed, then the deed will transfer the property to the beneficiaries on the death of the last joint tenant. A later conveyance by one owner does not affect the beneficiary designation of the other owner or owners.
- If the owners hold title as tenants by the entirety (a special form of ownership available only to married couples), then a deed by only one owner is invalid. Both spouses must sign in order for the TOD deed to be valid.
- If multiple beneficiaries are named in the TOD deed, then the consequences depend on what is specified in the deed. Our Deed Generator gives several options for dealing with the consequences of transfers to multiple beneficiaries and what happens if a beneficiary dies before the owner.

Situations Where Transfer-on-Death Deeds Cannot Be Used

Because a TOD deed form becomes effective upon death, non-living owners cannot use a TOD deed. If the property is owned by a business, trust, or any other owner other than a living person, the TOD deed cannot be used.

Some states prohibit the use of a power of attorney to create a TOD deed. Section 32-17-14-11(a)(2) of the Indiana Transfer on Death Property Act allows an Indiana TOD deed to be signed by an owner's "legal representative," which presumably would include an agent under a power of attorney. But because the deed must be signed and recorded before death, a TOD deed could not be signed by an owner's legal representative (for example, an executor of the owner's estate) after the owner's death.

How to Create an Indiana Transfer-on-Death Deed

Indiana TOD deeds are authorized by the Transfer on Death Property Act, which includes specific requirements that a deed must meet to qualify as a TOD deed. These requirements include:

- The TOD deed must include the language required to create the transfer that takes effect at death. Code § 32-17-14-11(f).
- The TOD deed must be signed by the owner or the owner's legal representative. Code § 32-17-14-11(a).
- The TOD deed must be recorded with the recorder of deeds in the county where the property is located before the owner's death. Code § 32-17-14-11(a)(2), (b).
- The deed must meet other requirements that apply to other Indiana deed forms, including a valid legal description.

The deeds created by our Deed Generator were attorney-designed with each requirement in mind. Each deed is customized based on the answers provided in the interview and comes with step-by-step instructions for signing and notarizing the deed and completing the transfer with the county recorder's office.

Forms

Recording requested by:

When recorded mail to and mail tax statements to:

Space above this line for recorder's use

Indiana Transfer on Death Deed

(Beneficiary Deed)

I, ______________________, with a mailing address of ________________________ ______________________________________ (hereinafter referred to as the "Owner") being of competent mind and having the legal capacity to execute this document, as owner transfer on death to ______________________ with a mailing address of ______ ____ (hereinafter referred to as the "Primary Beneficiary") as grantee beneficiary, the following described interest in real estate:

____

____

____

____

____

____

____

Legal description of the property (including square, suffix, and lot number)

If the Primary Beneficiary does not survive me, I designate ______________________ with a mailing address of ____ _________ (hereinafter referred to as the "Alternate Beneficiary") as grantee beneficiary.

This Transfer on Death Deed is revocable. It does not transfer any ownership until the death of the owner. It revokes all prior beneficiary designations by this owner for this

interest in real estate. The grantor has the right to withdraw or rescind this deed at any time. Any beneficiaries named in this deed are hereby advised that this deed may be withdrawn or rescinded whether or not money or any other consideration was paid or given.

Owner's Name	Primary Beneficiary's Name	Alternate Beneficiary's Name
Owner's Signature	Primary Beneficiary's Signature	Alternate Beneficiary's Signature
Date	Date	Date

Notary Acknowledgment

State of ____________________

County of __________________

The foregoing was acknowledged before me this ____ day of ________________, by the undersigned, ________________, who is personally known to me or satisfactorily proven to me to be the person whose name is subscribed to the within instrument.

____

Printed Name of Notary Public

____

Signature of Notary Public

My commission expires: __________________ (seal)

Indiana Transfer on Death Deed Revocation Form

Recording requested by (name):

____

When recorded mail to
and mail tax statements to:

____

____

____

____

Recorder's Use Only

REVOCATION OF REVOCABLE TRANSFER ON DEATH DEED

This document is exempt from documentary transfer tax under Rev. & Tax. Code § 11930. This document is exempt from preliminary change of ownership report under Rev. & Tax. Code § 480.3.

Assessor's Parcel No.:

____

Declaration of Exemption From Gov't Code § 27388.1 Fee

☐ Transfer is exempt from fee per GC § 27388.1(a)(2):
  ☐ recorded concurrently "in connection with" transfer subject to Documentary Transfer Tax
  ☐ recorded concurrently "in connection with" a transfer of residential dwelling to an owner-occupier
☐ Transfer is exempt from fee per GC 27388.1(a)(1):
  ☐ Fee cap of $225.00 reached ☐ Not related to real property

IMPORTANT NOTICE: THIS FORM MUST BE RECORDED TO BE EFFECTIVE

This revocation form MUST be RECORDED before your death or it will not be effective. This revocation form only affects a transfer on death deed that YOU made. A transfer on death deed made by a co-owner of your property is not affected by this revocation form. A co-owner who wants to revoke a transfer on death deed that he/she made must complete and RECORD a SEPARATE revocation form.

PROPERTY DESCRIPTION

Print the legal description of the property affected by this revocation:

____

____

____

REVOCATION

I, ______________________________, am the transferor under the Revocable TOD deed dated ______________ and recorded on ______________ as Instrument No. ____________ in Book/Reel ________, Page/Image ________, of Official Records of ______________________________ County, Indiana, which named as beneficiary(ies) ______________________________
____.

I hereby revoke any TOD deed to transfer the described property that I executed before executing this form, including the TOD deed described above.

SIGNATURE AND DATE

Sign and print your name below (your name should exactly match the name shown on your title documents):

Date: ____________________

____
(Signature of declarant)

____
(Typed or written name of declarant)

Notary Acknowledgment

State of ____________________

County of __________________

The foregoing was acknowledged before me this ____ day of ________________, by the undersigned, ________________, who is personally known to me or satisfactorily proven to me to be the person whose name is subscribed to the within instrument.

____

Printed Name of Notary Public

____

Signature of Notary Public

My commission expires: __________________ (seal)

Kansas

Table of Contents

Kansas Transfer on Death Deed

What is a Transfer on Death Deed?

A transfer-on-death (TOD) deed, also called a beneficiary deed, looks like a regular deed used to transfer real estate. But there's a crucial divide: It doesn't take effect until your death. You are free to change your mind and revoke the deed at any time during your life.

For Land, Home, Certain types of oil gas and mineral rights, and Royalties thereof:

A TOD is a document that can be prepared and signed at any time.

- It directs the transfer of your interest in property to another person at the moment of your death.
- It doesn't avoid creditors or SRS Estate Recovery. It doesn't avoid taxes (although only very large estates are taxed in Kansas now).
- It doesn't transfer ownership until your death, so you don't cause possible Medicaid Transfer of Asset penalties.
- You still own your property, so you can sell it at any time.
- Property owned in joint tenancy with right of survivorship is fully transferred to the surviving owner, upon the death of one owner.

Note: You must give an exact legal description of the property, so obtaining a copy of your deed is best.

For Car, Recreational or Other vehicle:

- Transfer on Death Form – this is a label you can have added to your car title.
- It is best to do with when pay your annual vehicle registration.
- Work with the County Treasurer or Tag office to complete the paperwork.
- The vehicle will be transferred to them upon the proof of death of all owners.
- This must be done for each vehicle owned.

Making it official:

A TOD for Land, home, or mineral and oil rights should be filed with the Recorder of Deeds in the county where the real estate is located.

A small fee is included for recording the deed.

You will need a full description of your real estate.

A TOD for Vehicles can be recorded by taking the title to the County Treasurer in the owner's county of residence and paying a fee.

The grantor need not inform the recipient or get their approval to be able to record a TOD.

What are the benefits of a Transfer on Death Deed?

- A TOD allows you to transfer ownership of property after death by naming a recipient and bypassing the probate process. Even if you choose a beneficiary of a piece of property in your will, it will still need to be probated.
- A TOD however will not go through the probate system and transfers the property without the need for court and clerical fees.
- TOD do not replace wills. It is still a good idea to have a valid will in place to properly give out your estate.
- A TOD has a place within an estate plan along with a will but should not replace a will totally.
- A benefit of the TOD is that, because the recipient has no interest in the property until the owner dies, the recipient's creditors cannot reach the property.

In contrast with the transfer of property under a revocable trust or a will, the transfer of property through a TOD deed is much less costly. In some states the cost of probate is great, and in any state a probate proceeding will cost more than the fees related to a TOD deed.

What are possible drawbacks of Transfer on Death Deeds?

A downside of TOD deeds is that people may use them without consulting a lawyer and may make legal mistakes. An owner might name one beneficiary but neglect to arrange for the possibility that the recipient predeceases the owner.

Revoking a TOD?

To revoke a TOD, it must be done formally and in writing.

Simply denying a TOD in a will is not enough to undo the TOD.

Forms

Recording requested by:

When recorded mail to and mail tax statements to:

Space above this line for recorder's use

Kansas Transfer on Death Deed

(Beneficiary Deed)

I, ______________________, with a mailing address of ________________________ ______________________________________ (hereinafter referred to as the "Owner") being of competent mind and having the legal capacity to execute this document, as owner transfer on death to _____________________ with a mailing address of ______ ____ (hereinafter referred to as the "Primary Beneficiary") as grantee beneficiary, the following described interest in real estate:

____

____

____

____

____

____

____

Legal description of the property (including square, suffix, and lot number)

If the Primary Beneficiary does not survive me, I designate ______________________ with a mailing address of ____ _________ (hereinafter referred to as the "Alternate Beneficiary") as grantee beneficiary.

This Transfer on Death Deed is revocable. It does not transfer any ownership until the death of the owner. It revokes all prior beneficiary designations by this owner for this

interest in real estate. The grantor has the right to withdraw or rescind this deed at any time. Any beneficiaries named in this deed are hereby advised that this deed may be withdrawn or rescinded whether or not money or any other consideration was paid or given.

____________________ Owner's Name	____________________ Primary Beneficiary's Name	____________________ Alternate Beneficiary's Name
____________________ Owner's Signature	____________________ Primary Beneficiary's Signature	____________________ Alternate Beneficiary's Signature
____________________ Date	____________________ Date	____________________ Date

Notary Acknowledgment

State of ____________________

County of __________________

The foregoing was acknowledged before me this ____ day of ________________, by the undersigned, ________________, who is personally known to me or satisfactorily proven to me to be the person whose name is subscribed to the within instrument.

____
Printed Name of Notary Public

____
Signature of Notary Public

My commission expires: __________________ (seal)

Kansas Transfer on Death Deed Revocation Form

Recording requested by (name):

____

When recorded mail to
and mail tax statements to:

____

____

____

____

Recorder's Use Only

REVOCATION OF REVOCABLE TRANSFER ON DEATH DEED

This document is exempt from documentary transfer tax under Rev. & Tax. Code § 11930. This document is exempt from preliminary change of ownership report under Rev. & Tax. Code § 480.3.

Assessor's Parcel No.:

____

Declaration of Exemption From Gov't Code § 27388.1 Fee

☐ Transfer is exempt from fee per GC § 27388.1(a)(2):
- ☐ recorded concurrently "in connection with" transfer subject to Documentary Transfer Tax
- ☐ recorded concurrently "in connection with" a transfer of residential dwelling to an owner-occupier

☐ Transfer is exempt from fee per GC 27388.1(a)(1):
- ☐ Fee cap of $225.00 reached ☐ Not related to real property

IMPORTANT NOTICE: THIS FORM MUST BE RECORDED TO BE EFFECTIVE

This revocation form MUST be RECORDED before your death or it will not be effective. This revocation form only affects a transfer on death deed that YOU made. A transfer on death deed made by a co-owner of your property is not affected by this revocation form. A co-owner who wants to revoke a transfer on death deed that he/she made must complete and RECORD a SEPARATE revocation form.

PROPERTY DESCRIPTION

Print the legal description of the property affected by this revocation:

____

____

____

REVOCATION

I, ______________________, am the transferor under the Revocable TOD deed dated ____________ and recorded on ____________ as Instrument No. __________ in Book/Reel ________, Page/Image ________, of Official Records of ______________________ County, Kansas, which named as beneficiary(ies) ______________________________

____.

I hereby revoke any TOD deed to transfer the described property that I executed before executing this form, including the TOD deed described above.

SIGNATURE AND DATE

Sign and print your name below (your name should exactly match the name shown on your title documents):

Date: ________________

____
(Signature of declarant)

____
(Typed or written name of declarant)

Notary Acknowledgment

State of ____________________

County of __________________

The foregoing was acknowledged before me this ____ day of ________________, by the undersigned, ________________, who is personally known to me or satisfactorily proven to me to be the person whose name is subscribed to the within instrument.

____
Printed Name of Notary Public

____
Signature of Notary Public

My commission expires: __________________ (seal)

Maine

Table of Contents

Maine now allows you to leave real estate with transfer-on-death deeds, also called beneficiary deeds. You sign and record the deed now, but it doesn't take effect until your death. You can revoke the deed or sell the property at any time; the beneficiary you name on the deed has no rights until your death.

How do you transfer a deed when someone dies?

In most cases, the surviving owner or heir obtains the title to the home, the former owner's death certificate, a notarized affidavit of death, and a preliminary change of ownership report form. When all these are gathered, the transfer gets recorded, the fees are paid, and the county issues a new title deed

Understanding the Transfer on Death Deed

If you own real property and are looking for a way to avoid probate, you need to understand the benefits of a transfer on death deed. This simple document may help you to simply and inexpensively avoid probate for real estate.

How a TOD Deed Works

In a TOD deed, the current owner designates one or more persons as beneficiary. The beneficiary automatically becomes the owner of the property when the current owner dies. A beneficiary can be an individual or an organization such as a charity. In some states a TOD deed is referred to as a beneficiary deed, TOD instrument or deed upon death.

Advantages of a TOD Deed

Following are a few benefits of the TOD deed compared with other methods of transferring property upon death:

Transfer by Will

Even with a Will, the property must go through probate to be transferred to the new owner. A TOD deed avoids probate.

Joint Ownership

Having someone on the deed as a joint owner with rights of survivorship will avoid probate. Upon the death of one owner, title automatically goes to the surviving joint owner or owners. But all joint owners have equal rights in the property. Therefore, selling or mortgaging the property will require the agreement of all joint owners. With a TOD deed, you keep full control of the property.

Transfer to a Living Trust

While transferring property to a living trust can avoid probate without sacrificing control, setting up a trust requires a more complicated document than a TOD deed. If an attorney prepares the document, creating a living trust will be significantly more expensive than a TOD deed. But for large estates with various types of property, a comprehensive estate plan that includes a living trust may be advantageous.

Other advantages of a TOD deed may include:

Maintaining homestead advantages. Many states offer asset protection and taxation benefits for a person's principal residence. These benefits may be lost with certain types of ownership transfers, but not with a TOD deed.

Tax savings

Designating a beneficiary is not an immediate transfer, so no federal gift tax is owed. The beneficiary acquires ownership on the current owner's date of death. If the beneficiary later sells the property, any capital gain will be based upon the value of the property at the original owner's date of death, not the value when the original owner acquired the property.

Maintaining Medicaid Eligibility

If a person applying for Medicaid has made a gift of property within a certain period before applying, that gift may delay the receipt of benefits. Upon a Medicaid recipient's death, the government may seek reimbursement from the recipient's probate estate. A TOD deed is not usually considered a gift of the property, nor is the property part of the probate estate subject to reimbursement.

Creating a Transfer on Death Deed

As with any real estate deed, the document must comply with state law. All real estate deeds must include certain information, such as the names of the grantor (current owner) and grantee (beneficiary), legal description of the property, signature of the grantor, and legally required witness and notary provisions. Other requirements may include minimum type size and formatting to allow space for recording stamps.

Special language must be used to create a TOD deed, clearly stating the name of the beneficiary, who is usually referred to as the "grantee beneficiary," and that transfer will take place upon the death of the current owner.

Prior to the death of the current owner, the TOD deed must be recorded in the property records of the county where the property is located. This is simply a matter of taking the original TOD deed to the county public records office — usually the county clerk or register of deeds — and paying a small fee. The records clerk will take the deed, stamp it to indicate the date it was received, take whatever other action is necessary to have it officially entered in the county records and return the original to you.

How does property get transferred after death?

In most states, the property will completely avoid Probate and be transferred directly to the surviving owner. This process is completed through a legal arrangement called joint tenancy with right of survivorship. ... When one spouse dies, the property can automatically transfer ownership to the other spouse.

Forms

Recording requested by:

When recorded mail to and mail tax statements to:

Space above this line is for recorder's use

Maine Transfer on Death Deed

(Beneficiary Deed)

I, ________________________, with a mailing address of ______________________________

______________________________________ (hereinafter referred to as the "Owner") being of competent mind and having the legal capacity to execute this document, as owner transfer on death to ____________________ with a mailing address of ______________________________

______________________________________ (hereinafter referred to as the "Primary Beneficiary") as a grantee beneficiary, the following described interest in the real estate:

____

____

____

Legal description of the property (including square, suffix, and lot number)

If the Primary Beneficiary does not survive me, I designate ______________________________

with a mailing address of ____

_______________ (hereinafter referred to as the "Alternate Beneficiary") as grantee beneficiary.

This Transfer on Death Deed is revocable. It does not transfer any ownership until the death of the owner. It revokes all prior beneficiary designations by this owner for this interest in real estate. The grantor has the right to withdraw or rescind this deed at any time. Any beneficiaries' names in this deed are hereby advised that this deed may be withdrawn or rescinded whether or not money or any other consideration was paid or given.

____________________	____________________	____________________
Owner's Name	Primary Beneficiary's Name	Alternate Beneficiary's Name
____________________	____________________	____________________
Owner's Signature	Primary Beneficiary's Signature	Alternate Beneficiary's Signature
____________________	____________________	____________________
Date	Date	Date

Notary Acknowledgement

State of _______________

County of _____________

The foregoing was acknowledged before me this ____ day of ______________, by the undersigned, ____________________, who is personally known to me or satisfactorily proven to me to be the person whose name is subscribed to the within instrument.

____

Printed Name of Notary Public

____

Signature of Notary Public

My commission expires: __________________ (seal)

Maine Transfer on Death Deed Revocation Form

Recording requested by (name):

____

When recorded mail to
and mail tax statements to:

____

____

____

____

Recorder's Use Only

REVOCATION OF REVOCABLE TRANSFER ON DEATH DEED

This document is exempt from documentary transfer tax under Rev. & Tax. Code § 11930. This document is exempt from preliminary change of ownership report under Rev. & Tax. Code § 480.3.

Assessor's Parcel No.: ____________________________________

Declaration of Exemption From Gov't Code § 27388.1 Fee

- ☐ Transfer is exempt from fee per GC § 27388.1(a)(2):
  - ☐ recorded concurrently "in connection with" transfer subject to Documentary Transfer Tax
  - ☐ recorded concurrently "in connection with" a transfer of residential dwelling to an owner-occupier
- ☐ Transfer is exempt from fee per GC 27388.1(a)(1):
  - ☐ Fee cap of $225.00 reached ☐ Not related to real property

IMPORTANT NOTICE: THIS FORM MUST BE RECORDED TO BE EFFECTIVE

This revocation form MUST be RECORDED before your death or it will not be effective. This revocation form only affects a transfer on death deed that YOU made. A transfer on death deed made by a co-owner of your property is not affected by this revocation form. A co-owner who wants to revoke a transfer on death deed that he/she made must complete and RECORD a SEPARATE revocation form.

PROPERTY DESCRIPTION

Print the legal description of the property affected by this revocation:

____

____

____

REVOCATION

I, ___________________________________, am the transferor under the Revocable TOD deed dated ________________ and recorded on ________________ as Instrument No. ______________ in Book/Reel ________, Page/Image ________, of Official Records of ____________________________________ County, Maine, which named as beneficiary(ies) ____.

I hereby revoke any TOD deed to transfer the described property that I executed before executing this form, including the TOD deed described above.

SIGNATURE AND DATE

Sign and print your name below (your name should exactly match the name shown on your title documents):

Date: ______________________ ____

(Signature of declarant)

____

(Typed or written name of declarant)

ACKNOWLEDGMENT

A Notary Public or other officer completing this certificate verifies only the identity of the individual who signed the document to which this certificate is attached, and not the truthfulness, accuracy, or validity of that document.

State of Maine)
County of ____________________)

On ________________________ before me, ________________________________
(insert name and title of the officer)

Personally appeared

____

who proved to me on the basis of satisfactory evidence to be the person(s) whose name(s) is/are subscribed to the within instrument and acknowledged to me that she/he/they executed the same in his/her/their authorized capacity(ies), and by his/her/their signature(s) on the instrument the person(s), or the entity upon behalf of which the person(s) acted, executed the instrument.

I certify under PENALTY OF PERJURY under the laws of the State of Maine that the foregoing paragraph is true and correct.

Witness me hand and official seal. **(Seal)**

Signature ______________________________________

Michigan

Table of Contents

Michigan does not allow **real estate** to be **transferred** with **transfer-on-death deeds**. There is a type of **deed** available in **Michigan** known as an enhanced life estate **deed**, or "Lady Bird" **deed**, that functions like a **transfer-on-death deed**. This type of **deed** is not common.

Lady Bird Deeds

A "Lady Bird" deed offers a simple way to transfer real estate at your death, without probate. If you're shopping around for a way to avoid probate for your house or other real estate, you may run across something called a "Lady Bird" deed. It offers a simple, inexpensive way to transfer real estate at your death, without probate.

A Lady Bird deed may be a good idea if you think you might need Medicaid, the joint state-federal program that helps many Americans with nursing home costs. It may help preserve your eligibility for Medicaid and keep assets in the family that otherwise would be taken by the state to repay the cost of Medicaid benefits you receive during your life. These deeds have some drawbacks, however, and they are used only in a few states.

How a Lady Bird Deed Works

These deeds are also called "enhanced life estate" deeds. With a standard life estate deed, you could name a beneficiary to inherit your property while you keep ownership of it for your lifetime, but with significant restrictions. You wouldn't have the right to sell or mortgage the property, and you might also be liable to the beneficiary you named if you greatly decreased the value of the property—for example, let a house fall into serious disrepair.

By contrast, an enhanced life estate deed (the Lady Bird deed), lets you: avoid probate of the property keep the right to use and profit from the property for your lifetime keep the right to sell the property at any time avoid making a gift that might be subject to federal gift tax avoid jeopardizing your eligibility for Medicaid in some states, prevent the property from being sold, after your death, to repay the cost of Medicaid benefits you received

Alternatives to Lady Bird Deeds

These deeds aren't used in most states, but estate planners sometimes use them in a few states, including Florida, Michigan, and Texas. If you're interested in using one, you should talk to a local lawyer, to see whether it is authorized by law where you live and whether it's a good idea in your particular situation. Local custom can be important; in some places, title companies may be reluctant to insure property transferred this way.

In states that specifically authorize transfer-on-death deeds, that may be a simpler and more readily accepted way to avoid probate and also get the Medicare-related benefits of a Lady Bird deed.

And Where Did That Name Come From?

Finally, if you're wondering how the deed got its odd name, it's not because President Lyndon Johnson ever used this kind of deed to transfer property to his wife, Lady Bird. According to Texas Tech law professor Gerry Beyer, the Florida lawyer who created the deed in the 1980s used the names of the Johnson family in an example showing how the deed worked—and the name stuck.

A Michigan lady bird deed form allows a person to retain control over Michigan real estate during his or her life and automatically transfer the real estate at his or her death. The property transfer occurs automatically at the prior owner's death, avoiding probate.

Michigan lady bird deeds work by dividing ownership into lifetime and future interests. When a person creates a lady bird deed, she transfers property to herself for the rest of her life. This creates the lifetime interest, called a *life estate*. The person who holds a life estate is called the *life tenant*.

The deed also identifies at least one other party—called a *remainderman* or *remainder beneficiary*—to inherit the real estate at death. The life estate deed may designate multiple remainder beneficiaries, and the remainder beneficiaries may include people, trusts, or organizations.

During the life tenant's life, the life tenant retains control of the property. This control includes the right to sell, gift, mortgage, or otherwise dispose of the property without the life tenant's involvement.

At the life tenant's death, the title transfers to the remainder beneficiaries. The transfer happens automatically, without the need to probate the property. Michigan is one of only five states that recognizes lady bird deeds. The other states include Florida, Texas, Vermont, and West Virginia.

Other Names for Michigan Lady Bird Deeds

Although this deed is most commonly known as a *lady bird deed*, the technical name is *enhanced life estate deed*. The deed is "enhanced" in the sense that, unlike a traditional life estate deed, it provides the life tenant with retained control over the property. These deeds are also called *ladybird deeds*, with no space between "lady" and "bird."

Benefits of Michigan Lady Bird Deeds

Michigan lady bird deeds have several benefits that make them ideal planning tools for Michigan property owners that want to transfer real estate at death without going through probate.

Avoiding Michigan Probate.

Most people that use Michigan lady bird deeds do so to avoid probate. A properly drafted Michigan lady bird deed will pass automatically to the remainder beneficiaries on the death of the life tenant, without the need to probate the property. Many benefits described below—such as tax savings and Medicaid planning—depend on the probate avoidance feature.

1. Retaining Control. Given a choice, most people would prefer to keep control of their property while they are still alive. As discussed below, traditional life estate deeds forfeit control. A Michigan lady bird deed avoids this problem by giving the owner (life tenant) retained control to sell, mortgage, or gift the property without involving the remainder beneficiaries.

2. Medicaid Asset Protection. The Michigan Department of Health & Human Services—the agency that that administers Michigan's Medicaid program—has expressly approved the use of lady bird deeds. Because property transferred by lady bird deed is not part of the probate estate, it is not subject to Medicaid recovery after the owner's death. A transfer by lady bird deed is not considered a "divestment" when calculating the Medicaid penalty period for purposes of qualifying for nursing home care.

4. Retaining Homestead Exemption. Because a Michigan lady bird deed does not transfer ownership until death, it does not affect the owner's homestead (principal residence) exemption. Property that qualifies for homestead exemption before the transfer continues to be eligible for homestead exemption after the transfer.

5. Saving Property Taxes. A Michigan lady bird deed is not considered a *transfer of ownership* for property tax purposes. This means that the transfer will not cause a reassessment of the property or trigger an "uncapping" of the taxable value of the property.

6. Saving Legal Fees. A living trust provides many of the same benefits as a lady bird deed but requires additional cost and complication. A lady bird deed can accomplish many of the same objectives as a living trust—including retaining control during life and avoiding probate at death—without the complication of a living trust.

Relationship of Lady Bird Deed Form to Warranty of Title

The designation of a deed as a *lady bird deed* (or *enhanced life estate deed*) deals exclusively with the estate planning feature (control during life and probate avoidance at death). Other deeds are named after the warranty of title they provide. These types of deeds include quitclaim deeds, covenant deeds, and warranty deeds.

Because the names for these kinds of deeds are based on different features, a single deed may be appropriately called by multiple names. For example, a deed can be both a lady bird deed and a quitclaim deed.

Comparison of Michigan Lady Bird Deeds to Traditional Life Estate Deeds

The Michigan lady bird deed form is a spin on the traditional life estate deed form. Regular life estate deeds have historically been the go-to instrument for transferring property automatically at death. But traditional life estate deeds have a significant drawback: Loss of control. A person who conveys property using a conventional life estate deed cannot change her mind without involving the remainder beneficiary.

Example: Ashley creates a conventional life estate deed that transfers her home to Ashley as the life tenant Brett as the remainder beneficiary. The next year, while Ashley is still alive, she decides that she wants to sell her home and buy a different one. Because Ashley used a traditional life estate deed form, she cannot sell her home without Brett's consent. If Brett is unwilling or unable to sign (due to disability for example), Ashley cannot transfer the property.

In this scenario, most people prefer to retain control of property during life. This loss of control is a significant reason life estate deeds are rarely used. Lady bird deeds fix this problem. Like a traditional life estate deed, a lady bird deed automatically transfers property at death. But the *enhanced* feature of a lady bird deed also gives the original owner the right to change his or her mind without involving the remainder beneficiaries.

Comparison of Michigan Lady Bird Deed to Living Trust

Sometimes a living trust can be an alternative to a Michigan lady bird deed. Like a lady bird deed, a living trust allows the transferor to retain control during life and avoid probate at death. But living trusts are, by comparison, relatively expensive. An attorney is often needed to draft the trust instrument and related documents, and the deed is still required to transfer the property into the trust. A lady bird deed can avoid this expense and hassle.

How to Create a Michigan Lady Bird Deed

Although lady bird deeds have their roots in common law, the most common type of Michigan lady bird deed form is based on Michigan Title Standards (6th Edition), available on the Michigan state bar's website. Standard 9.3 states:

The holder of a life estate, coupled with an absolute power to dispose of the fee estate by inter vivos conveyance, can convey a fee simple estate during the lifetime of the holder. If the power is not exercised, the gift over becomes effective.

This standard is important because of the role of title insurance in real estate transactions. As a practical matter, whether a deed is valid depends on whether a title insurance company will recognize the deed. The reason that lady bird deeds are not used in other states is that title insurance companies in those states don't recognize them. This is not a problem in Michigan since the Michigan Title Standards explicitly recognize lady bird deeds.

Michigan lady bird deeds must meet the requirements of other deeds. These requirements include:

- A valid legal description;
- The warranty of title provided by the deed;
- A statement of the consideration provided, if any;
- Margins and spacing that meet the requirements of Michigan's recording laws;
- Signature and notary acknowledgments that comply with Michigan law; and
- The form of co-ownership if multiple remainder beneficiaries are named.
- Like other deeds, lady bird deeds are valid when signed and delivered and should be recorded as soon as possible.

When preparing a Michigan lady bird deed, it is important to use correct language and format. Failure to do so could cause additional recording costs or refusal to register the deed. In some situations, improper drafting can invalidate the transfer or require costly court proceedings to straighten out title issues. The lady bird deeds prepared by our Deed Generator were designed by attorneys to meet all Michigan requirements.

Forms

Recording requested by

When recorded mail to and mail tax statements to:

Space above this line for recorder's use

Michigan Transfer on Death Deed

(Beneficiary Deed)

I, ______________________, with a mailing address of ________________________ ______________________________________ (hereinafter referred to as the "Owner") being of competent mind and having the legal capacity to execute this document, as owner transfer on death to ______________________ with a mailing address of ______ ____ (hereinafter referred to as the "Primary Beneficiary") as grantee beneficiary, the following described interest in real estate:

____

____

____

____

____

____

____

Legal description of the property (including square, suffix, and lot number)

If the Primary Beneficiary does not survive me, I designate ______________________ with a mailing address of ____ _________ (hereinafter referred to as the "Alternate Beneficiary") as grantee beneficiary.

This Transfer on Death Deed is revocable. It does not transfer any ownership until the death of the owner. It revokes all prior beneficiary designations by this owner for this

interest in real estate. The grantor has the right to withdraw or rescind this deed at any time. Any beneficiaries named in this deed are hereby advised that this deed may be withdrawn or rescinded whether or not money or any other consideration was paid or given.

______________________	______________________	______________________
Owner's Name	Primary Beneficiary's Name	Alternate Beneficiary's Name
______________________	______________________	______________________
Owner's Signature	Primary Beneficiary's Signature	Alternate Beneficiary's Signature
______________________	______________________	______________________
Date	Date	Date

Notary Acknowledgment

State of ____________________

County of __________________

The foregoing was acknowledged before me this ____ day of ________________, by the undersigned, ________________, who is personally known to me or satisfactorily proven to me to be the person whose name is subscribed to the within instrument.

____
Printed Name of Notary Public

____
Signature of Notary Public

My commission expires: __________________ (seal)

Michigan Lady Bird Deed Revocation Form

Recording requested by (name): ________________________________ When recorded mail to and mail tax statements to: ________________________________ ________________________________ ________________________________ ________________________________	Recorder's Use Only

REVOCATION OF REVOCABLE LADY BIRD DEED

This document is exempt from documentary transfer tax under Rev. & Tax. Code § 11930. This document is exempt from preliminary change of ownership report under Rev. & Tax. Code § 480.3.

Assessor's Parcel No.: ________________________________

Declaration of Exemption From Gov't Code § 27388.1 Fee

☐ Transfer is exempt from fee per GC § 27388.1(a)(2):
- ☐ recorded concurrently "in connection with" transfer subject to Documentary Transfer Tax
- ☐ recorded concurrently "in connection with" a transfer of residential dwelling to an owner-occupier

☐ Transfer is exempt from fee per GC 27388.1(a)(1):
- ☐ Fee cap of $225.00 reached ☐ Not related to real property

IMPORTANT NOTICE: THIS FORM MUST BE RECORDED TO BE EFFECTIVE

This revocation form MUST be RECORDED before your death or it will not be effective. This revocation form only affects a transfer on death deed that YOU made. A transfer on death deed made by a co-owner of your property is not affected by this revocation form. A co-owner who wants to revoke a transfer on death deed that he/she made must complete and RECORD a SEPARATE revocation form.

PROPERTY DESCRIPTION

Print the legal description of the property affected by this revocation:

____

____

____

REVOCATION

I, ________________________________, am the transferor under the Revocable Lady Bird deed dated ________________ and recorded on ________________ as Instrument No. ______________ in Book/Reel ________, Page/Image ________, of Official Records of ______________________________________ County Michigan, which named as beneficiary(ies) ____.

I hereby revoke any Lady Bird deed to transfer the described property that I executed before executing this form, including the Lady Bird deed described above.

SIGNATURE AND DATE

Sign and print your name below (your name should exactly match the name shown on your title documents):

Date: ____________________

____
(Signature of declarant)

____
(Typed or written name of declarant)

Notary Acknowledgment

State of ____________________

County of __________________

The foregoing was acknowledged before me this ____ day of ________________, by the undersigned, ________________, who is personally known to me or satisfactorily proven to me to be the person whose name is subscribed to the within instrument.

____

Printed Name of Notary Public

____

Signature of Notary Public

My commission expires: __________________ (seal)

Minnesota

Table of Contents

Transfer on Death Deed

A transfer-on-death deed (TODD) allows for the transfer of title of real property to a named beneficiary at the death of the owner, or the last to die of multiple owners.

Is a transfer on death deed a good idea?

If you'd like to avoid having your property going through the probate process, it's a good idea to look into a transfer on death deed. A transfer on death deed allows you to select a beneficiary who will receive your property, but only when you've passed away.

What does a transfer on death deed do?

A Transfer on Death Deed lets you keep all ownership rights to the property during your lifetime, so you can sell it or use is as collateral on a loan. When you die, your property interest passes to the person you named in the Transfer on Death Deed (the "beneficiary") without any probate action.

Do you pay taxes on transfer on death?

The amount that's in a TOD account at the time of your death is not taxable under federal law to the person who receives the account, although it may be taxable to your estate. If your beneficiary or the account are in a state with an inheritance tax, he may have to pay that.

Is transfer on death considered an inheritance?

Because TOD accounts are still part of the decedent's estate (although not the probate estate that the Last Will establishes), they may be subject to income, estate and/or inheritance tax. TOD accounts are also not out of reach for the decedent's creditors or other relatives.

How does a TOD account work?

So, how do Transfer on Death accounts work? A TOD account automatically transfers the assets to a named beneficiary, when the account holder dies. Your son is the beneficiary for the TOD account. When you die, the account's assets are transferred directly to him without having to go through probate.

Are transfer on death deeds revocable?

The transfer on death deed is fully revocable before the death of the real property owner.

What is the difference between POD and TOD?

A POD account is very similar to a transfer-on-death (TOD) arrangement but deals with a person's bank assets instead of their stocks, bonds, mutual funds, or other investment assets. 2 Both POD and TOD agreements offer quick means of dispersing assets, as both avoid the probate process, which can take several months.

Does transfer on death avoid estate tax?

Estate Taxes

When someone dies and their property transfers to their beneficiaries, the federal government impose an estate tax on the value of all that property. Since the transfer on death account is not a trust, it does not help you avoid or minimize estate taxes.

Does a TOD supersede a will?

A TOD designation supersedes a will. For bank accounts, you can set up a similar account known as payable-on-death, sometimes referred to as a Totten trust. Your beneficiaries can't touch the account while you're alive, and you're free to change beneficiaries or close the accounts at any time.

Can I withdraw money from my own TOD account?

This account is wholly owned by both spouses while they're both alive. As a result, a creditor of one spouse could make a claim against the entire account, without any approval or say from the other spouse. Either spouse could also withdraw all the money in the account and not tell the other.

What is the difference between beneficiary and transfer on death?

A beneficiary form states who will directly inherit the asset at your death. Under a TOD arrangement, you keep full control of the asset during your lifetime and pay taxes on any income the asset generates as you own it outright. TOD arrangements require minimal paperwork to establish.

Is a TOD a retirement account?

Understanding Transfer on Death (TOD)

Individual retirement accounts, 401(k)s, and other retirement accounts are TOD. The Uniform Transfer on Death Securities Registration Act lets owners name beneficiaries for their stocks, bonds, or brokerage accounts. The process is similar to a payable-on-death bank account.

Can a TOD be contested?

But whatever you do, a lawsuit to challenge a TOD Deed must be filed within three years of the property owner's death. The bottom line: you have the right to contest a TOD Deed, just as you can a Will or Trust, but in many cases that will be no easy task

Can a POA add a TOD?

The transfer on death deed statute specifically prohibits an agent acting under a power of attorney from creating a transfer on death deed.

What states allow transfer on death accounts?

States that allow TOD deeds are Alaska, Arizona, Arkansas, California, Colorado, District of Columbia, Hawaii, Illinois, Indiana, Kansas, Maine, Minnesota, Mississippi, Missouri, Montana, Nebraska, Nevada, New Mexico, North Dakota, Ohio, Oklahoma, Oregon, South Dakota, Texas, Utah, Virginia, Washington, West Virginia.

What happens if TOD beneficiary dies?

In the event that there are no living beneficiaries, life insurance policies, TOD and POD accounts will go to the decedent's estate. If the beneficiary outlives the person creating the estate plan, but dies before receiving the gift, the gift will go to the probate estate of the deceased beneficiary.

Can you put a TOD on a joint account?

TOD becomes effective for joint accounts if both owners pass away simultaneously. Joint and TOD registration generally allow an account to pass outside the probate estate, enabling the surviving owner or beneficiaries to avoid the time and expense of that process for this account.

Does transfer on death trump a will?

If you leave a transfer on death account to a beneficiary but also put in your will that you leave that specific account to someone else, the documentation will supersede your will. The account creates a contract. Your will is not a contract and, therefore, the asset will not pass according to your will.

Forms

Recording requested by:

When recorded mail to and mail tax statements to:

Space above this line for recorder's use

Minnesota Transfer on Death Deed
(Beneficiary Deed)

I, ______________________, with a mailing address of ________________________ ______________________________________ (hereinafter referred to as the "Owner") being of competent mind and having the legal capacity to execute this document, as owner transfer on death to ______________________ with a mailing address of _____ ____ (hereinafter referred to as the "Primary Beneficiary") as grantee beneficiary, the following described interest in real estate:

____

____

____

____

____

____

____

Legal description of the property (including square, suffix, and lot number)

If the Primary Beneficiary does not survive me, I designate ______________________ with a mailing address of ____ _________ (hereinafter referred to as the "Alternate Beneficiary") as grantee beneficiary.

This Transfer on Death Deed is revocable. It does not transfer any ownership until the death of the owner. It revokes all prior beneficiary designations by this owner for this

interest in real estate. The grantor has the right to withdraw or rescind this deed at any time. Any beneficiaries named in this deed are hereby advised that this deed may be withdrawn or rescinded whether or not money or any other consideration was paid or given.

______________________ Owner's Name	______________________ Primary Beneficiary's Name	______________________ Alternate Beneficiary's Name
______________________ Owner's Signature	______________________ Primary Beneficiary's Signature	______________________ Alternate Beneficiary's Signature
______________________ Date	______________________ Date	______________________ Date

Notary Acknowledgment

State of ____________________

County of __________________

The foregoing was acknowledged before me this ____ day of ________________, by the undersigned, ________________, who is personally known to me or satisfactorily proven to me to be the person whose name is subscribed to the within instrument.

____
Printed Name of Notary Public

____
Signature of Notary Public

My commission expires: __________________ (seal)

Minnesota Transfer on Death Deed Revocation Form

Recording requested by (name):

____

When recorded mail to
and mail tax statements to:

____

____

____

____

Recorder's Use Only

REVOCATION OF REVOCABLE TRANSFER ON DEATH DEED

This document is exempt from documentary transfer tax under Rev. & Tax. Code § 11930. This document is exempt from preliminary change of ownership report under Rev. & Tax. Code § 480.3.

Assessor's Parcel No.:

____

Declaration of Exemption From Gov't Code § 27388.1 Fee

☐ Transfer is exempt from fee per GC § 27388.1(a)(2):
  ☐ recorded concurrently "in connection with" transfer subject to Documentary Transfer Tax
  ☐ recorded concurrently "in connection with" a transfer of residential dwelling to an owner-occupier

☐ Transfer is exempt from fee per GC 27388.1(a)(1):
  ☐ Fee cap of $225.00 reached ☐ Not related to real property

IMPORTANT NOTICE: THIS FORM MUST BE RECORDED TO BE EFFECTIVE

This revocation form MUST be RECORDED before your death or it will not be effective. This revocation form only affects a transfer on death deed that YOU made. A transfer on death deed made by a co-owner of your property is not affected by this revocation form. A co-owner who wants to revoke a transfer on death deed that he/she made must complete and RECORD a SEPARATE revocation form.

PROPERTY DESCRIPTION

Print the legal description of the property affected by this revocation:

____

____

____

REVOCATION

I, ____________________________, am the transferor under the Revocable TOD deed dated ______________ and recorded on ______________ as Instrument No. ______________ in Book/Reel ________, Page/Image ________, of Official Records of ______________________________ County Minnesota, which named as beneficiary(ies) ____.

I hereby revoke any TOD deed to transfer the described property that I executed before executing this form, including the TOD deed described above.

SIGNATURE AND DATE

Sign and print your name below (your name should exactly match the name shown on your title documents):

Date: ____________________

____
(Signature of declarant)

____
(Typed or written name of declarant)

Notary Acknowledgment

State of ____________________

County of __________________

The foregoing was acknowledged before me this ____ day of ________________, by the undersigned, ________________, who is personally known to me or satisfactorily proven to me to be the person whose name is subscribed to the within instrument.

____
Printed Name of Notary Public

____
Signature of Notary Public

My commission expires: __________________ (seal)

Mississippi

Table of Contents

Until recently, Mississippi law did not recognize transfer-on-death deeds. However, with the passage of SB 2851, the Mississippi legislature created statutory guidelines for "Transfer on Death Deeds" in Mississippi. SB 2851 was signed into law on June 29, 2020, by Governor Reeves and became effective July 1, 2020. The "Mississippi Real Property Transfer on Death Act" provides the requirements for using a transfer on death deed ("TODD") in Mississippi.

What is a TODD?

A TODD is a legal document that transfers an individual's interest in real property to one or more designated beneficiaries effective at the transferor's death. The TODD requires the property owner (the "transferor") to name a person (the "beneficiary") to whom the property will automatically transfer at the death of the transferor. The creation and filing of a TODD does not impact the rights of the transferor while living. In other words, the transferor retains all rights and control over the property, including the right to sell, transfer, encumber, and use the property. A TODD does not change ownership of or rights to the property until the death of the transferor.

Who can execute a TODD?

In order to execute a valid TODD, the transferor must have the capacity to make a contract. A TODD cannot be created through the use of a power of attorney, unless the power of attorney expressly authorizes it.

What can be transferred by a TODD?

Any real property in Mississippi may be transferred by a TODD.

What must be included in a TODD?

A TODD must contain the essential elements of a recordable deed and must also state the transfer of real property to a designated beneficiary (or beneficiaries) is to take place at the death of the transferor. Unlike other deeds, there is no requirement that a deed be delivered to or accepted by the beneficiary. A TODD is effective if executed by the grantor and filed, without any action by or even knowledge of a beneficiary.

What must be done with a TODD?

In order to be effective, a TODD must be executed and recorded before the transferor's death in the land records in the official records of the chancery clerk of the county where the property is located. If the TODD is not recorded prior to death, it is not effective.

Can a TODD be revoked?

Unlike other deeds, a TODD is revocable. In order for a transferor to revoke a TODD, the transferor must file an instrument of revocation expressly revoking the TODD or may execute and file a subsequent TODD that revokes all or part of the prior TODD either by expressly revoking or by inconsistency between the two TODDs. Any subsequent revocation must be recorded prior to the transferor's death in order to be effective. A will does not revoke or supersede a transfer-on-death deed. If a transferor and a designated beneficiary were married when a TODD was created and subsequently divorce, the TODD is revoked only if the final judgment of divorce is recorded in the land records where the TODD is recorded prior to the death of the transferor. The mere fact that a divorce occurred would not revoke the TODD.

What other rights are affected by a TODD?

Certain property transfers can impact rights of a transferor. Here is how a TODD may or may not impact the most common of these rights:

- A TODD does not affect the transferor's right to claim the property as their homestead.
- A TODD does not affect any property tax exemptions afforded to the transferor (i.e. over 65 years old exemption).
- A TODD does not affect the rights of creditors of the transferor.
- A TODD does not trigger a "due on sale" or similar clause in a mortgage or other type of loan document.
- A TODD does not subject the property to claims of a creditor of the beneficiary.

Because a TODD does not transfer ownership of the property until the death of the transferor, the property receives a step-up in basis adjustment at the transferor's death.

Since the TODD is not a completed gift until the death of the transferor, it is not considered a taxable event for the purposes of gift taxes.

What action must the beneficiary take at the transferor's death?

At the death of the transferor, a beneficiary must record an affidavit of death in the deed records in order to become the legal owner of the property.

What are the pros of a TODD?

A TODD can be attractive as a means to transfer ownership of real property quickly and affordably without going through the probate process. A TODD allows the transferor to keep control over the property during his or her lifetime and allows the transferor to revoke the TODD at any time.

What are the cons of a TODD?

Because TODDs are so new, there is simply not very much law related to these instruments, which may lead to uncertainty for lawyers and clients alike. One potential downside of a TODD is the recording requirement for both the TODD itself and any revocation of the TODD. If a transferor fails to properly record the document prior to his or her death, it is ineffective and that could lead to unintended consequences at the transferor's death. Another potential downside is that people may not understand the concept that a TODD trumps a will if both address the same property, which again could lead to unintended consequences is a TODD was executed in addition to a will. Finally, and probably most importantly, is that a TODD is subject to claims of creditors and estate taxes. Thus, before the designated beneficiary may rely on the deed, they must either probate the transferor's estate or wait, in the case of claims of unsecured creditors, 3 years and 90 days, or in the case of federal estate taxes, 10 years.

Forms

Recording requested by:

When recorded mail to and mail tax statements to:

Space above this line for recorder's use

Mississippi Transfer on Death Deed
(Beneficiary Deed)

I, ______________________, with a mailing address of _________________________ ______________________________________ (hereinafter referred to as the "Owner") being of competent mind and having the legal capacity to execute this document, as owner transfer on death to ______________________ with a mailing address of ______ ____ (hereinafter referred to as the "Primary Beneficiary") as grantee beneficiary, the following described interest in real estate:

____

____

____

____

____

____

____

Legal description of the property (including square, suffix, and lot number)

If the Primary Beneficiary does not survive me, I designate ______________________ with a mailing address of ____ _________ (hereinafter referred to as the "Alternate Beneficiary") as grantee beneficiary.

This Transfer on Death Deed is revocable. It does not transfer any ownership until the death of the owner. It revokes all prior beneficiary designations by this owner for this

interest in real estate. The grantor has the right to withdraw or rescind this deed at any time. Any beneficiaries named in this deed are hereby advised that this deed may be withdrawn or rescinded whether or not money or any other consideration was paid or given.

Owner's Name	Primary Beneficiary's Name	Alternate Beneficiary's Name
Owner's Signature	Primary Beneficiary's Signature	Alternate Beneficiary's Signature
Date	Date	Date

Notary Acknowledgment

State of ____________________

County of __________________

The foregoing was acknowledged before me this ____ day of ________________, by the undersigned, ________________, who is personally known to me or satisfactorily proven to me to be the person whose name is subscribed to the within instrument.

____
Printed Name of Notary Public

____
Signature of Notary Public

My commission expires: __________________ (seal)

Mississippi Transfer on Death Deed Revocation Form

Recording requested by (name):

____

When recorded mail to
and mail tax statements to:

____

____

____

____

Recorder's Use Only

REVOCATION OF REVOCABLE TRANSFER ON DEATH DEED

This document is exempt from documentary transfer tax under Rev. & Tax. Code § 11930. This document is exempt from preliminary change of ownership report under Rev. & Tax. Code § 480.3.

Assessor's Parcel No.:

____

Declaration of Exemption From Gov't Code § 27388.1 Fee

☐ Transfer is exempt from fee per GC § 27388.1(a)(2):
☐ recorded concurrently "in connection with" transfer subject to Documentary Transfer Tax
☐ recorded concurrently "in connection with" a transfer of residential dwelling to an owner-occupier
☐ Transfer is exempt from fee per GC 27388.1(a)(1):
☐ Fee cap of $225.00 reached ☐ Not related to real property

IMPORTANT NOTICE: THIS FORM MUST BE RECORDED TO BE EFFECTIVE

This revocation form MUST be RECORDED before your death or it will not be effective. This revocation form only affects a transfer on death deed that YOU made. A transfer on death deed made by a co-owner of your property is not affected by this revocation form. A co-owner who wants to revoke a transfer on death deed that he/she made must complete and RECORD a SEPARATE revocation form.

PROPERTY DESCRIPTION

Print the legal description of the property affected by this revocation:

____

____

____

REVOCATION

I, _________________________________, am the transferor under the Revocable TOD deed dated ________________ and recorded on ________________ as Instrument No. ______________ in Book/Reel ________, Page/Image ________, of Official Records of ______________________________________ County, Nevada, which named as beneficiary(ies) ____ ____.

I hereby revoke any TOD deed to transfer the described property that I executed before executing this form, including the TOD deed described above.

SIGNATURE AND DATE

Sign and print your name below (your name should exactly match the name shown on your title documents):

Date: _____________________ ____

(Signature of declarant)

____

(Typed or written name of declarant)

Notary Acknowledgment

State of ____________________

County of __________________

The foregoing was acknowledged before me this ____ day of ________________, by the undersigned, ________________, who is personally known to me or satisfactorily proven to me to be the person whose name is subscribed to the within instrument.

____

Printed Name of Notary Public

____

Signature of Notary Public

My commission expires: __________________ (seal)

Missouri

Table of Contents

Does a transfer on death deed avoid creditors?

A revocable TOD deed does not avoid the owner's creditors. Creditors may seek collection against the designated beneficiaries as to secured and unsecured obligations of the original owner. A revocable TOD deed, if incorrect, cannot be resolved informally after the owner's death without tax consequences.

Missouri Beneficiary Deed Form

The Missouri beneficiary deed form allows property to be automatically transferred to a new owner when the current owner dies, without the need to go through probate. It also gives the current owner retained control over the property, including the right to change his or her mind about the transfer.

Is a transfer on death deed a good idea?

If you'd like to avoid having your property going through the probate process, it's a good idea to look into a transfer on death deed. A transfer on death deed allows you to select a beneficiary who will receive your property, but only when you've passed away.

Can a TOD be contested?

But whatever you do, a lawsuit to challenge a TOD Deed must be filed within three years of the property owner's death. The bottom line: you have the right to contest a TOD Deed, just as you can a Will or Trust, but in many cases that will be no easy task.

What is the difference between POD and TOD?

A POD account is very similar to a transfer-on-death (TOD) arrangement but deals with a person's bank assets instead of their stocks, bonds, mutual funds, or other investment assets. 2 Both POD and TOD agreements offer quick means of dispersing assets, as both avoid the probate process, which can take several months.

Do you pay taxes on transfer on death?

The amount that's in a TOD account at the time of your death is not taxable under federal law to the person who receives the account, although it may be taxable to your estate. If your beneficiary or the account are in a state with an inheritance tax, he may have to pay that.

Is transfer on death considered an inheritance?

Because TOD accounts are still part of the decedent's estate (although not the probate estate that the Last Will establishes), they may be subject to income, estate and/or inheritance tax. TOD accounts are also not out of reach for the decedent's creditors or other relatives.

Does TOD override a will?

A TOD designation supersedes a will. Once you're dead, your beneficiaries receive these assets by filling out forms provided by the financial institution and providing a certified copy of your death certificate.

Can I withdraw money from my own TOD account?

This account is wholly owned by both spouses while they're both alive. As a result, a creditor of one spouse could make a claim against the entire account, without any approval or say from the other spouse. Either spouse could also withdraw all the money in the account and not tell the other.

What happens if a TOD beneficiary dies?

In the event that there are no living beneficiaries, life insurance policies, TOD and POD accounts will go to the decedent's estate. If the beneficiary outlives the person creating the estate plan, but dies before receiving the gift, the gift will go to the probate estate of the deceased beneficiary.

Can a POA add a TOD?

The transfer on death deed statute specifically prohibits an agent acting under a power of attorney from creating a transfer on death deed.

Does transfer on death avoid estate tax?

Estate Taxes

When someone dies and their property transfers to their beneficiaries, the federal government impose an estate tax on the value of all that property. Since the transfer on death account is not a trust, it does not help you avoid or minimize estate taxes.

What are the tax consequences of a transfer on death deed?

Tax Implications of Transfer on Death Deeds

Keep in mind that as long as you're alive, TOD Deeds have no impact on (or benefit for) your Beneficiary. He or she has no legal rights to the property until after you pass away. That means you pay the property taxes on it until you die.

What states allow transfer on death accounts?

States that allow TOD deeds are Alaska, Arizona, Arkansas, California, Colorado, District of Columbia, Hawaii, Illinois, Indiana, Kansas, Maine, Minnesota, Mississippi, Missouri, Montana, Nebraska, Nevada, New Mexico, North Dakota, Ohio, Oklahoma, Oregon, South Dakota, Texas, Utah, Virginia, Washington, West Virginia.

Can a TOD account have multiple beneficiaries?

TOD Account Beneficiaries

TOD account holders can name multiple beneficiaries and divide assets any way they like. However, the beneficiaries have no access or rights to a TOD account while its owner is alive.

What does TOD mean in a will?

Transfer on death

On a nonretirement account, designating a beneficiary or beneficiaries establishes a transfer on death (TOD) registration for the account. For an individual account, a TOD registration generally allows ownership of the account to be transferred to the designated beneficiary upon your death.

Is a TOD a retirement account?

Understanding Transfer on Death (TOD)

Individual retirement accounts, 401(k)s, and other retirement accounts are TOD. The Uniform Transfer on Death Securities Registration Act lets owners name beneficiaries for their stocks, bonds, or brokerage accounts. The process is similar to a payable-on-death bank account.

How does a transfer on death account work?

A TOD account automatically transfers the assets to a named beneficiary, when the account holder dies. Let's say you have a savings account with $100,000 in it. Your son is the beneficiary for the TOD account. When you die, the account's assets are transferred directly to him without having to go through probate.

How do you do a TOD?

How to Prepare a Transfer-on-Death Deed

Get a Deed Form or Prepare Your Own. You can buy a state-specific TOD deed form for your state or type up your own document. ...

Name the Beneficiary. ...

Describe the Property. ...

Sign the Deed. ...

Record the Deed.

What is the benefit of a transfer on death account?

The principal advantage includes avoiding probate. Because you name a beneficiary for your Transfer on Death account (TOD), the account passes to the beneficiary at your death, without the need for probating your will with respect to that account.

Do transfer on death accounts get stepped up basis?

Do assets in a TOD account receive a "step up" (or "step down") in cost basis when the account owner dies? Yes. Securities held in TOD accounts receive a new cost basis as of the account owner's date of death using the same income tax rules that apply at the death of an individual.

What is a TOD bank account?

A transfer on death (TOD) account is a type of beneficiary designation that names recipient beneficiaries to receive the assets of the account at the time of the account holder's death, without the assets going through probate.

Are transfer on death deeds revocable?

The transfer on death deed is fully revocable before the death of the real property owner.

Are TOD accounts included in estate?

Transferring control

Because TOD accounts are still part of the decedent's estate (although not the probate estate that the Last Will establishes), they may be subject to income, estate and/or inheritance tax. TOD accounts are also not out of reach for the decedent's creditors or other relatives.

Forms

Recording requested by:

When recorded mail to and mail tax statements to:

Space above this line for recorder's use

Missouri Transfer on Death Deed
(Beneficiary Deed)

I, ______________________, with a mailing address of ________________________ ______________________________________ (hereinafter referred to as the "Owner") being of competent mind and having the legal capacity to execute this document, as owner transfer on death to ______________________ with a mailing address of ______ ____ (hereinafter referred to as the "Primary Beneficiary") as grantee beneficiary, the following described interest in real estate:

____

____

____

____

____

____

Legal description of the property (including square, suffix, and lot number)

If the Primary Beneficiary does not survive me, I designate ______________________ with a mailing address of ____ _________ (hereinafter referred to as the "Alternate Beneficiary") as grantee beneficiary.

This Transfer on Death Deed is revocable. It does not transfer any ownership until the death of the owner. It revokes all prior beneficiary designations by this owner for this

interest in real estate. The grantor has the right to withdraw or rescind this deed at any time. Any beneficiaries named in this deed are hereby advised that this deed may be withdrawn or rescinded whether or not money or any other consideration was paid or given.

______________________	______________________	______________________
Owner's Name	Primary Beneficiary's Name	Alternate Beneficiary's Name
______________________	______________________	______________________
Owner's Signature	Primary Beneficiary's Signature	Alternate Beneficiary's Signature
______________________	______________________	______________________
Date	Date	Date

Notary Acknowledgment

State of ____________________

County of __________________

The foregoing was acknowledged before me this ____ day of ________________, by the undersigned, ________________, who is personally known to me or satisfactorily proven to me to be the person whose name is subscribed to the within instrument.

____
Printed Name of Notary Public

____
Signature of Notary Public

My commission expires: __________________ (seal)

Missouri Transfer on Death Deed Revocation Form

Recording requested by (name):

____

When recorded mail to
and mail tax statements to:

____

____

____

____

Recorder's Use Only

REVOCATION OF REVOCABLE TRANSFER ON DEATH DEED

This document is exempt from documentary transfer tax under Rev. & Tax. Code § 11930. This document is exempt from preliminary change of ownership report under Rev. & Tax. Code § 480.3.

Assessor's Parcel No.: ____________________________________

Declaration of Exemption From Gov't Code § 27388.1 Fee

- ☐ Transfer is exempt from fee per GC § 27388.1(a)(2):
  - ☐ recorded concurrently "in connection with" transfer subject to Documentary Transfer Tax
  - ☐ recorded concurrently "in connection with" a transfer of residential dwelling to an owner-occupier
- ☐ Transfer is exempt from fee per GC 27388.1(a)(1):
  - ☐ Fee cap of $225.00 reached ☐ Not related to real property

IMPORTANT NOTICE: THIS FORM MUST BE RECORDED TO BE EFFECTIVE

This revocation form MUST be RECORDED before your death or it will not be effective. This revocation form only affects a transfer on death deed that YOU made. A transfer on death deed made by a co-owner of your property is not affected by this revocation form. A co-owner who wants to revoke a transfer on death deed that he/she made must complete and RECORD a SEPARATE revocation form.

PROPERTY DESCRIPTION

Print the legal description of the property affected by this revocation:

____

____

____

REVOCATION

I, ________________________________, am the transferor under the Revocable TOD deed dated _________________ and recorded on _________________ as Instrument No. _______________ in Book/Reel _________, Page/Image _________, of Official Records of ____ County Missouri, which named as beneficiary(ies) ____.

I hereby revoke any TOD deed to transfer the described property that I executed before executing this form, including the TOD deed described above.

SIGNATURE AND DATE

Sign and print your name below (your name should exactly match the name shown on your title documents):

Date: ______________________

____
(Signature of declarant)

____
(Typed or written name of declarant)

Notary Acknowledgment

State of ____________________

County of __________________

The foregoing was acknowledged before me this ____ day of ________________, by the undersigned, ________________, who is personally known to me or satisfactorily proven to me to be the person whose name is subscribed to the within instrument.

____
Printed Name of Notary Public

____
Signature of Notary Public

My commission expires: __________________ (seal)

Montana

Table of Contents

A Transfer on Death Deed allows owners of real property in Montana to transfer it at death to one or more designated beneficiaries without probate. Describes how to transfer a Certificate of Title, also known as the title, for a motor vehicle to the deceased's legal heirs.

Does Montana allow beneficiary deeds?

Beneficiary deeds allow owners of real property in Montana to transfer at death without probate their property to one or more beneficiaries. Beneficiary deeds as a way for people to transfer at death their real property (located in Montana) to one or more beneficiaries without probate.

How does a TOD account work?

So, how do Transfer on Death accounts work? A TOD account automatically transfers the assets to a named beneficiary, when the account holder dies. Your son is the beneficiary for the TOD account. When you die, the account's assets are transferred directly to him without having to go through probate.

What is the difference between beneficiary and transfer on death?

A beneficiary form states who will directly inherit the asset at your death. Under a TOD arrangement, you keep full control of the asset during your lifetime and pay taxes on any income the asset generates as you own it outright. TOD arrangements require minimal paperwork to establish.

Can I withdraw money from my own TOD account?

This account is wholly owned by both spouses while they're both alive. As a result, a creditor of one spouse could make a claim against the entire account, without any approval or say from the other spouse. Either spouse could also withdraw all the money in the account and not tell the other.

Understanding Transfer on Death (TOD)

Individual retirement accounts, 401(k)s, and other retirement accounts are TOD. The Uniform Transfer on Death Securities Registration Act lets owners name beneficiaries for their stocks, bonds, or brokerage accounts. The process is similar to a payable-on-death bank account.

Montana Code Annotated 2019

TITLE 72. ESTATES, TRUSTS, AND FIDUCIARY RELATIONSHIPS

CHAPTER 6. NONPROBATE TRANSFERS ON DEATH

Part 4. Uniform Real Property Transfer on Death Act

What does the Transfer on Death (TOD) deed do?

When you die, this deed transfers the described property, subject to any liens or mortgages (or other encumbrances) on the property at your death. Probate is not required. The TOD deed has no effect until you die. You can revoke it at any time. You are also free to transfer the property to someone else during your lifetime. If you do not own any interest in the property when you die, this deed will have no effect.

How do I make a TOD deed? Complete this form. Have it acknowledged before a notary public or other individual authorized by law to take acknowledgments. Record the form in each county where any part of the property is located. The form has no effect unless it is acknowledged and recorded before your death.

Can I change my mind before I record the TOD deed?

Yes. If you have not yet recorded the deed and want to change your mind, simply tear up or otherwise destroy the deed.

How do I "record" the TOD deed?

Take the completed and acknowledged form to the office of the county clerk and recorder of the county where the property is located. Follow the instructions given by the county clerk and recorder to make the form part of the official property records. If the property is in more than one county, you should record the deed in each county.

Can I later revoke the TOD deed if I change my mind?

Yes. You can revoke the TOD deed. No one, including the beneficiaries, can prevent you from revoking the deed.

How do I revoke the TOD deed after it is recorded? There are three ways to revoke a recorded TOD deed:

(1) Complete and acknowledge a revocation form and record it in each county where the property is located.

(2) Complete and acknowledge a new TOD deed that disposes of the same property and record it in each county where the property is located.

(3) Transfer the property to someone else during your lifetime by a recorded deed that expressly revokes the TOD deed. You may not revoke the TOD deed by will.

I am being pressured to complete this form. What should I do? Do not complete this form under pressure. Seek help from a trusted family member, friend, or lawyer.

Do I need to tell the beneficiaries about the TOD deed? No, but it is recommended. Secrecy can cause later complications and might make it easier for others to commit fraud.

I have other questions about this form. What should I do? This form is designed to fit some but not all situations. If you have other questions, you are encouraged to consult a lawyer.

History: En. Sec. 98, Ch. 313, L. 2019.

Forms

Recording requested by:

When recorded mail to and mail tax statements to:

Space above this line for recorder's use

Montana Transfer on Death Deed

(Beneficiary Deed)

I, ______________________, with a mailing address of ________________________ ______________________________________ (hereinafter referred to as the "Owner") being of competent mind and having the legal capacity to execute this document, as owner transfer on death to ______________________ with a mailing address of ______ ____ (hereinafter referred to as the "Primary Beneficiary") as grantee beneficiary, the following described interest in real estate:

____

____

____

____

____

____

Legal description of the property (including square, suffix, and lot number)

If the Primary Beneficiary does not survive me, I designate ________________________ with a mailing address of ____ _________ (hereinafter referred to as the "Alternate Beneficiary") as grantee beneficiary.

This Transfer on Death Deed is revocable. It does not transfer any ownership until the death of the owner. It revokes all prior beneficiary designations by this owner for this

interest in real estate. The grantor has the right to withdraw or rescind this deed at any time. Any beneficiaries named in this deed are hereby advised that this deed may be withdrawn or rescinded whether or not money or any other consideration was paid or given.

Owner's Name	Primary Beneficiary's Name	Alternate Beneficiary's Name
Owner's Signature	Primary Beneficiary's Signature	Alternate Beneficiary's Signature
Date	Date	Date

Notary Acknowledgment

State of ____________________

County of __________________

The foregoing was acknowledged before me this ____ day of ________________, by the undersigned, ________________, who is personally known to me or satisfactorily proven to me to be the person whose name is subscribed to the within instrument.

____
Printed Name of Notary Public

____
Signature of Notary Public

My commission expires: __________________ (seal)

Montana Transfer on Death Deed Revocation Form

Recording requested by (name):

____

When recorded mail to
and mail tax statements to:

____

____

____

____

Recorder's Use Only

REVOCATION OF REVOCABLE TRANSFER ON DEATH DEED

This document is exempt from documentary transfer tax under Rev. & Tax. Code § 11930. This document is exempt from preliminary change of ownership report under Rev. & Tax. Code § 480.3.

Assessor's Parcel No.: ___________________________________

Declaration of Exemption From Gov't Code § 27388.1 Fee

- ☐ Transfer is exempt from fee per GC § 27388.1(a)(2):
  - ☐ recorded concurrently "in connection with" transfer subject to Documentary Transfer Tax
  - ☐ recorded concurrently "in connection with" a transfer of residential dwelling to an owner-occupier
- ☐ Transfer is exempt from fee per GC 27388.1(a)(1):
  - ☐ Fee cap of $225.00 reached ☐ Not related to real property

IMPORTANT NOTICE: THIS FORM MUST BE RECORDED TO BE EFFECTIVE

This revocation form MUST be RECORDED before your death or it will not be effective. This revocation form only affects a transfer on death deed that YOU made. A transfer on death deed made by a co-owner of your property is not affected by this revocation form. A co-owner who wants to revoke a transfer on death deed that he/she made must complete and RECORD a SEPARATE revocation form.

PROPERTY DESCRIPTION

Print the legal description of the property affected by this revocation:

____

____

____

REVOCATION

I, ______________________________, am the transferor under the Revocable TOD deed dated ______________ and recorded on ______________ as Instrument No. ______________ in Book/Reel ________, Page/Image ________, of Official Records of ______________________________ County Montana, which named as beneficiary(ies) ______________________________
____.

I hereby revoke any TOD deed to transfer the described property that I executed before executing this form, including the TOD deed described above.

SIGNATURE AND DATE

Sign and print your name below (your name should exactly match the name shown on your title documents):

Date: ____________________

____
(Signature of declarant)

____
(Typed or written name of declarant)

Notary Acknowledgment

State of ____________________

County of __________________

The foregoing was acknowledged before me this ____ day of _________________, by the undersigned, _________________, who is personally known to me or satisfactorily proven to me to be the person whose name is subscribed to the within instrument.

____

Printed Name of Notary Public

____

Signature of Notary Public

My commission expires: ___________________ (seal)

Nebraska

Table of Contents

If you'd like to avoid having your property going through the probate process, it's a good idea to look into a transfer on death deed. A transfer on death deed allows you to select a beneficiary who will receive your property, but only when you've passed away.

Does Nebraska have transfer on death deeds?

Nebraska has adopted a new method of transferring ownership of real estate upon the death of the owner. Effective January 1, 2013, we may now use a revocable transfer on death deed ("TOD Deed") in Nebraska. The TOD Deed will operate in a similar fashion to a pay.

How do I set up a transfer on death?

All you need to do is fill out a simple form, provided by the bank, naming the person you want to inherit the money in the account at your death. As long as you are alive, the person you named to inherit the money in a payable-on-death (POD) account has no rights to it.

How do I fill out a TOD form?

Get a Deed Form or Prepare Your Own. You can buy a state-specific TOD deed form for your state or type up your own document. Name the Beneficiary. Describe the Property. Sign the Deed. Record the Deed.

Can a TOD account have multiple beneficiaries?

TOD account holders can name multiple beneficiaries and divide assets any way they like. However, the beneficiaries have no access or rights to a TOD account while its owner is alive. Those beneficiaries can also be changed at any time, so long as the TOD account holder is deemed mentally competent.

Transfer-on-death deeds for real estate

You can leave Nebraska real estate with a transfer-on-death deed. You'll need to prepare a new deed, naming a beneficiary, and then record it with the local land records office. The TOD beneficiary doesn't have any rights to the property until after your death.

Is transfer on death considered an inheritance?

Because TOD accounts are still part of the decedent's estate (although not the probate estate that the Last Will establishes), they may be subject to income, estate and/or inheritance tax. TOD accounts are also not out of reach for the decedent's creditors or other relatives.

What is the difference between transfer on death and beneficiary?

Transfer on death applies to certain assets that have a named beneficiary. The beneficiaries (or a spouse) receive the assets without having to go through probate. Beneficiaries of the TOD don't have access to the assets prior to the owner's death.

Do you pay taxes on transfer on death?

The amount that's in a TOD account at the time of your death is not taxable under federal law to the person who receives the account, although it may be taxable to your estate. If your beneficiary or the account are in a state with an inheritance tax, he may have to pay that.

Is a trust better than a TOD?

With a trust, you can avoid unintended outcomes more easily than with a TOD asset. In addition, if you have multiple assets that you would have designated as "transfer on death," keeping them in a trust allows you to change beneficiary designations by changing the beneficiaries of the trust

Can a TOD account be contested?

In other words, you can challenge a TOD Deed on many of the same bases used to challenge a Trust or Will. The bottom line: you have the right to contest a TOD Deed, just as you can a Will or Trust, but in many cases that will be no easy task.

What is the difference between POD and TOD?

A POD account is very similar to a transfer-on-death (TOD) arrangement but deals with a person's bank assets instead of their stocks, bonds, mutual funds, or other investment assets.

Both POD and TOD agreements offer quick means of dispersing assets, as both avoid the probate process, which can take several months.

Does a TOD supersede a will?

A TOD designation supersedes a will. For bank accounts, you can set up a similar account known as payable-on-death, sometimes referred to as a Totten trust. Your beneficiaries can't touch the account while you're alive, and you're free to change beneficiaries or close the accounts at any time.

Does transfer on death avoid estate tax?

When someone dies and their property transfers to their beneficiaries, the federal government impose an estate tax on the value of all that property. Since the transfer on death account is not a trust, it does not help you avoid or minimize estate taxes.

What happens if a TOD beneficiary dies?

In the event that there are no living beneficiaries, life insurance policies, TOD and POD accounts will go to the decedent's estate. If the beneficiary outlives the person creating the estate plan, but dies before receiving the gift, the gift will go to the probate estate of the deceased beneficiary.

Can I withdraw money from my own TOD account?

This account is wholly owned by both spouses while they're both alive. As a result, a creditor of one spouse could make a claim against the entire account, without any approval or say from the other spouse. Either spouse could also withdraw all the money in the account and not tell the other.

Forms

Recording requested by:

When recorded mail to and mail tax statements to:

Space above this line for recorder's use

Nebraska Transfer on Death Deed
(Beneficiary Deed)

I, ______________________, with a mailing address of ______________________ ______________________________________ (hereinafter referred to as the "Owner") being of competent mind and having the legal capacity to execute this document, as owner transfer on death to ______________________ with a mailing address of ______ ____ (hereinafter referred to as the "Primary Beneficiary") as grantee beneficiary, the following described interest in real estate:

____

____

____

____

____

____

____

Legal description of the property (including square, suffix, and lot number)

If the Primary Beneficiary does not survive me, I designate ______________________ with a mailing address of ____ _________ (hereinafter referred to as the "Alternate Beneficiary") as grantee beneficiary.

This Transfer on Death Deed is revocable. It does not transfer any ownership until the death of the owner. It revokes all prior beneficiary designations by this owner for this

interest in real estate. The grantor has the right to withdraw or rescind this deed at any time. Any beneficiaries named in this deed are hereby advised that this deed may be withdrawn or rescinded whether or not money or any other consideration was paid or given.

______________________	______________________	______________________
Owner's Name	Primary Beneficiary's Name	Alternate Beneficiary's Name
______________________	______________________	______________________
Owner's Signature	Primary Beneficiary's Signature	Alternate Beneficiary's Signature
______________________	______________________	______________________
Date	Date	Date

Notary Acknowledgment

State of ____________________

County of __________________

The foregoing was acknowledged before me this ____ day of ________________, by the undersigned, ________________, who is personally known to me or satisfactorily proven to me to be the person whose name is subscribed to the within instrument.

____
Printed Name of Notary Public

____
Signature of Notary Public

My commission expires: __________________ (seal)

Nebraska Transfer on Death Deed Revocation Form

Recording requested by (name):

____

When recorded mail to
and mail tax statements to:

____

____

____

____

Recorder's Use Only

REVOCATION OF REVOCABLE TRANSFER ON DEATH DEED

This document is exempt from documentary transfer tax under Rev. & Tax. Code § 11930. This document is exempt from preliminary change of ownership report under Rev. & Tax. Code § 480.3.

Assessor's Parcel No.:

____

Declaration of Exemption From Gov't Code § 27388.1 Fee

☐ Transfer is exempt from fee per GC § 27388.1(a)(2):
 ☐ recorded concurrently "in connection with" transfer subject to Documentary Transfer Tax
 ☐ recorded concurrently "in connection with" a transfer of residential dwelling to an owner-occupier

☐ Transfer is exempt from fee per GC 27388.1(a)(1):
 ☐ Fee cap of $225.00 reached ☐ Not related to real property

IMPORTANT NOTICE: THIS FORM MUST BE RECORDED TO BE EFFECTIVE

This revocation form MUST be RECORDED before your death or it will not be effective. This revocation form only affects a transfer on death deed that YOU made. A transfer on death deed made by a co-owner of your property is not affected by this revocation form. A co-owner who wants to revoke a transfer on death deed that he/she made must complete and RECORD a SEPARATE revocation form.

PROPERTY DESCRIPTION

Print the legal description of the property affected by this revocation:

____

____

____

REVOCATION

I, ______________________________, am the transferor under the Revocable TOD deed dated ______________ and recorded on ______________ as Instrument No. ____________ in Book/Reel ________, Page/Image ________, of Official Records of ______________________________ County Nebraska, which named as beneficiary(ies) ______________________________
____.

I hereby revoke any TOD deed to transfer the described property that I executed before executing this form, including the TOD deed described above.

SIGNATURE AND DATE

Sign and print your name below (your name should exactly match the name shown on your title documents):

Date: ____________________

____
(Signature of declarant)

____
(Typed or written name of declarant)

Notary Acknowledgment

State of ____________________

County of __________________

The foregoing was acknowledged before me this ____ day of ________________, by the undersigned, ________________, who is personally known to me or satisfactorily proven to me to be the person whose name is subscribed to the within instrument.

____
Printed Name of Notary Public

____
Signature of Notary Public

My commission expires: __________________ (seal)

Nevada

Table of Contents

Nevada Transfer on Death Deed

Nevada's statutory transfer on death instrument for real property is called a deed upon death. It is governed by NRS 111.655-111.699 (2013), inclusive, and incorporates the Uniform Real Property Transfer on Death Act into its text. Like other transfer on death deeds, THE EXECUTED DEED, AS WELL AS ANY CHANGES OR REVOCATIONS, MUST BE RECORDED IN THE COUNTY WHERE THE LAND IS LOCATED, DURING THE OWNER'S NATURAL LIFE.

Transfer on death deeds/deeds upon death make it possible for owners of real estate in Nevada to convey their land to one or more designated beneficiaries after their death, with no need to subject the property to probate distribution. Significantly, transfers included in deeds upon death are not affected by directions included in wills. As such, these deeds comprise only one part of a regularly updated overall estate plan.

When correctly executed and recorded, a deed upon death only contains a potential future interest in the property, so there is no requirement to pay consideration or to give notice to any named beneficiary. In addition, the owner retains absolute control over the property, including the right to change beneficiary designations, revoke the deed, sign sales, rental, or mortgage agreements, and use the land in any other lawful way without penalty.

After the owner's death, the surviving beneficiary claims the property by recording an affidavit of death of grantor, along with an official copy of the owner's death certificate. Alternately, if the beneficiary is unable or unwilling to accept the transfer, the statutes provide a method to disclaim it.

Overall, Nevada's deed upon death offers a flexible tool for estate planning. Because each circumstance is unique, take the time to fully understand the benefits and drawbacks that accompany these documents, including the potential impact on taxes, benefit eligibility and repayment, and other financial concerns. Contact a local attorney with specific questions or for complex situations.

Problems with Deeds on Death, Transfer on Death Deeds or Beneficiary Deeds

When a person dies owning real property in his or her name, probate may be required in order to transfer that property to the heirs of the deceased person.

Because of the costs, delays and hassles associated with going through probate in the State of Nevada, many people desire to transfer, or to at least structure the future transfer of, their real property, and prior to their deaths.

Common methods of probate avoidance for real estate include the following:

1. Hold real property with a right of survivorship, either in joint tenancy or as community property;
2. Convey outright title to real estate by way of pre-death gift;
3. Establish a living revocable trust or other type of trust, to own and hold real property; or
4. Use a beneficiary deed, deed upon death, or transfer on death deed (all synonyms referring to the same instrument) to make the transfer of real estate effective upon death.

While using a joint tenancy or other titling options with rights of survivorship is sometimes to referred to as the "Poor Man's Estate Plan" or "Home Spun Estate Planning", this article will focus on the particulars and problems with using beneficiary deeds in Las Vegas, Henderson, Clark County and other parts of the State of Nevada.

In 2011, the State of Nevada passed the Uniform Real Property Transfer on Death Act, which can be found at NRS 111.655 to 111.699 (the "Deed upon Death Act"). In pertinent part, the Deed on Death Act allows for the recordation of a deed which will effectively transfer the real property to the named beneficiary upon the death of the grantor.

These deeds are revocable, so that if the grantor changes their mind, they may revoke the conveyance. To be effective these Beneficiary Deeds must be recorded prior to the death of the grantor.

It should be noted that Transfer on Death Deeds do not "show up" on the Clark County Assessor's website until someone files an Affidavit of Death (upon the passing of the grantor), but such instruments do "show up" on the Clark County Recorder's website.

While Deeds upon Death may initially appear to be less expensive than establishing and using a revocable trust, there are many downsides which ought to be considered prior to going down the Transfer on Death route.

Transfer on death forms or deed upon death forms

Forms for beneficiary deeds are readily available online but may prove unreliable. Unless a grantor uses the correct language, as required by the Deed upon Death Act, the transfer will not be effective.

Difficult to get title insurance

Many title insurance companies are refusing to issue a title insurance policy until the new owner has owned the property for at least eighteen (18) months after the grantor's death. This is because under Nevada law creditors of the decedent have eighteen months to file claims against the estate and would have priority claim on any assets belonging to the estate, including of course, the real property subject to a beneficiary deed. See #3 below.

If, in such case, the beneficiary desires to sell the property soon after the grantor's death, especially to a non-cash buyer, the new buyer may have problems obtaining title insurance, and, therefore, may have problems borrowing money to buy the property, seeing how most mortgage companies require title insurance before making a loan.

It is possible that probate can be done to rectify this situation, but this, of course, defeats the purpose of the transfer on death deed which was to avoid probate.

Vulnerability to claims by grantor's creditors

The reason title insurance may not be obtainable in Nevada until 18 months following the grantor's death, as stated above in #2, is that NRS 111.689 allows the creditors of the grantor's probate estate to enforce their liabilities against a property transferred pursuant to a deed upon death for up to 18 months following the grantor's death.

The executor/personal representative of the decedent's estate can of course petition the probate court for this 18-month creditor period to be shortened, however, it would require the opening of probate, which is obviously negates the major reason for trying to use a beneficiary deed in the first place!

With transfers of property to trusts, on the other hand, this creditor claim period may be shortened to just 120 days, upon publishing of the appropriate notice to creditors. This is four and one-half times faster than if a deed upon death is used.

On a related note, in 2019 the Nevada legislature updated NRS 164.025 to require that such notice to creditors of a decedent owning an interest in a trust publish such notice to both creditors of the trust AND the settlor of the trust, whereas before, only notice to the creditors of the trust was required.

Vulnerability to claims by beneficiary's creditors

As the creditors of the grantor may have increased opportunity to attach the real estate being transferred by way of beneficiary deed, so also might the creditors of the beneficiary be able to attack the property upon the death of the grantor.

For example, in the event a beneficiary is going through a divorce, bankruptcy, insolvency or has a large judgment against them, the related creditors in those actions may be able to legally attach and take the value of such real property.

The homestead declaration and exemption may be of little use to a beneficiary, unless they decide to occupy the property as their primary residence, and unless they meet the required residency waiting requirements.

Many beneficiaries, however, decide to sell the property or place it into service as a rental property, once the original owner dies.

Real Property Transfer Taxes

When the deed upon death is recorded, there is no real estate transfer fee at that time. However, when the grantor dies and the new owner (the beneficiary) files his "Death of Grantor Affidavit," as required by NRS 111.699, there will be a real property transfer tax due, unless the beneficiary and the grantor are not husband and wife or parent and child.

In the alternative, using a living revocable trust will help the beneficiary avoid the payment of real property transfer tax, regardless of the beneficiary's relationship to the grantor.

This is because by law in Nevada, transfers of real property to or from a trust, without consideration, are exempt from this transfer tax.

With that said, even if the grantor and beneficiary on a deed upon death are related in the ways stated above, proving such relation to the Clark County Assessor can be difficult to say the least, inasmuch as birth certificates, marriage certificates, and name change documents must be presented in original form and may be difficult to obtain.

Beneficiaries do not handle contingencies well

The transfer upon death deed does not provide for solutions to contingencies in the same way a revocable trust can. For example, a trust will generally specify that upon Mom's passing, any trust property, including real estate, will instead be distributed to Son, and if Son does not survive Mom, it is instead to be given to the children of Son.

Moreover, trusts can provided that distributions to minor children, or anyone else who may be incapacitated or vulnerable, will not be made until such beneficiaries attain certain ages, levels of education, or other benchmarks denoting maturity and sensibility.

Beneficiary deeds do not have these same capabilities built in and therefore, a transfer by deed upon death might be soon wasted or spent by a spendthrift child or otherwise vulnerable beneficiary. While trusts may cost a bit more in the beginning, they unusually provide greater flexibility and savings in the long run.

Transfer-on-Death Deed – Avoiding Probate in Nevada

How do you transfer title to your home after you die? In most instances, property can only be transferred through a trust or the probate process. As I've discussed previously, probate is usually not the desired approach as it takes time and money. You can put your property into a trust, but if that is your only significant asset, the cost and complexity may not be very appealing. Some people just add their children to the title while they are living. However, such an action is unwise as it amounts to a gift of an interest in real property which may be subject to gift tax. In addition, the property becomes subject to the child's creditors, thereby putting the homeowner at risk of a foreclosure. These problems can be avoided in states which have enacted transfer-on-death deeds. In Nevada and twelve (12) other states (Arizona, Colorado, Kansas, Missouri, Nevada, New Mexico, Ohio, Arkansas, Wisconsin, Montana, Minnesota, Indiana and Oklahoma) a property owner can transfer real property by executing a transfer-on-death deed, known as a Deed Effective Upon Death in Nevada. In such a deed, the owner lists a beneficiary or beneficiaries in a deed and records that deed while living. The benefit of the deed is that is effective immediately upon death, transferring ownership upon presentation of a certified copy of the owner's death certificate. This means that the property does not go through probate, and it is not available to pay the owner's creditors. These deeds are also revocable, so that the owner can refinance or sell the property or change the beneficiary at any time.

Forms

Recording requested by:

When recorded mail to and mail tax statements to:

Space above this line for recorder's use

Nevada Transfer on Death Deed
(Beneficiary Deed)

I, ______________________, with a mailing address of ______________________ __________________________________ (hereinafter referred to as the "Owner") being of competent mind and having the legal capacity to execute this document, as owner transfer on death to ____________________ with a mailing address of ______ ____ (hereinafter referred to as the "Primary Beneficiary") as grantee beneficiary, the following described interest in real estate:

____

____

____

____

____

____

Legal description of the property (including square, suffix, and lot number)

If the Primary Beneficiary does not survive me, I designate ______________________ with a mailing address of ____ _________ (hereinafter referred to as the "Alternate Beneficiary") as grantee beneficiary.

This Transfer on Death Deed is revocable. It does not transfer any ownership until the death of the owner. It revokes all prior beneficiary designations by this owner for this

interest in real estate. The grantor has the right to withdraw or rescind this deed at any time. Any beneficiaries named in this deed are hereby advised that this deed may be withdrawn or rescinded whether or not money or any other consideration was paid or given.

Owner's Name	Primary Beneficiary's Name	Alternate Beneficiary's Name
Owner's Signature	Primary Beneficiary's Signature	Alternate Beneficiary's Signature
Date	Date	Date

Notary Acknowledgment

State of ____________________

County of __________________

The foregoing was acknowledged before me this ____ day of ________________, by the undersigned, ________________, who is personally known to me or satisfactorily proven to me to be the person whose name is subscribed to the within instrument.

____

Printed Name of Notary Public

____

Signature of Notary Public

My commission expires: __________________ (seal)

Nevada Transfer on Death Deed Revocation Form

Recording requested by (name):

____

When recorded mail to
and mail tax statements to:

____

____

____

____

Recorder's Use Only

REVOCATION OF REVOCABLE TRANSFER ON DEATH DEED

This document is exempt from documentary transfer tax under Rev. & Tax. Code § 11930. This document is exempt from preliminary change of ownership report under Rev. & Tax. Code § 480.3.

Assessor's Parcel No.:

____

Declaration of Exemption From Gov't Code § 27388.1 Fee

☐ Transfer is exempt from fee per GC § 27388.1(a)(2):
- ☐ recorded concurrently "in connection with" transfer subject to Documentary Transfer Tax
- ☐ recorded concurrently "in connection with" a transfer of residential dwelling to an owner-occupier

☐ Transfer is exempt from fee per GC 27388.1(a)(1):
- ☐ Fee cap of $225.00 reached ☐ Not related to real property

IMPORTANT NOTICE: THIS FORM MUST BE RECORDED TO BE EFFECTIVE

This revocation form MUST be RECORDED before your death or it will not be effective. This revocation form only affects a transfer on death deed that YOU made. A transfer on death deed made by a co-owner of your property is not affected by this revocation form. A co-owner who wants to revoke a transfer on death deed that he/she made must complete and RECORD a SEPARATE revocation form.

PROPERTY DESCRIPTION

Print the legal description of the property affected by this revocation:

____

____

____

REVOCATION

I, ______________________________, am the transferor under the Revocable TOD deed dated ______________ and recorded on ______________ as Instrument No. ____________ in Book/Reel ________, Page/Image ________, of Official Records of ______________________________ County Nevada, which named as beneficiary(ies) ____.

I hereby revoke any TOD deed to transfer the described property that I executed before executing this form, including the TOD deed described above.

SIGNATURE AND DATE

Sign and print your name below (your name should exactly match the name shown on your title documents):

Date: ____________________

____
(Signature of declarant)

____
(Typed or written name of declarant)

Notary Acknowledgment

State of ____________________

County of __________________

The foregoing was acknowledged before me this ____ day of ________________, by the undersigned, ________________, who is personally known to me or satisfactorily proven to me to be the person whose name is subscribed to the within instrument.

____
Printed Name of Notary Public

____
Signature of Notary Public

My commission expires: __________________ (seal)

New Mexico

Table of Contents

New Mexico Transfer on Death Deed

On January 1, 2014, New Mexico joined with eleven other states to enact the Uniform Real Property Transfer on Death Act (URPTODA), found at Sections 45-6-401 through 45-6-417 NMSA 1978 (2014). This enhances and adds clarity to the previous transfer on death statute already in force in the state.

A transfer on death deed (TODD) under the new law is defined by the Uniform Law Commission as an instrument that provides owners of real estate in New Mexico with a simple process for the non-probate transfer of real estate. The act allows an owner of real property to designate a beneficiary who will automatically receive the property upon the owner's death, without the need to include it in the decedent's probate estate. Instead, the property passes by means of a recorded TODD. During the owner's lifetime, the beneficiary of a TOD deed has no interest in the property and the owner retains full power to transfer or encumber the property, or even to revoke the deed outright.

New Mexico's version of the URPTODA sets out the rules and provides forms for both the deed and its revocation. To be valid, the TODD must meet three requirements (45-6-409):

1) it must contain the essential elements and formalities of a properly recordable inter vivos deed;

2) it must state that the transfer to the designated beneficiary is to occur at the transferor's death; and

3) it must be recorded before the transferor's death in the public records with the clerk of the county where the property is located.

TODDs represent a potential future interest, conveying whatever rights, if any, the owner retains in the property at the time of death. So, unlike inter vivos deeds ("traditional" documents such as warranty or quitclaim deeds), a TODD does not require notice, delivery, acceptance, or consideration (45-6-410).

The transferor (owner) under a TODD must meet the same standards for capacity as someone who executes a will, but the deed is not affected by the terms of the deceased owner's will. For example, Mary executes and records a TODD leaving her house and land to Bob, and then leaves the same property to Joe in her will. In most cases, Bob gets the land and Joe gets nothing.

If Mary actually wanted to leave the land to Joe, she could execute and record a revocation of the transfer to Bob, then record a new TODD in Joe's name. Alternately, she could sell the land to someone else entirely, and include a statement in the deed, revoking all or part of any previously recorded TODDs. See Section 45-6-411 for more information.

TODDs also offer some flexibility to beneficiaries. If the recipient is unable or unwilling to accept the transfer, Section 45-6-414 authorizes a beneficiary to disclaim all or part of his/her interest as provided by the Uniform Disclaimer of Property Interests Act [Chapter 45, Article 2, Part 11 NMSA 1978].

Overall, New Mexico's statutory transfer on death deed is a flexible estate planning tool that allows owners of real property in the state to convey a potential future interest in real property to one or more beneficiaries. The transfer may be changed or revoked at any time during the owner's life, simply by recording the appropriate documents. Each situation is unique, so carefully review all the benefits and drawbacks of this and any other real estate decisions. Seek legal counsel for help with specific questions or complex situations.

Is a transfer on death deed a good idea?

If you'd like to avoid having your property going through the probate process, it's a good idea to look into a transfer on death deed. A transfer on death deed allows you to select a beneficiary who will receive your property, but only when you've passed away.

Probate court proceedings (during which a deceased person's assets are transferred to the people who inherit them) can be long, costly, and confusing. It's no wonder so many people take steps to spare their families the hassle. Different states, however, offer different ways to avoid probate. Here are your options in New Mexico.

Living trusts

In New Mexico, you can make a living trust to avoid probate for virtually any asset you own—real estate, bank accounts, vehicles, and so on. You need to create a trust document (it's similar to a will), naming someone to take over as trustee after your death (called a successor trustee). Then—and this is crucial—you must transfer ownership of your property to yourself as the trustee of the trust. Once all that's done, the property will be controlled by the terms of the trust. At your death, your successor trustee will be able to transfer it to the trust beneficiaries without probate court proceedings.

Joint ownership

If you own property jointly with someone else, and this ownership includes the "right of survivorship," then the surviving owner automatically owns the property when the other owner dies. No probate will be necessary to transfer the property, although of course it will take some paperwork to show that title to the property is held solely by the surviving owner.

In New Mexico, this form of joint ownership is available:

Joint tenancy.

Property owned in joint tenancy automatically passes to the surviving owners when one owner dies. No probate is necessary. Joint tenancy often works well when couples (married or not) acquire real estate, vehicles, bank accounts or other valuable property together. In New Mexico, each owner, called a joint tenant, must own an equal share.

Payable-on-death designations for bank accounts

In New Mexico, you can add a "payable-on-death" (POD) designation to bank accounts such as savings accounts or certificates of deposit. You still control all the money in the account—your POD beneficiary has no rights to the money, and you can spend it all if you want. At your death, the beneficiary can claim the money directly from the bank, without probate court proceedings.

Transfer-on-death registration for securities

New Mexico lets you register stocks and bonds in transfer-on-death (TOD) form. People commonly hold brokerage accounts this way. If you register an account in TOD (also called beneficiary) form, the beneficiary you name will inherit the account automatically at your death. No probate court proceedings will be necessary; the beneficiary will deal directly with the brokerage company to transfer the account.

Transfer-on-death deeds for real estate

New Mexico allows you to leave real estate with transfer-on-death deeds, also called beneficiary deeds. You sign and record the deed now, but it doesn't take effect until your death. You can revoke the deed or sell the property at any time; the beneficiary you name on the deed has no rights until your death. N.M. Stat. § 45-6-401 and following.

Transfer-on-death registration for vehicles

New Mexico does not allow transfer-on-death registration of vehicles.

Simplified probate procedures

Even if you don't do any planning to avoid probate, your estate may qualify for New Mexico's simplified "small estate" probate procedures. For more details, see Probate Shortcuts. For more on avoiding probate, see 8 Ways to Avoid Probate, by Mary Randolph (Nolo).

Forms

Recording requested by: When recorded mail to and mail tax statements to:	

Space above this line for recorder's use

New Mexico Transfer on Death Deed
(Beneficiary Deed)

I, ______________________, with a mailing address of ______________________ ______________________________________ (hereinafter referred to as the "Owner") being of competent mind and having the legal capacity to execute this document, as owner transfer on death to ______________________ with a mailing address of ______ ____ (hereinafter referred to as the "Primary Beneficiary") as grantee beneficiary, the following described interest in real estate:

____

____

____

____

____

____

Legal description of the property (including square, suffix, and lot number)

If the Primary Beneficiary does not survive me, I designate ______________________ with a mailing address of ____ _________ (hereinafter referred to as the "Alternate Beneficiary") as grantee beneficiary.

This Transfer on Death Deed is revocable. It does not transfer any ownership until the death of the owner. It revokes all prior beneficiary designations by this owner for this

interest in real estate. The grantor has the right to withdraw or rescind this deed at any time. Any beneficiaries named in this deed are hereby advised that this deed may be withdrawn or rescinded whether or not money or any other consideration was paid or given.

______________________	______________________	______________________
Owner's Name	Primary Beneficiary's Name	Alternate Beneficiary's Name
______________________	______________________	______________________
Owner's Signature	Primary Beneficiary's Signature	Alternate Beneficiary's Signature
______________________	______________________	______________________
Date	Date	Date

Notary Acknowledgment

State of ____________________

County of __________________

The foregoing was acknowledged before me this ____ day of ________________, by the undersigned, ________________, who is personally known to me or satisfactorily proven to me to be the person whose name is subscribed to the within instrument.

____

Printed Name of Notary Public

____

Signature of Notary Public

My commission expires: __________________ (seal)

New Mexico Transfer on Death Deed Revocation Form

Recording requested by (name):

____

When recorded mail to
and mail tax statements to:

____

____

____

____

Recorder's Use Only

REVOCATION OF REVOCABLE TRANSFER ON DEATH DEED

This document is exempt from documentary transfer tax under Rev. & Tax. Code § 11930. This document is exempt from preliminary change of ownership report under Rev. & Tax. Code § 480.3.

Assessor's Parcel No.:

____

Declaration of Exemption From Gov't Code § 27388.1 Fee

☐ Transfer is exempt from fee per GC § 27388.1(a)(2):
- ☐ recorded concurrently "in connection with" transfer subject to Documentary Transfer Tax
- ☐ recorded concurrently "in connection with" a transfer of residential dwelling to an owner-occupier

☐ Transfer is exempt from fee per GC 27388.1(a)(1):
- ☐ Fee cap of $225.00 reached ☐ Not related to real property

IMPORTANT NOTICE: THIS FORM MUST BE RECORDED TO BE EFFECTIVE

This revocation form MUST be RECORDED before your death or it will not be effective. This revocation form only affects a transfer on death deed that YOU made. A transfer on death deed made by a co-owner of your property is not affected by this revocation form. A co-owner who wants to revoke a transfer on death deed that he/she made must complete and RECORD a SEPARATE revocation form.

PROPERTY DESCRIPTION

Print the legal description of the property affected by this revocation:

____

____

____

REVOCATION

I, ______________________, am the transferor under the Revocable TOD deed dated ____________ and recorded on ____________ as Instrument No. ____________ in Book/Reel ________, Page/Image ________, of Official Records of ______________________ County, New Mexico, which named as beneficiary(ies) ____.

I hereby revoke any TOD deed to transfer the described property that I executed before executing this form, including the TOD deed described above.

SIGNATURE AND DATE

Sign and print your name below (your name should exactly match the name shown on your title documents):

Date: ____________________

____
(Signature of declarant)

____
(Typed or written name of declarant)

Notary Acknowledgment

State of ____________________

County of __________________

The foregoing was acknowledged before me this ____ day of ________________, by the undersigned, ________________, who is personally known to me or satisfactorily proven to me to be the person whose name is subscribed to the within instrument.

____
Printed Name of Notary Public

____
Signature of Notary Public

My commission expires: __________________ (seal)

North Dakota

Table of Contents

In 2011, North Dakota enacted the Uniform Real Property Transfer on Death Act, found in the North Dakota Century Code (NDCC) at Chapter 30.1-32.1.

According to this statute, owners of North Dakota real property may transfer property to one or more beneficiaries effective, at the transferor's death, by lawfully executing and recording a transfer on death deed in the county or counties where the property is located (NDCC 32.1-02). The instruments must contain all the information required for traditional deeds, as well as a statement that the transfer will occur at the owner's death (30.1-32.1-06).

This transfer is no testamentary, meaning it is not included in the owner's will (30.1-32.1-04). As a result, it does not require probate distribution. Even so, best practices dictate that the will and any other transfers should not contain any conflicting instructions.

Deeds under this law allow the owners to retain absolute ownership of and control over the land until death, including the ability to cancel or change the beneficiary designation, and to sell the property outright to someone else (30.1-32.1-09). Because the transfer is revocable (30.1-32.1-03), there is no obligation to notify the beneficiary or to collect consideration (money) for the potential future interest (30.1-32.1-07).

When the transferor dies, the beneficiary gains ownership of the property with no warranties of title, and subject to any mortgages, encumbrances, and agreements in place during the owner's life. (30.1-32.1-10).

Overall, transfer on death deeds are a convenient, flexible tool for a comprehensive estate plan. North Dakota Transfer of Death Deed Forms Have Been Updated as Recently as
Thursday March 25, 2021.

What is a transfer on a Death Deed?

A transfer-on-death deed is an important tool in estate planning. It allows a person to leave property or assets to someone without leaving a full formal will. This means that the probate process, and in some cases inheritance taxes, can be avoided. It also simplifies the process when the death occurs.

What is transfer upon death?

Transfer on death (TOD) is a legal agreement by an account owner for their investment account that transfers the ownership of certain assets in the account to named beneficiaries upon the account holder's death, bypassing probate.

Is a transfer on Death Deed signed and notarize?

Once it is created, a transfer on death deed needs to be **signed and recorded** to be legally valid. The exact signing requirements vary from state to state, however, most states require the property owner making the transfer deed to sign the document as well as have it notarized.

Can I complete and file a transfer on death Deed?

A Transfer on Death Deed, also referred to as TODD, is a legal document that must be prepared before the homeowner or property owner dies. When a property owner files a Transfer on Death Deed, it is equivalent to naming a beneficiary or new property owner upon the current property owner's death. Minnesota offers the Transfer on Death Deed form as a PDF file that you can download, complete and then submit.

Does a transfer on Death Deed supersede a will?

No. The statute specifically states that a Will may not revoke or supersede a transfer on death deed. If you wish to revoke the deed, it will be necessary for you to sign with transfer on death expressly revokes the prior one or specifies that the property should pass to someone else.

What is bank payable on death form?

A Totten trust (also referred to as a "Payable on Death" account) is a form of trust in the United States in which one party (the settlor or "grantor" of the trust) places money in a bank account or security with instructions that upon the settlor's death, whatever is in that account will pass to a named beneficiary.

Is transfer on death account taxable?

However, it doesn't avoid taxes. In fact, transfer on death accounts are exposed to all the same income and capital gains taxes when the account owner is alive, as well as estate and inheritance taxes upon the owner's death.

North Dakota Transfer on Death Deeds Defined Authority

Pursuant to, N.D.C.C. 30.1-32.1-02 an *individual* may transfer *property,* to one or more *beneficiaries,* effective at *the transferor's* death, by a *transfer on death deed.*

The above definition contemplates five separate requirements for an effective *North Dakota transfer on death deed*:

1. An *individual transferor* having the proper legal capacity;
2. North Dakot*a real proper*ty;
3. One or more qualified *beneficiaries;*
4. A qualifying *North Dakota transfer on death deed* document; and
5. A *transfer* of North Dakota *real property* taking effect at the death of the *individual transferor.*

Transferor

Under N.D.C.C. 30.1-32.1-01, the term "*transferor*" is defined to mean: *an individual,* who makes *a North Dakota transfer on death deed.*

Legal Capacity

N.D.C.C. 30.1-32.1-05 identifies the legal capacity which is required of a *transferor* in order to execute a *North Dakota transfer on death deed,* by providing as follows:

The capacity required to make or revoke a *transfer on death deed* is the same as the capacity required to make a will.

Joint Tenants

The *Uniform Real Property Transfer on Death Act* official commentary corresponding to N.D.C.C. 30.1-32.1-02 declares that the term *individual* is not limited to a singular person, but also includes a multiple number of persons. Such official commentary provides an example, which identifies that: more than one person – including spouses who own real property as joint tenants, can execute *a transfer on death deed.*

Pursuant to N.D.C.C. 30.1-32.1-10(3), any *surviving joint tenant* will have ownership priority over any *surviving beneficiary* identified in a North Dakota *transfer on death deed*

Owner

The term *"owner"* is not defined by *North Dakota's* version of the Uniform Real Property Transfer on Death Act – although to a certain extent, its meaning can be inferred from the statutory definition of a *"joint owner".*

Joint Owner

Under N.D.C.C. 30.1-32.1-01, the term *"joint owner"* is defined to mean an *individual,* who owns property concurrently with one or more other *individuals*, with a right of survivorship.

The term *"joint owner"* includes: *a joint tenant,* and t*enant by the entirety* – describing a form of ownership in land restricted to married persons.

Both the *joint tenancy* and the *tenancy by the entirety* forms of ownership recognize all co- owners as a unified whole.

However, since N.D.C.C. 47-02-05 identifies that North Dakota does not otherwise recognize *tenancy by the entirety,* the term *"joint owner"* must be limited under N.D.C.C. 30.1-32.1-01 to *a joint tenant* –and not *a tenant by the entirety.*

Joint Tenancy Interest

N.D.C.C. 47-02-06 defines the term *joint tenancy interest – or joint interest* – in the following manner: A joint interest is one owned by several persons in equal shares by a title created by a single will or transfer, when expressly declared in the will or transfer to be a joint tenancy, or when granted or devised to executors or trustees as joint tenants.

At common law, each *joint tenant* owns an undivided interest in the whole estate – not merely a fractional interest in the estate and is a member of a group which collectively owns the entire estate. Unlike a *tenant in common, a joint tenant* has a right of survivorship.

Therefore, when one *joint tenant* dies: the remaining *joint tenant(s)* retain ownership of the entire estate, the former *joint tenancy interest* of the deceased co-tenant is extinguished, and nothing passes by reason of death to the heirs or devisees of the deceased *joint tenant.*

Tenant in Common

N.D.C.C. 30.1-32.1-01 identifies that the term *"joint owner"* specifically excludes a *tenant in common.* N.D.C.C. 47-02-08 defines the term *interest in common* – which is perhaps equivalent to tenant *in common* – in the following manner:

An interest in common is one owned by several persons not in joint ownership or partnership. Every interest created in favor of several persons in their own right is an interest in common, unless acquired by them in partnership for partnership purposes, or unless declared in its creation to be a joint tenancy.

Unlike a *joint tenant,* each *tenant in common* has: a distinct undivided, separate interest in the property, with no right of survivorship. Upon the death of a *tenant in common*, such co-tenant's separate interest in the property will either: pass by succession to that co-tenant's heirs under the laws of intestate succession, or devolve to that co-tenant's Will devisees.

North Dakota Transfer on Death Deeds Defined – Property

Under N.D.C.C. 30.1-32.1-01, the term *"property"* is defined to mean: *An interest in North Dakota real property,* which is transferable upon the death of the owner. The Uniform Real Property Transfer on Death Act official commentary corresponding to N.D.C.C. 30.1-32.1-02 identifies that a "*transferor* "will be able to specify in the *transfer on death deed:* the nature and extent of the *property rights* transferred – whether: surface rights, mineral rights, or both surface rights, and mineral rights, and the property *rights* reserved – if any – whether: surface rights, or mineral rights. North Dakota Mineral rights constitute real property interests, as do surface rights.

Therefore, the *property* which may be transferred by a North Dakota *transfer on death deed* can be limited to either: surface rights, or mineral rights.

Beneficiary

Under N.D.C.C. 30.1-32.1-01, the term *"beneficiary"* is defined to mean: a person that actually receives *property,* under a North Dakota *transfer on death deed.*

However, the complete version of the Uniform Real Property Transfer on Death Act provides definition for the term *person* – which definition is not included in North Dakota's version of the Uniform Real

Property Transfer on Death Act, and identifies estates, trusts, and various government and business entities as *persons.*

The corresponding Uniform Real Property Transfer on Death Act official commentary associates the definition of the term *person,* with the definition of the term *beneficiary,* since the complete version of the *Uniform Real Property Transfer on Death Act* provides a definition for the term *person.*

Therefore, the Uniform Real Property Transfer on Death Act official commentary identifies that a *beneficiary* can be any *person* including a trustee of a revocable trust. It could be argued that by excluding estates, trusts, and various government and business entities from the definition of a *person*, North Dakota intended to exclude estates, trusts, and various government and business entities from the term *beneficiary.*

By failing to provide a definition for the term *person,* North Dakota's version of the Uniform Real Property Transfer on Death Act creates some uncertainty as to whether a *beneficiary* can be anyone other than an individual person.

Therefore, estates, trusts, and various government and business entities may not be permitted to be *beneficiaries* under a North Dakota *transfer on death deed.*

Designated Beneficiary

Under N.D.C.C. 30.1-32.1-01, the term "*designated beneficiary*" is defined to mean: a person, designated to receive property, in a North Dakota *transfer on death deed.*

However, the complete version of the Uniform Real Property Transfer on Death Act provides a definition for the term *person*, and associates that definition with the definition for the term *designated beneficiary.* Therefore, the corresponding Uniform Real Property Transfer on Death Act official commentary identifies that a *designated beneficiary* can be any person – including a trustee of a revocable trust.

The definition of a *designated beneficiary* contemplates a person who: and he nature and extent of the *property rights* transferred whether is designated to receive such property, upon the death of the transferor pursuant to a North Dakota *transfer on death deed* which remains revocable until death – rather than the person(s) who actually receive the property.

Recording Requirements

N.D.C.C. 30.1-32.1-06 identifies the recording requirements for an effective North Dakota *transfer on death deed*, by providing in part as follows. A *transfer on death deed* must_be recorded before the transferor's death in the public records in the office of the county recorder of the county where the property is located.

Therefore, if a North Dakota *transfer on death deed* is not recorded properly before the death of the *transferor*, it will not be effective to transfer title to the *designated beneficiary* upon the death of the *transferor*.

North Dakota Primary and Contingent Designated Beneficiaries

The Uniform Real Property Transfer on Death Act official commentary corresponding to N.D.C.C. 30.1-32.1-02 identifies that the "*transferor* "will be able to designate in a *transfer on death deed* one or more primary beneficiaries who will have rights to the *transferor's* property if such *beneficiary* or *beneficiaries* survive the *transferor.*

Such official commentary corresponding to N.D.C.C. 30.1-32.1-02 also provides that one or more contingent beneficiaries will have rights to the *transferor's* property if, such *beneficiary* or *beneficiaries* survive the *transferor,* but one or more of the primary beneficiaries do not.

Forms

Recording requested by:

When recorded mail to and mail tax statements to:

Space above this line for recorder's use

North Dakota Transfer on Death Deed
(Beneficiary Deed)

I, ______________________, with a mailing address of ____ (hereinafter referred to as the "Owner") being of competent mind and having the legal capacity to execute this document, as owner transfer on death to ______________________ with a mailing address of ____ (hereinafter referred to as the "Primary Beneficiary") as grantee beneficiary, the following described interest in real estate:

____

____

____

____

____

____

____

Legal description of the property (including square, suffix, and lot number)

If the Primary Beneficiary does not survive me, I designate ______________________ with a mailing address of ____ _________ (hereinafter referred to as the "Alternate Beneficiary") as grantee beneficiary.

This Transfer on Death Deed is revocable. It does not transfer any ownership until the death of the owner. It revokes all prior beneficiary designations by this owner for this

interest in real estate. The grantor has the right to withdraw or rescind this deed at any time. Any beneficiaries named in this deed are hereby advised that this deed may be withdrawn or rescinded whether or not money or any other consideration was paid or given.

Owner's Name	Primary Beneficiary's Name	Alternate Beneficiary's Name
Owner's Signature	Primary Beneficiary's Signature	Alternate Beneficiary's Signature
Date	Date	Date

Notary Acknowledgment

State of ____________________

County of ___________________

The foregoing was acknowledged before me this ____ day of ________________, by the undersigned, ________________, who is personally known to me or satisfactorily proven to me to be the person whose name is subscribed to the within instrument.

____
Printed Name of Notary Public

____
Signature of Notary Public

My commission expires: ___________________ (seal)

North Dakota Transfer on Death Deed Revocation Form

Recording requested by (name):

____

When recorded mail to
and mail tax statements to:

____

____

____

____

Recorder's Use Only

REVOCATION OF REVOCABLE TRANSFER ON DEATH DEED

This document is exempt from documentary transfer tax under Rev. & Tax. Code § 11930. This document is exempt from preliminary change of ownership report under Rev. & Tax. Code § 480.3.

Assessor's Parcel No.: ____________________________________

Declaration of Exemption From Gov't Code § 27388.1 Fee

- ☐ Transfer is exempt from fee per GC § 27388.1(a)(2):
  - ☐ recorded concurrently "in connection with" transfer subject to Documentary Transfer Tax
  - ☐ recorded concurrently "in connection with" a transfer of residential dwelling to an owner-occupier
- ☐ Transfer is exempt from fee per GC 27388.1(a)(1):
  - ☐ Fee cap of $225.00 reached ☐ Not related to real property

IMPORTANT NOTICE: THIS FORM MUST BE RECORDED TO BE EFFECTIVE

This revocation form MUST be RECORDED before your death or it will not be effective. This revocation form only affects a transfer on death deed that YOU made. A transfer on death deed made by a co-owner of your property is not affected by this revocation form. A co-owner who wants to revoke a transfer on death deed that he/she made must complete and RECORD a SEPARATE revocation form.

PROPERTY DESCRIPTION

Print the legal description of the property affected by this revocation:

____

____

____

REVOCATION

I, ______________________________, am the transferor under the Revocable TOD deed dated ______________ and recorded on ______________ as Instrument No. _____________ in Book/Reel ________, Page/Image ________, of Official Records of ____________________________________ County North Dakota, which named as beneficiary(ies) ____.

I hereby revoke any TOD deed to transfer the described property that I executed before executing this form, including the TOD deed described above.

SIGNATURE AND DATE

Sign and print your name below (your name should exactly match the name shown on your title documents):

Date: ____________________

____
(Signature of declarant)

____
(Typed or written name of declarant)

Notary Acknowledgment

State of ____________________

County of __________________

The foregoing was acknowledged before me this ____ day of ________________, by the undersigned, ________________, who is personally known to me or satisfactorily proven to me to be the person whose name is subscribed to the within instrument.

____

Printed Name of Notary Public

____

Signature of Notary Public

My commission expires: __________________ (seal)

Ohio

Table of Contents

Does Ohio have transfer on death deeds?

In August of 2000, Ohio became one of only a handful of states that allowed what is commonly called a transfer on death deed or TOD deed. A transfer on death deed allowed an owner of real estate to create a deed with a beneficiary designation naming who would inherit the real estate on death.

Ohio law allows individuals who do not need the estate administration benefits of a trust agreement to avoid Probate on the transfer of real property by executing a legal document called a Transfer-On-Death ("TOD") Designation Affidavit.

Is a transfer on death deed a good idea?

If you'd like to avoid having your property going through the probate process, it's a good idea to look into a transfer on death deed. A transfer on death deed allows you to select a beneficiary who will receive your property, but only when you've passed away.

What is the difference between an Ohio survivorship deed and a transfer on death designation affidavit?

Survivorship Deeds contain special language that enables the property to transfer to the surviving owner(s) upon the deceased owner's death.

A Transfer-On-Death Designation Affidavit allows the owner of Ohio real estate to designate one or more beneficiaries of the property.

Do you pay taxes on transfer on death?

Keep in mind that as long as you're alive, TOD Deeds have no impact on (or benefit for) your beneficiary. He or she has no legal rights to the property until after you pass away.
That means you pay the property taxes on it until you die.

Is transfer on death considered an inheritance?

Because TOD accounts are still part of the decedent's estate (although not the probate estate that the Last Will establishes), they may be subject to Income, estate and/or inheritance tax. TOD accounts are also not out of reach for the decedent's creditors or other relatives.

Can I withdraw money from my own TOD account?

This account is wholly owned by both spouses while they're both alive. As a result, a creditor of one spouse could make a claim against the entire account, without any approval or say from the other spouse. Either spouse could also withdraw all the money in the account and not tell the other.

How much does it cost to do a TOD?

You must record a TOD deed within 60 days, or it becomes invalid.

Record the TOD deed in the county where the property is located.

The Recorder's Office charges a recording fee (currently $21/first page plus $3 for additional pages).

Are transfer on death deeds revocable?

The transfer on death deed is fully revocable before the death of the real property owner.

Can a transfer on death deed go to a trust?

Having someone on the deed as a joint owner with rights of survivorship will avoid probate. Upon the death of one owner, title automatically goes to the surviving joint owner or owners. With a TOD deed, you keep full control of the property transfer to a living trust.

Can transfer on death be contested?

Because transfer-on-death beneficiary deeds do not become effective until you pass away, someone can challenge the validity of the deed after you die or beneficiaries and family members can sue each other to take the property entirely. In this case, a court proceeding may be required to resolve the issue.

How do I transfer a deed after death in Ohio?

Avoid probate and pass on your Ohio real estate with a simple transfer-on-death deed

Fill in information about you and the TOD beneficiary.

Provide a description of the property.

Check over the completed deed.

Sign the deed in front of a notary public

How to Prepare a Transfer-on-Death Deed

Get a Deed Form or Prepare Your Own. You can buy a state-specific TOD deed form for your state or type up your own document.

Name the Beneficiary.

Describe the Property.

Sign the Deed.

Record the Deed.

How does a TOD account work?

A TOD account automatically transfers the assets to a named beneficiary, when the account holder dies. Let's say you have a savings account with $100,000 in it. Your son is the beneficiary for the TOD account. When you die, the account's assets are transferred directly to him without having to go through probate.

What is the difference between TOD and beneficiary?

A beneficiary form states who will directly inherit the asset at your death. Under a TOD arrangement, you keep full control of the asset during your lifetime and pay taxes on any income the asset generates as you own it outright. TOD arrangements require minimal paperwork to establish.

Does a TOD Supersede a will?

A TOD designation supersedes a will. For bank accounts, you can set up a similar account known as payable-on-death, sometimes referred to as a Totten trust. Your beneficiaries can't touch the account while you're alive, and you're free to change beneficiaries or close the accounts at any time.

Do you have to pay taxes on POD accounts?

The value of a POD account generally will not be included in your taxable income because bequests aren't taxable as income. Any income earned by the POD account prior to the date the bequeathed died is reported on their final income tax return.

Is a TOD account part of an estate?

Because TOD accounts are still part of the decedent's estate (although not the probate estate that the Last Will establishes), they may be subject to income, estate and/or inheritance tax. TOD accounts are also not out of reach for the decedent's creditors or other relatives.

Are TOD accounts taxable to the beneficiary?

The amount that's in a TOD account at the time of your death is not taxable under federal law to the person who receives the account, although it may be taxable to your estate. If your beneficiary or the account are in a state with an inheritance tax, he may have to pay that.

Can you put a TOD on a joint account?

TOD becomes effective for joint accounts if both owners pass away simultaneously. Joint and TOD registration generally allow an account to pass outside the probate estate, enabling the surviving owner or beneficiaries to avoid the time and expense of that process for this account.

What happens if you don't file taxes for a deceased person?

If you don't file taxes for the decedent and the estate promptly, the IRS can file a federal tax lien requiring you pay the decedent's income tax ahead of other bills. If the deceased passed on owing more than the estate can pay, the IRS can use the lien to demand money.

How do I remove someone from a deed in Ohio?

The only way to forcibly change the ownership status is through a legal action and the resultant court order. However, if an owner chooses to be removed from the deed, it is simply a matter of preparing a new deed transferring that owner's interest in the property.

What is the difference between a title and a deed?

A deed is an official written document declaring a person's legal ownership of a property, while a title refers to the concept of ownership rights.

Does a deed mean you own the house?

A house deed is the legal document that transfers ownership of the property from the seller to the buyer. In short, it's what ensures the house you just bought is legally yours.

What's more important deed or title?

A title is the legal right to use and modify the property how you see fit, or transfer interest or any portion that you own to others via a deed. A deed represents the right of the owner to claim the property. As opposed to the title, that describes who the ultimate holder of the property is.

What does being on the deed of a house mean?

The person whose name is on the deed has the title to the property. It's the deed that transfers title. On the deed, you'll find the property's legal description, including property or boundary lines. The deed identifies the grantor, or party transferring his interest in the property, and the grantee,

Forms

Recording requested by:

When recorded mail to and mail tax statements to:

Space above this line for recorder's use

Ohio Transfer on Death Deed

(Beneficiary Deed)

I, ______________________, with a mailing address of ________________________ ______________________________________ (hereinafter referred to as the "Owner") being of competent mind and having the legal capacity to execute this document, as owner transfer on death to ______________________ with a mailing address of ______ ____ (hereinafter referred to as the "Primary Beneficiary") as grantee beneficiary, the following described interest in real estate:

____

____

____

____

____

____

____

Legal description of the property (including square, suffix, and lot number)

If the Primary Beneficiary does not survive me, I designate ______________________ with a mailing address of ____ _________ (hereinafter referred to as the "Alternate Beneficiary") as grantee beneficiary.

This Transfer on Death Deed is revocable. It does not transfer any ownership until the death of the owner. It revokes all prior beneficiary designations by this owner for this

interest in real estate. The grantor has the right to withdraw or rescind this deed at any time. Any beneficiaries named in this deed are hereby advised that this deed may be withdrawn or rescinded whether or not money or any other consideration was paid or given.

______________________	______________________	______________________
Owner's Name	Primary Beneficiary's Name	Alternate Beneficiary's Name
______________________	______________________	______________________
Owner's Signature	Primary Beneficiary's Signature	Alternate Beneficiary's Signature
______________________	______________________	______________________
Date	Date	Date

Notary Acknowledgment

State of ____________________

County of __________________

The foregoing was acknowledged before me this ____ day of ________________, by the undersigned, ________________, who is personally known to me or satisfactorily proven to me to be the person whose name is subscribed to the within instrument.

____
Printed Name of Notary Public

____
Signature of Notary Public

My commission expires: __________________ (seal)

TRANSFER ON DEATH DESIGNATION AFFIDAVIT
[RC 5302.22]

STATE of OHIO
COUNTY of ________________

____, owner, with a marital status of__________________, now owner of record of the following real property located at ____ as recorded at Instrument No. _______________________________of __________ County deed records, with the following legal description:

Title of record to the above property is held by owner(s) as follows:

_____ Sole owner
_____ Tenant(s) in common
_____ Tenant(s) in survivorship
_____ Tenant(s) by the entireties

Hereby designates the following as transfer on death beneficiary to receive the owner's title to that property upon the death of the owner:
____.

________________________________, wife/husband of the owner, states that her/his dower rights are subordinate to the vesting of title to the real property in the transfer on death beneficiary designated herein.

Notary Acknowledgment

State of ____________________

County of __________________

The foregoing was acknowledged before me this ____ day of ________________, by the undersigned, ________________, who is personally known to me or satisfactorily proven to me to be the person whose name is subscribed to the within instrument.

____
Printed Name of Notary Public

____
Signature of Notary Public

My commission expires: __________________ (seal)

Ohio Transfer on Death Deed Revocation Form

Recording requested by (name):

____

When recorded mail to
and mail tax statements to:

____

____

____

____

Recorder's Use Only

REVOCATION OF REVOCABLE TRANSFER ON DEATH DEED

This document is exempt from documentary transfer tax under Rev. & Tax. Code § 11930. This document is exempt from preliminary change of ownership report under Rev. & Tax. Code § 480.3.

Assessor's Parcel No.:

____

Declaration of Exemption From Gov't Code § 27388.1 Fee

☐ Transfer is exempt from fee per GC § 27388.1(a)(2):
- ☐ recorded concurrently "in connection with" transfer subject to Documentary Transfer Tax
- ☐ recorded concurrently "in connection with" a transfer of residential dwelling to an owner-occupier

☐ Transfer is exempt from fee per GC 27388.1(a)(1):
- ☐ Fee cap of $225.00 reached ☐ Not related to real property

IMPORTANT NOTICE: THIS FORM MUST BE RECORDED TO BE EFFECTIVE

This revocation form MUST be RECORDED before your death or it will not be effective. This revocation form only affects a transfer on death deed that YOU made. A transfer on death deed made by a co-owner of your property is not affected by this revocation form. A co-owner who wants to revoke a transfer on death deed that he/she made must complete and RECORD a SEPARATE revocation form.

PROPERTY DESCRIPTION

Print the legal description of the property affected by this revocation:

____

____

____

REVOCATION

I, ______________________, am the transferor under the Revocable TOD deed dated ____________ and recorded on ____________ as Instrument No. ____________ in Book/Reel ________, Page/Image ________, of Official Records of ______________________ County Ohio, which named as beneficiary(ies) ______________________________

____.

I hereby revoke any TOD deed to transfer the described property that I executed before executing this form, including the TOD deed described above.

SIGNATURE AND DATE

Sign and print your name below (your name should exactly match the name shown on your title documents):

Date: ________________ ______________________________
(Signature of declarant)

____
(Typed or written name of declarant)

Notary Acknowledgment

State of ____________________

County of __________________

The foregoing was acknowledged before me this ____ day of ________________, by the undersigned, ________________, who is personally known to me or satisfactorily proven to me to be the person whose name is subscribed to the within instrument.

____
Printed Name of Notary Public

____
Signature of Notary Public

My commission expires: __________________ (seal)

Oklahoma

Table of Contents

How to do a transfer on death deed in Oklahoma?

You need to know:

TITLE: Title the property "Transfer-on-death" by making a new deed.

NAME: Name the person to get the land, home or mineral interest when the record owner dies on the new deed. This person is called the "beneficiary."

SIGN: Sign the deed before two witnesses and a notary.

What is a Transfer-On-Death Deed?

On November 1, 2008, Oklahoma's "No testamentary Transfer of Property Act" (Title 58 O.S. §§ 1251-1258) went into effect. This law allows a **"record owner"** to use a **"Transfer-On-Death Deed"** to name another person to receive his **real estate** without going through probate. This transfer **does not take effect** until the landowner's death. The person receiving the property (called the **beneficiary)** must take certain steps to make the transfer legal.

Terms to know

"Record owner" is the person whose interest in real estate is recorded in County Clerk's office where the real estate is located.

"Grantor" is the person who owns the land or home and who has a properly recorded deed or title to the land, home or mineral interest being transferred. A grantor is sometimes also called homeowner, landowner or oil, gas and mineral interest owner.

"Beneficiary" is the person to get the land, home or mineral interest when the **record owner** dies. This person is named on the new deed the **record owner** must file. This person is sometimes called a **"grantee."**

"Alternative beneficiary" is a second person named by the record owner to receive the property, only if the first person cannot. For example, if the **beneficiary** named to receive the property dies before the landowner dies, the property cannot be transferred as the owner wanted because of probate and real estate laws. There would have to be a probate to transfer the property to someone else.

"Revoke" means to change your mind. If you sign a Transfer-On-Death Deed and then later decide to leave the property to someone else, you have to sign and file a certain kind of form and then make a new Transfer-On-Death Deed.

"Joint Tenancy with Right of Survivorship" is co-ownership of property. Two or more people own the property together with exactly the same rights. Usually how married people own property. You still have to change the deed when one person dies, but usually do not have to go through probate to do this.

Who can use a Transfer on Death (or Beneficiary) Deed?

Anyone who owns a home, land or oil, gas or mineral interests can use a **Transfer-On-Death Deed**. This type of deed is used to transfer property to another person after someone dies, but without having to file an expensive or time-consuming probate case in the court.

What Types of Property (Real Estate) Can the Owner Transfer Using a Transfer-On-Death Deed?

Land

A Home

Certain types of oil, gas and mineral rights.

(Please consult an oil and gas attorney for further advice regarding oil, gas and mineral interests.)

The exclusive rights to drill for, produce, or otherwise gain possession of such substances.

The owner's right to a royalty, which is a percentage of profit from what is drilled or taken out of the land.

How Does an Owner Use a Transfer-On-Death Deed To Avoid Probate?

A record owner may use this type of deed to transfer property to a beneficiary to be effective after the record owner dies. Specific forms are required. You must follow the law for the transfer to be done correctly. Please ask a lawyer for advice!

The record owner must:

TITLE: Title the property "Transfer-on-death" by making a new deed.

NAME: Name the person to get the land, home or mineral interest when the record owner dies on the new deed. This person is called the "beneficiary."

SIGN: Sign the deed before two witnesses and a notary.

RECORD: Record the deed in the office of the County Clerk in the county where the real estate is located, before his or her death.

You need to know:

- The beneficiary does not have to pay the owner any money for the transfer-on-death deed to be legal.
- The owner is not required to tell or get approval from the person named to receive the property.
- The owner may change his mind and "revoke" the deed any time before he dies.
- The owner has to file a form to "revoke" and then file a new transfer-on-death deed.
- Writing something in a will does NOT revoke the transfer-on-death deed.
- The record owner should name a second person on the deed as an "alternative beneficiary," in case the person named dies before the record owner.

If no alternative is named and the first beneficiary dies before the owner, the transfer will not be effective under law. A probate will have to be filed to transfer title.

If you file a second transfer-on-death deed, that second deed makes any deed you filed before that invalid. You should file a form to "revoke" first and then sign a new deed.

Property owned by more than one person by "Joint Tenancy with Right of Survivorship" can be transferred by this kind of deed but will only be effective if the person who signed the transfer-on-death deed is the last of the joint owners to die.

The beneficiary will obtain the real estate subject to all conveyances, assignments, contracts, mortgages, liens and security pledges the record owner made during his lifetime. This may also include any conveyances of interest that are less than all of the record owner's interest in the property. To be sure what other interests the record owner had recorded on the property, you should search the title records on the property at the County Clerk's office.

How Does a Beneficiary Claim the Transfer-On-Death Property?

The Beneficiary must sign a form. The form must be filed with the County Clerk in the county where the real estate is located and the deed is recorded.

The form is called an Affidavit. An Affidavit is a form that has certain information and a sworn statement by you that are the beneficiary. It must be signed in front of a notary.

<u>The Affidavit must contain:</u>

1. The fact of the death of the record owner.
2. Whether or not the record owner and the beneficiary were husband and wife.
3. The legal description of the real estate.
4. If the beneficiary was not the record owner's spouse, the beneficiary, must attach with the Affidavit: A copy of the death certificate of the record owner. You can apply for a death certificate with this form at the OK Department of Vital Statistics (OKC),
5. A beneficiary must file a written Beneficiary's Affidavit to accept a Transfer-on-Death Deed within 9 months of the landowner's death or the property will revert to the deceased owner's estate.

REMEMBER:

A beneficiary will get title to the real estate subject to all conveyances, assignments, contracts, mortgages, liens and security pledges the record owner made during his lifetime. This may also include any conveyances of interest that are less than all of the record owner's interest in the property. You should search the title records on the property at the County Clerk's office so you know what other interests the owner recorded on the property.

How do I transfer a deed in Oklahoma?

Include the property address and its legal description and identify by name the grantor(s) and the grantee(s). Make copies of the deed and record the deed transfer with the assessor's office in the county where the property is located.17 Mar 2017

How do you avoid probate in Oklahoma?

In Oklahoma, you can make a living trust to avoid probate for virtually any asset you own—real estate, bank accounts, vehicles, and so on. You need to create a trust document (it's similar to a will), naming someone to take over as trustee after your death (called a successor trustee).

How much does an estate have to be worth to go to probate in Oklahoma?

Simplified Probate Procedures

You can use the simplified small estate process in Oklahoma if the value of the estate is $200,000 or less, if the deceased person has been dead for more than five years, or if he or she resided in another state at the time of death.

Is transfer on death considered an inheritance?

Because TOD accounts are still part of the decedent's estate (although not the probate estate that the Last Will establishes), they may be subject to income, estate and/or inheritance tax. TOD accounts are also not out of reach for the decedent's creditors or other relatives.18 Mar 2019

Do you pay taxes on transfer on death?

Tax Implications of Transfer on Death Deeds

Keep in mind that as long as you're alive, TOD Deeds have no impact on (or benefit for) your Beneficiary. He or she has no legal rights to the property until after you pass away. That means you pay the property taxes on it until you die.

Does transfer on death avoid estate tax?

Estate Taxes

When someone dies and their property transfers to their beneficiaries, the federal government impose an estate tax on the value of all that property. Since the transfer on death account is not a trust, it does not help you avoid or minimize estate taxes.

Can you withdraw money from a TOD account?

This account is wholly owned by both spouses while they're both alive. As a result, a creditor of one spouse could make a claim against the entire account, without any approval or say from the other spouse. Either spouse could also withdraw all the money in the account and not tell the other.

What happens if a TOD beneficiary dies?

In the event that there are no living beneficiaries, life insurance policies, TOD and POD accounts will go to the decedent's estate. If the beneficiary outlives the person creating the estate plan, but dies before receiving the gift, the gift will go to the probate estate of the deceased beneficiary.

Can you put a TOD on a joint account?

TOD becomes effective for joint accounts if both owners pass away simultaneously. Joint and TOD registration generally allow an account to pass outside the probate estate, enabling the surviving owner or beneficiaries to avoid the time and expense of that process for this account.

What type of account is a TOD?

What Is a TOD Account? A transfer on death (TOD) account automatically transfers its assets to a named beneficiary when the holder dies for example, if you have a savings account with $100,000 in it and name your son as its beneficiary that account would transfer to him upon your death.

Are bank accounts frozen upon death?

Will bank accounts be frozen? Banks and other financial institutions will freeze accounts that are titled in the decedent's name alone. You will need a tax release, death certificate, and Letters of Authority from probate court to have access to the account.

What happens if a beneficiary dies after the testator but before they inherited?

What happens when there is a predeceased beneficiary? When a beneficiary passes away before the testator their benefit from the estate will Lapse. This means that their death has rendered their gift void.

What happens if no one files probate?

If Probate is needed but you don't apply for it, the beneficiaries won't be able to receive their inheritance. Instead the deceased person's assets will be frozen and held in a state of limbo. No one will have the legal authority to access, sell or transfer them.

Can a bank release funds without probate?

Once the bank has all the necessary documents, the funds will usually be released within 10 to 15 working days. All banks have their own threshold for how much money they can release from a deceased person's account without a Grant of Probate.

Forms

Recording requested by: When recorded mail to and mail tax statements to:	

Space above this line for recorder's use

Oklahoma Transfer on Death Deed

(Beneficiary Deed)

I, ______________________, with a mailing address of ________________________ ______________________________________ (hereinafter referred to as the "Owner") being of competent mind and having the legal capacity to execute this document, as owner transfer on death to ______________________ with a mailing address of ______ ____ (hereinafter referred to as the "Primary Beneficiary") as grantee beneficiary, the following described interest in real estate:

____

____

____

____

____

____

____

Legal description of the property (including square, suffix, and lot number)

If the Primary Beneficiary does not survive me, I designate ______________________ with a mailing address of ____ _________ (hereinafter referred to as the "Alternate Beneficiary") as grantee beneficiary.

This Transfer on Death Deed is revocable. It does not transfer any ownership until the death of the owner. It revokes all prior beneficiary designations by this owner for this

interest in real estate. The grantor has the right to withdraw or rescind this deed at any time. Any beneficiaries named in this deed are hereby advised that this deed may be withdrawn or rescinded whether or not money or any other consideration was paid or given.

Owner's Name	Primary Beneficiary's Name	Alternate Beneficiary's Name
Owner's Signature	Primary Beneficiary's Signature	Alternate Beneficiary's Signature
Date	Date	Date

Notary Acknowledgment

State of ____________________

County of ___________________

The foregoing was acknowledged before me this ____ day of ________________, by the undersigned, ________________, who is personally known to me or satisfactorily proven to me to be the person whose name is subscribed to the within instrument.

____
Printed Name of Notary Public

____
Signature of Notary Public

My commission expires: ___________________ (seal)

Oklahoma Transfer on Death Deed Revocation Form

Recording requested by (name):

____

When recorded mail to
and mail tax statements to:

____

____

____

____

Recorder's Use Only

REVOCATION OF REVOCABLE TRANSFER ON DEATH DEED

This document is exempt from documentary transfer tax under Rev. & Tax. Code § 11930. This document is exempt from preliminary change of ownership report under Rev. & Tax. Code § 480.3.

Assessor's Parcel No.:

____

Declaration of Exemption From Gov't Code § 27388.1 Fee

☐ Transfer is exempt from fee per GC § 27388.1(a)(2):
- ☐ recorded concurrently "in connection with" transfer subject to Documentary Transfer Tax
- ☐ recorded concurrently "in connection with" a transfer of residential dwelling to an owner-occupier

☐ Transfer is exempt from fee per GC 27388.1(a)(1):
- ☐ Fee cap of $225.00 reached ☐ Not related to real property

IMPORTANT NOTICE: THIS FORM MUST BE RECORDED TO BE EFFECTIVE

This revocation form MUST be RECORDED before your death or it will not be effective. This revocation form only affects a transfer on death deed that YOU made. A transfer on death deed made by a co-owner of your property is not affected by this revocation form. A co-owner who wants to revoke a transfer on death deed that he/she made must complete and RECORD a SEPARATE revocation form.

PROPERTY DESCRIPTION

Print the legal description of the property affected by this revocation:

____

____

____

REVOCATION

I, ______________________________, am the transferor under the Revocable TOD deed dated ______________ and recorded on ______________ as Instrument No. ______________ in Book/Reel ________, Page/Image ________, of Official Records of ______________________________ County Oklahoma, which named as beneficiary(ies) ______________________________

______________________________.

I hereby revoke any TOD deed to transfer the described property that I executed before executing this form, including the TOD deed described above.

SIGNATURE AND DATE

Sign and print your name below (your name should exactly match the name shown on your title documents):

Date: ____________________

____
(Signature of declarant)

____
(Typed or written name of declarant)

Notary Acknowledgment

State of ____________________

County of __________________

The foregoing was acknowledged before me this ____ day of ________________, by the undersigned, ________________, who is personally known to me or satisfactorily proven to me to be the person whose name is subscribed to the within instrument.

____
Printed Name of Notary Public

____
Signature of Notary Public

My commission expires: __________________ (seal)

Oregon

Table of Contents

Transfer on Death Deed on Oregon

Effective January 1, 2012, Oregon law provides for a new form of deed known as a transfer on death (TOD) deed. These deeds allow an owner of real property to designate a beneficiary who will obtain title to that real property when the owner dies, without having to go through probate (subject to some exceptions)

Does Oregon recognize transfer on death deeds?

In 2012, Oregon began to allow transfer on death deeds for real property. It allows a very specific deed to be filed which automatically transfers title of the property to those listed as beneficiaries.

Is a transfer on death deed a good idea?

If you'd like to avoid having your property going through the probate process, it's a good idea to look into a transfer on death deed. A transfer on death deed allows you to select a beneficiary who will receive your property, but only when you've passed away

A Transfer on Death Deed trumps a will.

Later, you make a will leaving the same property to your spouse. When you die the property will pass to your child under the Transfer on Death Deed. If you want your spouse to inherit the property instead, you must change or cancel the old Transfer on Death Deed.

How do I transfer a deed in Oregon?

A conveyance of land in Oregon, or of any estate or interest therein located in Oregon, can be created, transferred, or declared by a deed in writing and should be signed by the person of lawful age (or their agent) from whom the estate or interest is intended to pass.

Do you pay taxes on transfer on death?

The amount that's in a TOD account at the time of your death is not taxable under federal law to the person who receives the account, although it may be taxable to your estate. If your beneficiary or the account are in a state with an inheritance tax, he may have to pay that.

Is transfer on death considered an inheritance?

Because TOD accounts are still part of the decedent's estate (although not the probate estate that the Last Will establishes), they may be subject to income, estate and/or inheritance tax. TOD accounts are also not out of reach for the decedent's creditors or other relatives.

Can a TOD account be contested?

Because transfer-on-death beneficiary deeds do not become effective until you pass away, someone can challenge the validity of the deed after you die. Or beneficiaries and family members can sue each other to take the property entirely. In this case, a court proceeding may be required to resolve the issue.

What is difference between POD and TOD?

A POD account is very similar to a transfer-on-death (TOD) arrangement but deals with a person's bank assets instead of their stocks, bonds, mutual funds, or other investment assets. 2Both POD and TOD agreements offer quick means of dispersing assets, as both avoid the probate process, which can take several months.

Does a TOD supersede a will?

A TOD designation supersedes a will. Once you're dead, your beneficiaries receive these assets by filling out forms provided by the financial institution and providing a certified copy of your death certificate.

When a deed is recorded in Oregon you must provide a statement of consideration?

Yes, Oregon law requires a warning to the grantee about ascertaining the land use status of the property. Oregon law requires that the statement of consideration state the actual monetary consideration for the transfer.

How do you avoid probate in Oregon?

In Oregon, you can make a living trust to avoid probate for virtually any asset you own—real estate, bank accounts, vehicles, and so on. You need to create a trust document (it's similar to a will), naming someone to take over as trustee after your death (called a successor trustee).

Can you withdraw money from a dead person's account?

Once a Grant of Probate has been awarded, the executor or administrator will be able to take this document to any banks where the person who has died held an account. They will then be given permission to withdraw any money from the accounts and distribute it as per instructions in the Will.

What happens if a TOD beneficiary dies?

In the event that there are no living beneficiaries, life insurance polic es, TOD and POD accounts will go to the decedent's estate. If the beneficiary outlives the person creating the estate plan, but dies before receiving the gift, the gift will go to the probate estate of the deceased beneficiary.

Can I put a TOD on my house?

Including California, TOD deeds are now permitted in 26 states and the District of Columbia. The TOD deed allows a person to leave his or her real property to a designated person or persons such as a family member, friend, life-long partner or other loved one without having to set up a living trust.

Can a POA add a TOD?

The POA retains access to any of the decedent's assets that name them as a joint owner or payable-on-death (POD) or transfer-on-death (TOD) beneficiary. Assets that commonly carry POD/TOD designations or can be jointly titled include life insurance proceeds, bank accounts, retirement accounts and brokerage accounts.

What type of account is a TOD?

What Is a TOD Account? A transfer on death (TOD) account automatically transfers its assets to a named beneficiary when the holder dies. For example, if you have a savings account with $10C,000 in it and name your son as its beneficiary, that account would transfer to him upon your death.

Does a TOD expire?

Yes, your Transfer on Death deed will remain valid as long as it is executed before January 1, 2022. However, with the uncertainty of the status of this law, there is no guarantee that future changes to the TOD deed law may not affect you.

What is transfer on death designation?

The transfer on death designation lets beneficiaries receive assets at the time of the person's death without going through probate. With TOD registration, the named beneficiaries have no access to or control over a person's assets as long as the person is alive.

How do I record a deed in Oregon?

Recording – A deed should be filed at the Recorder's Office in the County where the property is located (See List of County Offices). Required Disclosure (ORS 93.040) – This Statement must be written in all deeds filed in the State of Oregon.

How do you add a name to a deed in Oregon?

Step 1: Download the Oregon quitclaim deed form.

Step 2: Record the name and contact information of the person who is filling in the form, the "recorder." This goes in the "prepared by" section.

Step 3: Add the name and address of the person who will receive the form when it is recorded.

Forms

Recording requested by:

When recorded mail to and mail tax statements to:

Space above this line for recorder's use

Oregon Transfer on Death Deed

(Beneficiary Deed)

I, ______________________, with a mailing address of ________________________ ____ (hereinafter referred to as the "Owner") being of competent mind and having the legal capacity to execute this document, as owner transfer on death to ________________________ with a mailing address of ______ ____ (hereinafter referred to as the "Primary Beneficiary") as grantee beneficiary, the following described interest in real estate:

____

____

____

____

____

____

____

Legal description of the property (including square, suffix, and lot number)

If the Primary Beneficiary does not survive me, I designate ______________________ with a mailing address of ____ _________ (hereinafter referred to as the "Alternate Beneficiary") as grantee beneficiary.

This Transfer on Death Deed is revocable. It does not transfer any ownership until the death of the owner. It revokes all prior beneficiary designations by this owner for this

interest in real estate. The grantor has the right to withdraw or rescind this deed at any time. Any beneficiaries named in this deed are hereby advised that this deed may be withdrawn or rescinded whether or not money or any other consideration was paid or given.

Owner's Name	Primary Beneficiary's Name	Alternate Beneficiary's Name
Owner's Signature	Primary Beneficiary's Signature	Alternate Beneficiary's Signature
Date	Date	Date

Notary Acknowledgment

State of ____________________

County of __________________

The foregoing was acknowledged before me this ____ day of ________________, by the undersigned, ________________, who is personally known to me or satisfactorily proven to me to be the person whose name is subscribed to the within instrument.

____

Printed Name of Notary Public

____

Signature of Notary Public

My commission expires: __________________ (seal)

Oregon Transfer on Death Deed Revocation Form

Recording requested by (name):

____

When recorded mail to
and mail tax statements to:

____

____

____

____

Recorder's Use Only

REVOCATION OF REVOCABLE TRANSFER ON DEATH DEED

This document is exempt from documentary transfer tax under Rev. & Tax. Code § 11930. This document is exempt from preliminary change of ownership report under Rev. & Tax. Code § 480.3.

Assessor's Parcel No.:

____

Declaration of Exemption From Gov't Code § 27388.1 Fee

☐ Transfer is exempt from fee per GC § 27388.1(a)(2):
- ☐ recorded concurrently "in connection with" transfer subject to Documentary Transfer Tax
- ☐ recorded concurrently "in connection with" a transfer of residential dwelling to an owner-occupier

☐ Transfer is exempt from fee per GC 27388.1(a)(1):
- ☐ Fee cap of $225.00 reached ☐ Not related to real property

IMPORTANT NOTICE: THIS FORM MUST BE RECORDED TO BE EFFECTIVE

This revocation form MUST be RECORDED before your death or it will not be effective. This revocation form only affects a transfer on death deed that YOU made. A transfer on death deed made by a co-owner of your property is not affected by this revocation form. A co-owner who wants to revoke a transfer on death deed that he/she made must complete and RECORD a SEPARATE revocation form.

PROPERTY DESCRIPTION

Print the legal description of the property affected by this revocation:

____

____

____

REVOCATION

I, ______________________________, am the transferor under the Revocable TOD deed dated ______________ and recorded on ______________ as Instrument No. ____________ in Book/Reel ________, Page/Image ________, of Official Records of ______________________________ County Oregon, which named as beneficiary(ies) ______________________________

____.

I hereby revoke any TOD deed to transfer the described property that I executed before executing this form, including the TOD deed described above.

SIGNATURE AND DATE

Sign and print your name below (your name should exactly match the name shown on your title documents):

Date: ____________________

____
(Signature of declarant)

____
(Typed or written name of declarant)

Notary Acknowledgment

State of ____________________

County of __________________

The foregoing was acknowledged before me this ____ day of ________________, by the undersigned, ________________, who is personally known to me or satisfactorily proven to me to be the person whose name is subscribed to the within instrument.

____
Printed Name of Notary Public

____
Signature of Notary Public

My commission expires: __________________ (seal)

South Dakota

Table of Contents

South Dakota Transfer on Death Act

On July 1, 2014, South Dakota enacted the Real Property Transfer on Death Act, which provides for the transfer of real property in the event of death. The owner of real property creates and records a Transfer on Death Deed, which specifies the recipient to receive the real estate on the owner's death.

Is a transfer on death deed a good idea?

If you'd like to avoid having your property going through the probate process, it's a good idea to look into a transfer on death deed. A transfer on death deed allows you to select a beneficiary who will receive your property, but only when you've passed away.

Is transfer on death considered an inheritance?

Because TOD accounts are still part of the decedent's estate (although not the probate estate that the Last Will establishes), they may be subject to income, estate and/or inheritance tax. TOD accounts are also not out of reach for the decedent's creditors or other relatives.

Do you pay taxes on transfer on death?

The amount that's in a TOD account at the time of your death is not taxable under federal law to the person who receives the account, although it may be taxable to your estate. If your beneficiary or the account are in a state with an inheritance tax, he may have to pay that.

Is a TOD better than a will?

A will is more comprehensive than a TOD deed. It tells the authorities how to distribute your cash, investments and other types of belongings. This document can also provide instructions regarding the care of minors and pets. A transfer-on-death deed doesn't enable you to express all of your final wishes.

What is difference between POD and TOD?

A POD account is very similar to a transfer-on-death (TOD) arrangement but deals with a person's bank assets instead of their stocks, bonds, mutual funds, or other investment assets. 2 Both POD and TOD agreements offer quick means of dispersing assets, as both avoid the probate process, which can take several months.

Does a TOD supersede a will?

A TOD designation supersedes a will. Once you're dead, your beneficiaries receive these assets by filling out forms provided by the financial institution and providing a certified copy of

Can you withdraw money from a dead person's account?

Once a Grant of Probate has been awarded, the executor or administrator will be able to take this document to any banks where the person who has died held an account. They will then be given permission to withdraw any money from the accounts and distribute it as per instructions in the Will.

Can a TOD be contested?

But whatever you do, a lawsuit to challenge a TOD Deed must be filed within three years of the property owner's death. The bottom line: you have the right to contest a TOD Deed, just as you can a Will or Trust, but in many cases that will be no easy task

Can a POA add a TOD?

The POA retains access to any of the decedent's assets that name them as a joint owner or payable-on-death (POD) or transfer-on-death (TOD) beneficiary. Assets that commonly carry POD/TOD designations or can be jointly titled include life insurance proceeds, bank accounts, retirement accounts and brokerage accounts.

Can I put a TOD on my house?

Including California, TOD deeds are now permitted in 26 states and the District of Columbia. The TOD deed allows a person to leave his or her real property to a designated person or persons such as a family member, friend, life-long partner or other loved one without having to set up a living trust.

Forms

Recording requested by:

When recorded mail to and mail tax statements to:

Space above this line for recorder's use

South Dakota Transfer on Death Deed

(Beneficiary Deed)

I, ______________________, with a mailing address of ________________________ ______________________________________ (hereinafter referred to as the "Owner") being of competent mind and having the legal capacity to execute this document, as owner transfer on death to ______________________ with a mailing address of ______ ____ (hereinafter referred to as the "Primary Beneficiary") as grantee beneficiary, the following described interest in real estate:

____

____

____

____

____

____

____

Legal description of the property (including square, suffix, and lot number)

If the Primary Beneficiary does not survive me, I designate ______________________ with a mailing address of ____ _________ (hereinafter referred to as the "Alternate Beneficiary") as grantee beneficiary.

This Transfer on Death Deed is revocable. It does not transfer any ownership until the death of the owner. It revokes all prior beneficiary designations by this owner for this

interest in real estate. The grantor has the right to withdraw or rescind this deed at any time. Any beneficiaries named in this deed are hereby advised that this deed may be withdrawn or rescinded whether or not money or any other consideration was paid or given.

Owner's Name	Primary Beneficiary's Name	Alternate Beneficiary's Name
Owner's Signature	Primary Beneficiary's Signature	Alternate Beneficiary's Signature
Date	Date	Date

Notary Acknowledgment

State of ____________________

County of __________________

The foregoing was acknowledged before me this ____ day of ________________, by the undersigned, ________________, who is personally known to me or satisfactorily proven to me to be the person whose name is subscribed to the within instrument.

____
Printed Name of Notary Public

____
Signature of Notary Public

My commission expires: __________________ (seal)

South Dakota Transfer on Death Deed Revocation Form

Recording requested by (name):

____

When recorded mail to
and mail tax statements to:

____

____

____

____

Recorder's Use Only

REVOCATION OF REVOCABLE TRANSFER ON DEATH DEED

This document is exempt from documentary transfer tax under Rev. & Tax. Code § 11930. This document is exempt from preliminary change of ownership report under Rev. & Tax. Code § 480.3.

Assessor's Parcel No.:

____

Declaration of Exemption From Gov't Code § 27388.1 Fee

- ☐ Transfer is exempt from fee per GC § 27388.1(a)(2):
  - ☐ recorded concurrently "in connection with" transfer subject to Documentary Transfer Tax
  - ☐ recorded concurrently "in connection with" a transfer of residential dwelling to an owner-occupier
- ☐ Transfer is exempt from fee per GC 27388.1(a)(1):
  - ☐ Fee cap of $225.00 reached ☐ Not related to real property

IMPORTANT NOTICE: THIS FORM MUST BE RECORDED TO BE EFFECTIVE

This revocation form MUST be RECORDED before your death or it will not be effective. This revocation form only affects a transfer on death deed that YOU made. A transfer on death deed made by a co-owner of your property is not affected by this revocation form. A co-owner who wants to revoke a transfer on death deed that he/she made must complete and RECORD a SEPARATE revocation form.

PROPERTY DESCRIPTION

Print the legal description of the property affected by this revocation:

____

____

____

REVOCATION

I, _______________________, am the transferor under the Revocable TOD deed dated _____________ and recorded on _____________ as Instrument No. ___________ in Book/Reel ________, Page/Image ________, of Official Records of ______________________ County South Dakota, which named as beneficiary(ies)

____

____.

I hereby revoke any TOD deed to transfer the described property that I executed before executing this form, including the TOD deed described above.

SIGNATURE AND DATE

Sign and print your name below (your name should exactly match the name shown on your title documents):

Date: _______________

____
(Signature of declarant)

____
(Typed or written name of declarant)

Notary Acknowledgment

State of ____________________

County of __________________

The foregoing was acknowledged before me this ____ day of ________________, by the undersigned, ________________, who is personally known to me or satisfactorily proven to me to be the person whose name is subscribed to the within instrument.

____
Printed Name of Notary Public

____
Signature of Notary Public

My commission expires: __________________ (seal)

Texas

Table of Contents

What is a Transfer on Death Deed?

Texas state law allows real property owners to record a "Transfer on Death Deed" naming a beneficiary to own that real property after they die. With a properly recorded Transfer on Death Deed, you do not need to go through probate court to transfer real property.

I already have a will, so why would I want a Transfer on Death Deed?

Whether you have a will or not, your property will still have to go through the probate court system. A Transfer on Death Deed conveys property outside of probate. The avoidance of probate allows for you to avoid incurring court costs and administrative costs to deed the property to your beneficiary. Under current law, it also excludes the real property from Medicaid estate recovery.

Does a Transfer on Death Deed Replace a Will?

The Transfer on Death Deed does not replace a will. The will remains an important part of your estate plan. Your will may provide how property without beneficiary designations passes, and may provide what happens if all beneficiaries predecease you. Your will may allow you to provide in detail who gets items of personal property, including your motor vehicles, heirlooms, and furniture. You should consult an attorney about how a Transfer on Death Deed fits into your estate plan.

How do you transfer a deed after death in Texas?

Texas Legislature Creates New Way to Transfer Real Property Upon Death

Thanks to the 84th Legislature, Texans have a new, easy way to transfer real property to someone else upon their death. It does not involve going through probate court, which can be a lengthy and costly process. It also allows the owner to keep the exact same rights to the property that they've always had while they are alive – they can get the property tax exemption, use it as collateral on a loan, or sell the property as they like.

It works similarly to a life insurance policy or a payable on death bank account because the asset passes directly to the beneficiary named in the transfer on death deed outside the probate system when the owner dies.

While the transfer on death deed is a welcome benefit for all Texans, it brings substantial relief to our low-income homeowners. "The family home may be the only real asset they have, but the most common way to transfer title in Texas is often financially beyond their reach," said Harry Reasoner, Chair of the Texas Access to Justice Commission. "Many cannot afford to have a will prepared to properly transfer title to the property after they die, and even if a will exists, their heirs may not be able to afford to probate the will."

Failure to transfer clear title to property is a significant problem for low-income homeowners. The homes are often informally passed down to a family member, but that person is at risk of losing the home when clear title cannot be shown.

When a natural disaster strikes and a property has been informally handed down through generations, the people living there cannot qualify for FEMA benefits because they cannot show that they are the legal owners. The same is true for property tax exemptions.

These homes are often abandoned, causing blight and an invitation to crime to our neighborhoods.

Texas Supreme Court Chief Justice Nathan Hecht commented, "While it is always best to have a lawyer, millions of Texans cannot afford one. The transfer on death deed is a useful tool for low-income Texans to transfer clear title to property. It will help keep families in homes, which benefits the communities in which we live by keeping people off the street and reducing blight."

Now, people can convey clear title to their property by completing a transfer on death deed form, signing it in front of a notary, and filing it in the deed records office in the county where the property is located before they die at a cost of less than fifty dollars.

The Texas Access to Justice Commission has created a do-it-yourself Transfer on Death Deed Kit that includes forms and instructions for completing a transfer-on-death deed as well as a revocation form in the event that someone wants to cancel or change the transfer on death deed, and an affidavit of death that must be filed when the property owner dies. The kit is available on TexasLawHelp.org.

Does a Last Will & Testament Supersede Other Documents?

Your last will and testament doesn't necessarily designate who should receive every one of your assets after you die. It's possible you have already designated who receives certain assets in documents requiring the naming of beneficiaries, such as life insurance policies or retirement accounts. Accounts and property held jointly often pass to the surviving owner. These designations supersede your will. If you mistakenly leave these assets to a different beneficiary, they won't receive them.

Retirement Accounts

When you open a retirement account — whether a pension plan, employer-sponsored 401(k) or one of the various forms of Individual Retirement Accounts (IRA) — you must list beneficiaries. The same holds true for life insurance policies. When you die, these accounts bypass the probate process necessary for wills and your named beneficiaries inherit the funds.

Transfer-on-Death Accounts

A transfer-on-death account set up for your mutual funds or securities directs who receives the funds after your passing. A TOD designation supersedes a will. For bank accounts, you can set up a similar account known as payable-on-death, sometimes referred to as a Totten trust. Your beneficiaries can't touch the account while you're alive, and you're free to change beneficiaries or close the accounts at any time. Once you're dead, your beneficiaries receive these assets by filling out forms provided by the financial institution and providing a certified copy of your death certificate.

Transfer-on-Death Property

If you live in certain states, you can register your motor vehicles with a transfer-on-death option to a named beneficiary, as well as prepare real estate deeds with a TOD designation. Check with your state's motor vehicle department to see if this option is offered. As with other TOD accounts, you can revoke the deed or change beneficiaries during your lifetime. Deeds with a TOD beneficiary require notarizing and recording, just as any other such document.

Right of Survivorship

If you're married, it's likely you own your home with your spouse as "joint tenants with right of survivorship." You might own property titled as "tenancy by the entirety." Either means the surviving person owns the property. Joint tenancy with right of survivorship supersedes a will, as does any brokerage or bank accounts titled in this manner. Unlike TOD accounts, the person named in the joint bank or brokerage account with right of survivorship has full access to these funds while you are alive. That means there is always the possibility they could liquidate the account and withdraw all of the money. If there's a judgment against the person, creditors could go after the account.

You want to ensure that your assets go to the beneficiaries you intend. Contact an attorney to discuss your estate plans and go over the titling of all assets. Then, you'll rest assured that your estate affairs are in order.

When you're making your estate plan, what's the best way to leave your property to the people or organizations you want?

Start Your Transfer on Death Deed

While most of us know about a last will and testament, the assets that are included in your will can sometimes get tied up in probate. This can be a long and costly process and often prevents your loved ones from getting a hold of the things you left them for quite some time.

If you'd like to avoid having your property going through the probate process, it's a good idea to look into a transfer on death deed.

A transfer on death deed allows you to select a beneficiary who will receive your property, but only when you've passed away. The beneficiary will have no right to your property while you're alive and, if you own your home jointly, the transfer on death deed does not apply until all the owners have died. You can name alternate beneficiaries as well, in the event your beneficiary refuses your property or isn't around to receive it.

To make a transfer on death deed legal, you'll need to take it to the local county records office where the property is located. Of course, different localities will have different rules, so make sure you follow the instructions of your county recorder.

Here are a few other important notes about transfer on death deeds:
They can be revoked: You can either go to your county recorded and request a revocation form or create a new transfer on death deed that replaces the original.

The deed will include mortgages, liens, etc.: If you still owe money or your home or if a contractor has a lien on it, your beneficiary will inherit these responsibilities along with your property.

Lastly, note that a transfer on death deed cannot be used in every state. A transfer on death deed is one of the easiest ways to transfer property. If you live in one of the states listed above, it's a smart idea to consider including it in your estate plan. If you're not sure this is the right tool for you, you can always speak with an attorney who can help you sort this out

Transfer on Death Tax Implication

Receiving an inheritance can be an unexpected windfall. Although if you get stocks and securities through a transfer on death account, don't be surprised when your gift has a tax bill attached.

A transfer on death account is a popular estate planning tools designed to avoid probate by naming a beneficiary to a brokerage account. However, it doesn't avoid taxes. In fact, transfer on death accounts are exposed to all the same income and capital gains taxes when the account owner is alive, as well as estate and inheritance taxes upon the owner's death.

Before setting-up a transfer on death account, you should review the tax implications of these accounts.

Income Taxes

During your lifetime, you have full ownership and control of assets in a transfer on death account. You can manage the investments as you see fit, make additions or withdrawals, and even close the account if you wish. Since you receive all interest, dividends or other income, you're responsible for taxes on any income.

Estate Taxes

When someone dies and their property transfers to their beneficiaries, the federal government impose an estate tax on the value of all that property. Since the transfer on death account is not a trust, it does not help you avoid or minimize estate taxes. The IRS requires those passing in 2016 or later with estates exceeding $5.45 million in assets to pay estate taxes. Unless this threshold is reached, there is no IRS filing requirement.

Only a handful of states collect estate taxes. Of the states that impose their own tax, the value of the estate must exceed the tax exemption value before any taxes are owed.

Inheritance Taxes

An inheritance tax is a state-imposed tax that you pay when receiving money or property from a deceased person's estate. Fortunately, these taxes are almost a thing of the past. Only a handful of states still collect an inheritance tax. Those states with a tax, have a relatively high threshold before taxes are due. Unlike an estate tax, beneficiaries pay the inheritance tax and it is usually due shortly after funds are received by the beneficiary.

Depending on your relationship to the deceased, you may qualify for an exemption or reduction in the amount of inheritance tax owed. For example, most states exempt a spouse who inherits property from their deceased spouse.

Capital Gains Taxes

Transfer on death accounts may offer capital gains benefits. If you have appreciated stocks in your brokerage account and sold them before your death, you would owe a tax on any profits (capital gains) earned. Simply put, capital gains are the difference between the sale price of an investment and the original purchase price (the tax basis) of that investment.

When you created a transfer on death account by naming a beneficiary to your brokerage account, the laws sets the inheritor's tax basis as the value at the time of the previous owner's date of death.

For example, imagine you purchased 1,000 share of stock for $10 each. Several years later the stock is valued at $75 a share. If you sold the stock, you'd owe a capital gains tax on $65 profit per share or $65,000. With a transfer on death account, your beneficiary receives stock valued at $75 a share. If he sells the stock for that price, no capital gains is owed because he sold an asset valued at $75 for its face value.

Paying the Estate's Taxes with Account Funds

When you die death, your estate administrator will likely need to file your last tax return. If you owe estate or income taxes, these will need to be paid before distributions are made to your beneficiaries. Before you set up a transfer on death account, be sure there are other funds available to pay your final costs.

State law may require the beneficiary to contribute toward the payment of the estate tax or inheritance tax bill when the estate does not have other funds available. A few states allow you to place instructions in your will or living trust that require the transfer on death account beneficiary to use those funds to cover any tax liability.

Transfer on death accounts are an efficient, probate-avoiding method for distributing the securities you own. Since State law, rather than federal law, governs the way securities may be transferred at death, designing a tax-efficient estate plan is a challenge. Consulting with an experienced attorney can help prevent tax headaches down the road. Receive a free case review to better understand what works best for your situation.

Forms

Recording requested by:

When recorded mail to and mail tax statements to:

Space above this line for recorder's use

Texas Transfer on Death Deed

(Beneficiary Deed)

I, ______________________, with a mailing address of ______________________ ______________________________________ (hereinafter referred to as the "Owner") being of competent mind and having the legal capacity to execute this document, as owner transfer on death to ______________________ with a mailing address of _____ ____ (hereinafter referred to as the "Primary Beneficiary") as grantee beneficiary, the following described interest in real estate:

____

____

____

____

____

____

____

Legal description of the property (including square, suffix, and lot number)

If the Primary Beneficiary does not survive me, I designate ______________________ with a mailing address of ____ _________ (hereinafter referred to as the "Alternate Beneficiary") as grantee beneficiary.

This Transfer on Death Deed is revocable. It does not transfer any ownership until the death of the owner. It revokes all prior beneficiary designations by this owner for this

interest in real estate. The grantor has the right to withdraw or rescind this deed at any time. Any beneficiaries named in this deed are hereby advised that this deed may be withdrawn or rescinded whether or not money or any other consideration was paid or given.

____________________	____________________	____________________
Owner's Name	Primary Beneficiary's Name	Alternate Beneficiary's Name
____________________	____________________	____________________
Owner's Signature	Primary Beneficiary's Signature	Alternate Beneficiary's Signature
____________________	____________________	____________________
Date	Date	Date

Notary Acknowledgment

State of ____________________

County of __________________

The foregoing was acknowledged before me this ____ day of _______________, by the undersigned, ________________, who is personally known to me or satisfactorily proven to me to be the person whose name is subscribed to the within instrument.

____
Printed Name of Notary Public

____
Signature of Notary Public

My commission expires: __________________ (seal)

IMPORTANT NOTICE TO PROPERTY OWNER: Carefully read all instructions for this form. It is always best to talk to a lawyer before using this form. For privacy reasons, do not put your social security number or driver's license number on this form. Do not file these instructions.

REQUIRED:

- **Must Sign and Date Transfer on Death Deed In Front of a Notary.**
- **Must Record Transfer on Death Deed Before Your Death**: You must record (*file*) this deed before your death with the county clerk where the property is located or it will not be effective.

1. Property Owner(s) (Transferors) Making this Deed. *Enter your first, middle (if any), and last name here, along with your mailing address. If more than one person owns the property, all owners must list this information.*

______________________	______________________
Property Owner's Printed Name	Second Owner's Printed Name (If Applicable)
Mailing Address:	Mailing Address:
______________________	______________________
Address 1	*Address 1*
______________________	______________________
Address 2	*Address 2*
______________________	______________________
City State Zip	*City State Zip*

2. Legal Description of the Property. *The legal description is not the mailing or physical address of the property. The legal description is listed on the deed to the property, which you should have gotten when you became an owner. This information may also be available at the county clerk's office in the county where the property is located. Do NOT use the legal description listed on your property tax bill because it may be incorrect. IT IS VERY IMPORTANT THAT THIS INFORMATION IS CORRECT. If you are not absolutely sure, talk to a lawyer.*

Print legal description of the property.

3. Address of the Property (if any). *This is the physical address of the property. Include county.*

____

Address City County State Zip

4. Primary and Alternate Beneficiaries. **MUST CHECK AND COMPLETE A, B, OR C (Check ONE and ONLY ONE)**:
   - *A "beneficiary" is the person who you want to own the property when you die.*
   - *Section A: Fill out this section if you are married, and you and your spouse own the property together, and you want your spouse to own the property when you die.*
   - *Section B: Fill out this section if you are married and you own the property by yourself – your spouse doesn't own any part of it – and you want your spouse to own the property when you die.*
   - *Section C: Fill out this section in all other situations. See #4 in the detailed instructions to this form.*

☐ **A. Both Spouses Own the Property and Want to Leave to Surviving Spouse**: *Fill out this section if you are married, and you and your spouse own the property together, and you want your spouse to own the property when you die. Both spouses must sign the transfer on death deed.*

1) Primary Beneficiary is Surviving Spouse: The owners of this property are married to each other and are both signing this deed. If one of us dies and the other is living, the living spouse will be the sole owner of the property.

2) Alternate Beneficiary or Beneficiaries: *Enter the first, middle (if any), and last name of each person you want to get the property when both you and your spouse have died. This person(s) will be named the "beneficiary(ies)." You may list more than two beneficiaries by attaching a page with their name and mailing address.*

When we are both deceased, we want the following person(s) to own our property. This person(s) may or may not be our child, descendant, or a member of our family. If more than one alternate beneficiary is listed, they will own the property in equal shares.

______________________________	______________________________
Alternate Beneficiary *Print Name*	Second Alternate Beneficiary (Optional) *Print Name*
Mailing Address:	Mailing Address:
______________________________	______________________________
Address 1	*Address 1*
______________________________	______________________________
Address 2	*Address 2*
______________________________	______________________________
City *State* *Zip*	*City* *State* *Zip*

3) Transfer on Death: *If the alternate beneficiary is your child (or other descendant) or your brother or sister (or other descendant of either of your parents), you must choose an option below.*

At my death, I convey to (*give*) the primary beneficiary my interest in the property to have and hold forever. If my primary beneficiary does not survive me (*dies before I do*), I grant and convey (*give*) my interest in the property to my alternate beneficiary. If my alternate beneficiary is my child (or other descendant) or my brother or sister (or other descendant of either of my parents) AND an alternate beneficiary dies before I do, I grant and convey (*give*) my share to any living alternate beneficiary AND (choose by writing your initials in ONE blank ONLY):

______ (a) the deceased alternate beneficiary's share will pass to his/her surviving children or other descendants.

______ (b) no one else. I do not want the deceased alternate beneficiary's surviving children or other descendants to have a share of the property. If no primary or alternate beneficiary is alive when I die, this deed is canceled and has no force and effect, as if it had never been executed.

☐ **B. Only One Spouse Owns the Property**: *Fill out this section if you are married and you own all or part of the property by yourself – your spouse doesn't own any part of it – and you want your spouse to own the property when you die.*

1) Primary Beneficiary: I designate my spouse as the primary beneficiary if I die before my spouse:

Spouse's Printed Name: ______________________

Spouse's Mailing Address:

____
Address 1

____
Address 2

____
City *State* *Zip*

2) Alternate Beneficiary or Beneficiaries: *Enter the first, middle (if any), and last name of each person you want to get the property if your spouse dies before you. You may list more than two alternate beneficiaries by attaching a page with their name and mailing address.*

If my spouse dies before me, I want the following person(s) to own my property when I die. This person(s) may or may not be my child, descendant, or a member of my family. If more than one alternate beneficiary is listed, they will own the property in equal shares.

____
Alternate Beneficiary *Print Name*

Mailing Address:

____
Address 1

____
Address 2

____
City *State* *Zip*

____
Second Alternate Beneficiary (Optional) *Print Name*

Mailing Address:

____
Address 1

____
Address 2

____
City *State* *Zip*

3) Transfer on Death: *If the alternate beneficiary is your child (or other descendant) or your brother or sister (or other descendant of either of your parents), you must choose an option below.*

At my death, I convey to (*give*) the primary beneficiary my interest in the property to have and hold forever. If my primary beneficiary does not survive me (*dies before I do*), I grant and convey (*give*) my interest in the property to my alternate beneficiary. If my alternate beneficiary is my child (or other descendant) or my brother or sister (or other descendant of either of my parents) AND an alternate beneficiary dies before I do, I grant and convey (*give*) my share to any living alternate beneficiary AND (choose by writing your initials in ONE blank ONLY):

______ (a) the deceased alternate beneficiary's share will pass to his/her surviving children or other descendants.

______ (b) no one else. I do not want the deceased alternate beneficiary's surviving children or other descendants to have a share of the property. If no primary or alternate beneficiary is alive when I die, this deed is canceled and has no force and effect, as if it had never been executed.

☐ **C. Other:** *Fill out this section if neither section A or B apply to you, including if you are married and you do not want your share of the property to go to your spouse.*

1) Primary Beneficiary: *Enter the first, middle (if any), and last name of each person you want to get the property when you die. This person or people will be named the "beneficiary". You may list more than two primary beneficiaries by attaching a page with their name and mailing address.*

I want the following person(s) to own my property. This person(s) may or may not be my child, descendant, or a member of my family. If more than one primary beneficiary is listed, they will own the property in equal shares.

____

Primary Beneficiary *Print Name*

Mailing Address:

____

Address 1

____

Address 2

____

City *State* *Zip*

____

Second Primary Beneficiary (Optional) *Print Name*

Mailing Address:

____

Address 1

____

Address 2

____

City *State* *Zip*

2) Alternate Beneficiary or Beneficiaries: *Enter the first, middle (if any), and last name of each person you want to get the property if all primary beneficiaries die before you. You may list more than two alternate beneficiaries by attaching a page with their name and mailing address.*

If all the primary beneficiary or beneficiaries die before me, I want the following person(s) to own my property. If more than one alternate beneficiary is listed, they will own the property in equal shares:

____

Alternate Beneficiary
Print Name

Mailing Address:

____

Address 1

____

Address 2

____

City *State* *Zip*

____

Second Alternate Beneficiary (Optional)
Print Name

Mailing Address:

____

Address 1

____

Address 2

____

City *State* *Zip*

3) Transfer on Death: *If the primary or alternate beneficiary is your child (or other descendant) or your brother or sister (or other descendant of either of your parents), you must choose an option from each A and B below.*

At my death, I convey to (*give*) the primary beneficiary my interest in the property to have and hold forever.

A) If at least one Primary Beneficiary Survives Me (*dies after I do*):

If my primary beneficiary is my child (or other descendant) or my brother or sister (or other descendant of either of my parents) AND a primary beneficiary dies before I do, I grant and convey (*give*) my share to any living primary beneficiary AND (choose by writing your initials in ONE blank ONLY):

______ (a) the deceased primary beneficiary's share will pass to his/her surviving children or other descendants.

______ (b) no one else. I do not want the deceased primary beneficiary's surviving children or other descendants to have a share of the property.

B) If NO Primary Beneficiary Survives Me (*dies after I do*):

If my primary beneficiary is my child (or other descendant) or my brother or sister (or other descendant of either of my parents) AND all primary beneficiaries die before I do, I grant and convey (*give*) my share to (choose by writing your initials in ONE blank ONLY):

______ (a) the deceased primary beneficiary's share will pass to his/her surviving children or other descendants.

______ (b) the alternate beneficiary or beneficiaries. I do not want the deceased primary beneficiary's surviving children or other descendants to have a share of the property. If no primary beneficiary is alive when I die and I did not choose an alternate beneficiary, this deed is canceled and has no force and effect, as if it had never been executed.

C) If an Alternate Beneficiary Does Not Survive Me (*dies before I do*):

If my alternate beneficiary is my child (or other descendant) or my brother or sister (or other descendant of either of my parents) AND an alternate beneficiary dies before I do, I grant and convey (*give*) my share to any living alternate beneficiary AND (choose by writing your initials in ONE blank ONLY):

___________ (a) the deceased alternate beneficiary's share will pass to his/her surviving children or other descendants.

___________ (b) no one else. I do not want the deceased alternate beneficiary's surviving children or other descendants to have a share of the property. If no primary or alternate beneficiary is alive when I die, this deed is canceled and has no force and effect, as if it had never been executed.

5. Signature of Property Owner(s) Making this Deed: ***Do not sign or date below until you are in front of a notary public.***

______________________________	______________________________
Owner's Signature	*Second Owner's Signature (If Applicable)*
______________________________	______________________________
Date	*Date*

FOR NOTARY TO COMPLETE

Acknowledgement

STATE OF ____________________

COUNTY OF ___________________

This instrument was acknowledged before me on the ______ day of ______________, 20____, by ____.

____

Notary Public's Signature

After recording, please return to:

Owner's Name and Mailing Address

____

Name

____

Address 1

____

Address 2

____

City *State* *Zip*

IMPORTANT NOTICE TO PROPERTY OWNER:

- Carefully read all instructions for this form. You may want to talk to a lawyer before using this form.
- **The Cancellation Applies ONLY to the Portion of the Property Owned by the Person Signing this Cancellation.** For example: Joe and Sue own property together. They both sign and file a transfer on death deed naming Ann as the beneficiary. Sue changes her mind and files a cancellation of transfer on death deed but Joe doesn't. When Joe dies, Ann will get his share of the property but not Sue's share.
- **Must Record Cancellation Before Your Death**: You **must** file the completed Cancellation of Death Deed form with the county clerk where the property is located **before** your death. If you don't, the property will go to the person(s) listed as the primary or alternate beneficiaries in the transfer on death deed upon your death. NOTE: Tearing up or destroying your copy or the beneficiary's copy of the transfer on death deed will not cancel the deed.

1. Property Owner (Transferor) Making this Cancellation. *Enter your first, middle (if any), and last name here, along with your mailing address. If more than one person owns the property, each property owner who wants to cancel the transfer on death deed for their share of the property should complete a cancellation of transfer on death deed form.*

____
Property Owner's Printed Name
Owner's Mailing Address:

____
Address 1
____
Address 2
____
City *State* *Zip*

2. Legal Description of the Property. *Enter the legal description of the property exactly as it appears on the original transfer on death deed. IT IS VERY IMPORTANT THAT THIS INFORMATION IS CORRECT. If you are not absolutely sure, talk to a lawyer.*

Print legal description of the property.

3. Address of the Property (if any). *This is the physical address of the property. Include county.*

____
Address *City* *County* *State* *Zip Code*

4. Cancellation.

I cancel all my previous transfers of this property by transfer on death deed.

5. Printed Name and Signature of Owner (Transferor) Making this Cancellation. ***Do not sign your name or enter the date until you are standing in front of a notary.***

_________________________________ _________________________________

Owner's Signature Date

____

Owner's Printed Name

FOR NOTARY TO COMPLETE
Acknowledgement

STATE OF ____________________

COUNTY OF ____________________

This instrument was acknowledged before me by the above named Owner on the ______ day of _______________, 20____,

By ____.
Notary Public, State of ________

After recording, return to:

____

Owner's Name

Owner's Mailing Address:

____

Address 1

____

Address 2

____

City State Zip

Texas Transfer on Death Deed Revocation Form

Recording requested by (name):

____

When recorded mail to
and mail tax statements to:

____

____

____

____

Recorder's Use Only

REVOCATION OF REVOCABLE TRANSFER ON DEATH DEED

This document is exempt from documentary transfer tax under Rev. & Tax. Code § 11930. This document is exempt from preliminary change of ownership report under Rev. & Tax. Code § 480.3.

Assessor's Parcel No.:

____

Declaration of Exemption From Gov't Code § 27388.1 Fee

☐ Transfer is exempt from fee per GC § 27388.1(a)(2):
- ☐ recorded concurrently "in connection with" transfer subject to Documentary Transfer Tax
- ☐ recorded concurrently "in connection with" a transfer of residential dwelling to an owner-occupier

☐ Transfer is exempt from fee per GC 27388.1(a)(1):
- ☐ Fee cap of $225.00 reached ☐ Not related to real property

IMPORTANT NOTICE: THIS FORM MUST BE RECORDED TO BE EFFECTIVE

This revocation form MUST be RECORDED before your death or it will not be effective. This revocation form only affects a transfer on death deed that YOU made. A transfer on death deed made by a co-owner of your property is not affected by this revocation form. A co-owner who wants to revoke a transfer on death deed that he/she made must complete and RECORD a SEPARATE revocation form.

PROPERTY DESCRIPTION

Print the legal description of the property affected by this revocation:

____

____

____

REVOCATION

I, ______________________________, am the transferor under the Revocable TOD deed dated ______________ and recorded on ______________ as Instrument No. ______________ in Book/Reel ________, Page/Image ________, of Official Records of ______________________________ County Texas, which named as beneficiary(ies) ______________________________

____.

I hereby revoke any TOD deed to transfer the described property that I executed before executing this form, including the TOD deed described above.

SIGNATURE AND DATE

Sign and print your name below (your name should exactly match the name shown on your title documents):

Date: ____________________

____
(Signature of declarant)

____
(Typed or written name of declarant)

Notary Acknowledgment

State of ____________________

County of __________________

The foregoing was acknowledged before me this ____ day of ________________, by the undersigned, ________________, who is personally known to me or satisfactorily proven to me to be the person whose name is subscribed to the within instrument.

____

Printed Name of Notary Public

____

Signature of Notary Public

My commission expires: __________________ (seal)

Utah

Table of Contents

How a Utah TOD Deed Form Works

A Utah transfer-on-death deed form (often called a TOD deed form) is a new form of deed authorized by the Utah legislature on May 8, 2018. A Utah TOD deed form works much like a payable-on-death or transfer-on-death designation on a bank account. It allows the property owner to designate one or more beneficiaries to inherit the property at death. A TOD deed form has two primary benefits:

Probate Avoidance – The property described in a TOD deed form passes to the designated beneficiaries without probate. There is no need to hire a lawyer and go through the expense and hassle of a Utah probate proceeding.

Retained Control – A Utah property owner that makes a TOD deed retains complete control over the property during his or her lifetime. The owner can revoke the deed, name different beneficiaries, or sell, mortgage, or convey the property, all without the consent or even knowledge of the designated beneficiaries.

These benefits make a Utah TOD deed form an attractive option for Utah property owners that want to avoid probate without the expense and hassle of a living trust.

Other Names for Utah Transfer-on-Death Deeds

A Utah transfer-on-death deed is usually called a TOD deed or simply a TODD. In some states—including Arizona, Arkansas, Colorado, and Missouri—the same deed form is called a beneficiary deed. In others—like Nevada—it is called a deed upon death. And in Illinois, it is called a revocable transfer on death instrument. Each name refers to the same basic deed form created by statute to pass property to beneficiaries at an owner's death.

A handful of states recognize a similar type of deed called a lady bird deed. Although a lady bird deed often serves the same purpose as TOD deed, the two deeds are based in different sources of law and differ in important ways.

Benefits of Transfer-on-Death Deed Forms

A Utah TOD form has several important benefits that make it a popular estate planning tool for Utah property owners that want to leave property to beneficiaries outside of the probate process.

Avoiding Probate – As mentioned, probate avoidance is a primary benefit of a Utah TOD deed form. Although a person's will can leave property to beneficiaries at death, probate is usually necessary to pass clear title to real estate under a will. A TOD deed form avoids probate by creating a nontestamentary transfer, so probate is not required to pass property under a TOD deed form. Utah Code § 75-6-406.

Retained Control – An owner that uses a Utah TOD deed form keeps broad control over the property. During the owner's life, the deed creates no legal or equitable interest in the designated beneficiary. Utah Code § 75-6-412. An owner may always revoke a Utah transfer-on-death deed, even if the deed itself says otherwise. Utah Code § 76-6-406. These benefits allow the owner to keep broad control over the property, including the right to change his or her mind, name new beneficiaries, or sell, mortgage, or lease the property.

Continuity of Ownership – A Utah TOD deed form has little effect during the owner's life. This can have several important benefits: the property continues to qualify for homestead exemption under state law, does not result in a taxable transfer during the owner's life, and qualifies for a tax basis-step-up at the owner's death.

Less Expense and Hassle Than a Living Trust – Many benefits of a Utah TOD deed form could also be achieved with a living trust. Although there may be situations where a living trust is still a viable alternative, living trusts are more expensive to create and can create more hassle at the owner's death. By comparison, a TOD deed form provides a less expensive, hassle-free option.

We make it easy to create your own Utah Transfer-on-Death Deed. Just complete our user-friendly interview and our software will create a custom, ready-to-file Utah transfer-on-death deed that includes the right language based on choices you make in the interview. We also include customized, step-by-step instructions for completing the real estate transfer. Documents are delivered instantly.

Situations Where Transfer-on-Death Deeds Cannot Be Used

There are a few situations where a TOD deed form cannot be used. If the property owner is mentally incapacitated (due to dementia, for example), he or she cannot create a valid TOD deed. The Utah Uniform Real Property Transfer on Death Act requires the owner to have the same mental capacity required to make a will—a higher standard than applies to most contractual arrangements. Utah Code § 75-6-408.

A class gift is a gift to a class of beneficiaries. For example, a gift to "all of my children that survive me" would be considered a class gift. A TOD deed cannot be used to create a class gift. Utah Code § 75-6-405. The beneficiaries must be named in the deed and not simply described by class.

Relationship of Transfer-on-Death Deed Form to Warranty of Title

Key Term: Warranty of Title. Title issues can be caused by many things, including errors in the public record, unknown liens against the property, undisclosed prior conveyances, forged deeds, missing heirs or unprobated wills, or disputes about boundary lines or surveys. Title issues often require legal action to fix and can decrease the value of real estate. If the property has no title issues, it is said to have clear title. A warranty of title is a legal guarantee from the transferor to the transferee that there are no title issues. If a deed makes a warranty of title, the transferee can sue the transferor over any title issues.

A Utah TOD deed form conveys real estate with no warranty of title. The beneficiaries that inherit property under a TOD deed take the property "as is" and cannot sue the owner's estate if there are title problems associated with the property.

The lack of warranty of title is absolute and cannot be overridden by the deed. Even if the deed provides otherwise, a TOD deed form always conveys property with no warranty of title.

TOD Deeds and Multiple Owners or Multiple Beneficiaries

A Utah TOD deed may be signed by multiple owners. If the owners hold title as joint tenants with right of survivorship, the deed will not become effective until the death of the last surviving owner. If one owner dies but is survived by one or more other owners, the property will continue to belong to the surviving owner or owners with right of survivorship. The deed becomes effective only upon the death of the last owner. If multiple owners hold title as tenants in common, each TOD deed affects only that owner's interest and there is no right of survivorship.

If more than one owner makes a TOD deed, the revocation by one owner doesn't affect the deed as to the interest of the other owner. A deed of joint owners can only be revoked by all joint owners.

A Utah TOD deed may also convey property to multiple beneficiaries. Any interest left to multiple beneficiaries will give the beneficiaries equal and undivided interests in the property without right of survivorship unless the deed provides otherwise. This prevents the owner from leaving different percentage interests to different individuals. It also establishes a default rule that the beneficiaries that inherit the property each hold an interest as tenants in common. Each beneficiary simply inherits a share equal to the interest of each other beneficiary.

The rule just discussed deals with the treatment of beneficiaries who are alive and inherit the property after the owner's death. A different rule applies to beneficiaries who predecease the owner. Utah law is clear that a beneficiary that dies before the owner receives no interest in the property. The interest of any predeceased beneficiary will instead be transferred to the other beneficiaries in proportion to the interest that the other beneficiaries have in the remaining portion of the property.

How to Create a Utah Transfer-on-Death Deed

Utah TOD deeds are specifically authorized by the Utah Uniform Real Property Transfer on Death Act. The Act includes several specific requirements that must be met to create a valid TOD deed:

- With few exceptions, a Utah TOD deed must meet of the general requirements that apply to Utah deeds.
- The TOD deed must state specifically that the transfer will occur at the owner's death.
- The deed must be recorded before the owner's death in the public records in the county recorder's office of the county where the property is located.

Failure to meet these requirements could invalidate the deed or cause problems with recording.

.

Forms

Recording requested by:

When recorded mail to and mail tax statements to:

Space above this line is for recorder's use

Utah Transfer on Death Deed

(Beneficiary Deed)

I, __________________________, with a mailing address of ______________________________

____ (hereinafter referred to as the "Owner") being of competent mind and having the legal capacity to execute this document, as owner transfer on death to ____________________ with a mailing address of ______________________________

____ (hereinafter referred to as the "Primary Beneficiary") as a grantee beneficiary, the following described interest in the real estate:

____

____

____

Legal description of the property (including square, suffix, and lot number)

If the Primary Beneficiary does not survive me, I designate ______________________________

with a mailing address of ____

______________ (hereinafter referred to as the "Alternate Beneficiary") as grantee beneficiary.

This Transfer on Death Deed is revocable. It does not transfer any ownership until the death of the owner. It revokes all prior beneficiary designations by this owner for this interest in real estate. The grantor has the right to withdraw or rescind this deed at any time. Any beneficiaries' names in this deed are hereby advised that this deed may be withdrawn or rescinded whether or not money or any other consideration was paid or given.

____________________	____________________	____________________
Owner's Name	Primary Beneficiary's Name	Alternate Beneficiary's Name
____________________	____________________	____________________
Owner's Signature	Primary Beneficiary's Signature	Alternate Beneficiary's Signature
____________________	____________________	____________________
Date	Date	Date

Notary Acknowledgement

State of ________________

County of ______________

The foregoing was acknowledged before me this ____ day of _______________, by the undersigned, ______________________, who is personally known to me or satisfactorily proven to me to be the person whose name is subscribed to the within instrument.

____

Printed Name of Notary Public

____

Signature of Notary Public

My commission expires: ___________________ (seal)

Utah Transfer on Death Deed Revocation Form

Recording requested by (name): _______________________________ When recorded mail to and mail tax statements to: _______________________________ _______________________________ _______________________________ _______________________________	Recorder's Use Only

REVOCATION OF REVOCABLE TRANSFER ON DEATH DEED

This document is exempt from documentary transfer tax under Rev. & Tax. Code § 11930. This document is exempt from preliminary change of ownership report under Rev. & Tax. Code § 480.3.

Assessor's Parcel No.:

____

Declaration of Exemption From Gov't Code § 27388.1 Fee

- ☐ Transfer is exempt from fee per GC § 27388.1(a)(2):
  - ☐ recorded concurrently "in connection with" transfer subject to Documentary Transfer Tax
  - ☐ recorded concurrently "in connection with" a transfer of residential dwelling to an owner-occupier
- ☐ Transfer is exempt from fee per GC 27388.1(a)(1):
  - ☐ Fee cap of $225.00 reached ☐ Not related to real property

IMPORTANT NOTICE: THIS FORM MUST BE RECORDED TO BE EFFECTIVE

This revocation form MUST be RECORDED before your death or it will not be effective. This revocation form only affects a transfer on death deed that YOU made. A transfer on death deed made by a co-owner of your property is not affected by this revocation form. A co-owner who wants to revoke a transfer on death deed that he/she made must complete and RECORD a SEPARATE revocation form.

PROPERTY DESCRIPTION

Print the legal description of the property affected by this revocation:

____

____

____

REVOCATION

I, ______________________________, am the transferor under the Revocable TOD deed dated ______________ and recorded on ______________ as Instrument No. ____________ in Book/Reel _______, Page/Image _______, of Official Records of ______________________________ County, Utah, which named as beneficiary(ies) ____.

I hereby revoke any TOD deed to transfer the described property that I executed before executing this form, including the TOD deed described above.

SIGNATURE AND DATE

Sign and print your name below (your name should exactly match the name shown on your title documents):

Date: ___________________

____
(Signature of declarant)

____
(Typed or written name of declarant)

ACKNOWLEDGMENT

A Notary Public or other officer completing this certificate verifies only the identity of the individual who signed the document to which this certificate is attached, and not the truthfulness, accuracy, or validity of that document.

State of Utah)
County of ____________________)

On ________________________ before me, _________________________________
(insert name and title of the officer)

Personally appeared

____

who proved to me on the basis of satisfactory evidence to be the person(s) whose name(s) is/are subscribed to the within instrument and acknowledged to me that she/he/they executed the same in his/her/their authorized capacity(ies), and by his/her/their signature(s) on the instrument the person(s), or the entity upon behalf of which the person(s) acted, executed the instrument.

I certify under PENALTY OF PERJURY under the laws of the State of Utah that the foregoing paragraph is true and correct.

Witness me hand and official seal. **(Seal)**

Signature ____

Virginia

Table of Contents

Transfer on Death Deed of Virginia

A transfer on death deed is an instrument that allows owners of Virginia real estate to convey land to chosen beneficiaries without the need for a will or probate distribution (64.2-624).

Does Virginia have transfer on death deed?

Virginia allows you to leave real estate with transfer-on-death deeds, also called beneficiary deeds. You sign and record the deed now, but it doesn't take effect until your death. You can revoke the deed or sell the property at any time; the beneficiary you name on the deed has no rights until your death. Va.

Is a transfer on death deed a good idea?

If you'd like to avoid having your property going through the probate process, it's a good idea to look into a transfer on death deed. A transfer on death deed allows you to select a beneficiary who will receive your property, but only when you've passed away.

Does a transfer on death deed supersede a will?

A Transfer on Death Deed trumps a will. Later, you make a will leaving the same property to your spouse. When you die, the property will pass to your child under the Transfer on Death Deed. If you want your spouse to inherit the property instead, you must change or cancel the old Transfer on Death Deed.

Does a deed override a will in Virginia?

Generally, a deed will override the will.

Do you pay taxes on transfer on death?

The amount that's in a TOD account at the time of your death is not taxable under federal law to the person who receives the account, although it may be taxable to your estate. If your beneficiary or the account are in a state with an inheritance tax, he may have to pay that.

What is difference between POD and TOD?

A POD account is very similar to a transfer-on-death (TOD) arrangement but deals with a person's bank assets instead of their stocks, bonds, mutual funds, or other investment assets. 2 Both POD and TOD agreements offer quick means of dispersing assets, as both avoid the probate process, which can take several months.

Does a TOD supersede a will?

A TOD designation supersedes a will. Once you're dead, your beneficiaries receive these assets by filling out forms provided by the financial institution and providing a certified copy of your death certificate.

How much does probate cost in Virginia?

The following are taxes and fees applicable for probate: The state probate tax is 10 cents per $100 of the estate value at the time of death. The local probate tax is 3.33 cents (1/3 of 10 cents) per $100 of the estate value at the time of death.

How do I transfer a deed in Virginia?

How to Transfer Virginia Real Estate

Locate the most recent deed to the property.

Create the new deed.

Sign and notarize the new deed.

Record the deed in the land records of the clerk's office of the circuit court in the jurisdiction where the property is located.

Can you withdraw money from a dead person's account?

Once a Grant of Probate has been awarded, the executor or administrator will be able to take this document to any banks where the person who has died held an account. They will then be given permission to withdraw any money from the accounts and distribute it as per instructions in the Will.

Does transfer on death avoid estate tax?

Estate Taxes

When someone dies and their property transfers to their beneficiaries, the federal government impose an estate tax on the value of all that property. Since the transfer on death account is not a trust, it does not help you avoid or minimize estate taxes.

Can you put a TOD on a trust account?

A TOD beneficiary designation means "Transfer on Death". Some financial institutions also call this a POD designation (or "Pay on Death"). Usually, the people who name TOD beneficiaries on an account or transfer it to a Trust are trying to avoid probate.

What happens if a TOD beneficiary dies?

In the event that there are no living beneficiaries, life insurance policies, TOD and POD accounts will go to the decedent's estate. If the beneficiary outlives the person creating the estate plan, but dies before receiving the gift, the gift will go to the probate estate of the deceased beneficiary.

What assets go through probate in Virginia?

Probate assets can include vehicles, real estate, bank and brokerage accounts, and personal belongings (for example, jewelry, home furnishings, artwork, and collections). Life insurance proceeds that are payable to the estate (not a named beneficiary) are also probate assets.

Can you withdraw money from a dead person's account?

Once a Grant of Probate has been awarded, the executor or administrator will be able to take this document to any banks where the person who has died held an account. They will then be given permission to withdraw any money from the accounts and distribute it as per instructions in the Will.

Forms

Recording requested by:

When recorded mail to and mail tax statements to:

Space above this line for recorder's use

Virginia Transfer on Death Deed
(Beneficiary Deed)

I, ______________________, with a mailing address of ________________________ ______________________________________ (hereinafter referred to as the "Owner") being of competent mind and having the legal capacity to execute this document, as owner transfer on death to ______________________ with a mailing address of ______ ____ (hereinafter referred to as the "Primary Beneficiary") as grantee beneficiary, the following described interest in real estate:

____

____

____

____

____

____

____

Legal description of the property (including square, suffix, and lot number)

If the Primary Beneficiary does not survive me, I designate ______________________ with a mailing address of ____ _________ (hereinafter referred to as the "Alternate Beneficiary") as grantee beneficiary.

This Transfer on Death Deed is revocable. It does not transfer any ownership until the death of the owner. It revokes all prior beneficiary designations by this owner for this

interest in real estate. The grantor has the right to withdraw or rescind this deed at any time. Any beneficiaries named in this deed are hereby advised that this deed may be withdrawn or rescinded whether or not money or any other consideration was paid or given.

____________________	____________________	____________________
Owner's Name	Primary Beneficiary's Name	Alternate Beneficiary's Name
____________________	____________________	____________________
Owner's Signature	Primary Beneficiary's Signature	Alternate Beneficiary's Signature
____________________	____________________	____________________
Date	Date	Date

Notary Acknowledgment

State of ____________________

County of __________________

The foregoing was acknowledged before me this ____ day of ________________, by the undersigned, ________________, who is personally known to me or satisfactorily proven to me to be the person whose name is subscribed to the within instrument.

____

Printed Name of Notary Public

____

Signature of Notary Public

My commission expires: __________________ (seal)

Virginia Transfer on Death Deed Revocation Form

Recording requested by (name):

____

When recorded mail to
and mail tax statements to:

____

____

____

____

Recorder's Use Only

REVOCATION OF REVOCABLE TRANSFER ON DEATH DEED

This document is exempt from documentary transfer tax under Rev. & Tax. Code § 11930. This document is exempt from preliminary change of ownership report under Rev. & Tax. Code § 480.3.

Assessor's Parcel No.:

____

Declaration of Exemption From Gov't Code § 27388.1 Fee

☐ Transfer is exempt from fee per GC § 27388.1(a)(2):
- ☐ recorded concurrently "in connection with" transfer subject to Documentary Transfer Tax
- ☐ recorded concurrently "in connection with" a transfer of residential dwelling to an owner-occupier

☐ Transfer is exempt from fee per GC 27388.1(a)(1):
- ☐ Fee cap of $225.00 reached ☐ Not related to real property

IMPORTANT NOTICE: THIS FORM MUST BE RECORDED TO BE EFFECTIVE

This revocation form MUST be RECORDED before your death or it will not be effective. This revocation form only affects a transfer on death deed that YOU made. A transfer on death deed made by a co-owner of your property is not affected by this revocation form. A co-owner who wants to revoke a transfer on death deed that he/she made must complete and RECORD a SEPARATE revocation form.

PROPERTY DESCRIPTION

Print the legal description of the property affected by this revocation:

____

____

____

REVOCATION

I, ______________________, am the transferor under the Revocable TOD deed dated ______________ and recorded on ______________ as Instrument No. ____________ in Book/Reel ________, Page/Image ________, of Official Records of ______________________ County Virginia, which named as beneficiary(ies) ______________________________

____.

I hereby revoke any TOD deed to transfer the described property that I executed before executing this form, including the TOD deed described above.

SIGNATURE AND DATE

Sign and print your name below (your name should exactly match the name shown on your title documents):

Date: ________________

____
(Signature of declarant)

____
(Typed or written name of declarant)

Notary Acknowledgment

State of ____________________

County of __________________

The foregoing was acknowledged before me this ____ day of ________________, by the undersigned, ________________, who is personally known to me or satisfactorily proven to me to be the person whose name is subscribed to the within instrument.

____
Printed Name of Notary Public

____
Signature of Notary Public

My commission expires: __________________ (seal)

Vermont

Table of Contents

What is a Ladybird Deed in Vermont?

A lady bird deed is an estate planning tool that enables a Medicaid beneficiary to protect their home as an inheritance from their state's Medicaid Estate Recovery Program. A lady bird (ladybird) deed (also called an enhanced life estate deed, lady bird trust or a transfer on death deed) is a type of life estate deed.

In simple terms, a life estate is a form of co-ownership in a piece of property, and a deed is a document that legally transfers the property from one owner to another. For the purposes of Medicaid estate planning, a lady bird deed is specifically referring to one's primary home. In explanation of what this type of deed is, it is also important to discuss the topic of a traditional, or standard, life estate deed.

Ladybird Deeds

Ladybird Deeds are sometimes referred to as Enhanced Life Estate Deeds. A Ladybird Deed conveys a remainder interest which can be revoked during the property owner's lifetime. This allows the owner to sell, convey, mortgage and otherwise dispose of the property without sharing the proceeds with the person or persons designated to receive the remainder interest.

Advantages.

Perhaps the biggest advantage is probate avoidance. Because the deed transfers ownership without the need for probate, it is an attractive tool. Other advantages include:

<u>Low Cost</u>

The cost for a Ladybird Deed is much less than the cost of a trust. Because of the unique features of this type of deed, it may cost more to prepare than an ordinary deed.

No Immediate Doc Stamps

Documentary stamp taxes are not due on the recording of a Ladybird Deed, even for property encumbered by a mortgage, because there is no immediate transfer of ownership. However, documentary stamps are due upon the death of the person holding the life estate.

Medicaid Planning

Because the transfer is not a completed transfer of ownership, it is not considered to be a gift that would affect eligibility for public assistance. If the home has homestead status, the property will not be a "countable" asset when calculating Medicaid eligibility. Further, the ownership passes at the moment of death, avoiding the Florida Medicaid estate recovery rules. (Other states have statutes allowing for the recovery of Medicaid benefits against property owned by the Medicaid recipient, even ownership that passes through survivorship rights, including Ladybird deeds.)

Continued Homestead Exemption

The creation of a remainder interest does not change the present ownership and the owner remains eligible for the homestead exemption.

Stepped-up Basis for Determining Capital Gains Taxes

The persons who become the owners upon the current owner's death will receive the benefit of a "stepped-up basis" for purposes of calculating their capital gains taxes. This means that, like other inherited property, their tax basis is the value on the date of the owner's death, not the tax basis of the owner, which is usually much lower.

Disadvantages.

A Ladybird Deed is not without its drawbacks, including:

<u>Confusion</u>

Banks and title companies may not understand the non-vested nature of the remainder interest and require that the remaindermen join in a conveyance or a mortgage.

<u>Creditors</u>

A creditor's lien can attach to a remainder interest, creating a cloud on the title for the life tenant. For example, the IRS has indicated that a tax lien filed against a remainder interest does attach. (See The Fund Concept, Volume 39, July 2007, p. 77.) This means that if the life tenant sells the property, the lien against the remainder person must be paid.

It also unclear whether the owner's creditors can still make a claim against the property after the owner of the life estate dies. Without probate, creditor claims against a deceased owner may not be cleared until at least two years after the date of death.

<u>Homestead Devise Restrictions</u>

This type of deed should not be used by an owner with a spouse or minor child. If the owner is married and has no minor children, the deed could provide that the remainder interest in their homestead passes to their spouse in accordance with Article X, Section 4 of the Florida Constitution. The Constitution gives the surviving spouse and minor children rights in the home. A property owner who marries or has a minor child after creating the remainder interest must review their circumstances with their attorney to avoid unexpected results when they die.

<u>Unanticipated Circumstances</u>

Generally, the remaindermen are named, but it is difficult to provide for alternative distributions in the event a remaindermen predeceases the life tenant. A will or trust can be a better tool for planning for unexpected contingencies.

Estate Taxes

Tax clearances must still be obtained when a life tenant dies. An estate tax return may be required. For owners who pass away during 2013, there is an estate tax exemption of $5.25 million for S. citizens and permanent residents. The exemption is only $60,000 for nonresident aliens.

For noncitizens, the laws of other countries may impose a tax when there is a change in ownership, similar to our capital gains tax. Noncitizens should consult with a tax advisor in their home country before considering a Ladybird deed. In some cases, there are tax treaties that reduce or eliminate the taxes on S. property.

Changes

Where the owners later change their minds, special care should be taken, and some title insurance underwriters might require that the remaindermen quitclaim their interest. That means contacting the remaindermen to sign new deeds.

Title Insurance

Standard title insurance policies cover beneficiaries under a will or trust but typically do not cover persons who receive a gift of real property. It is likely that the remaindermen will not have the benefit of the existing title insurance policy.

Additional Work

The use of a Ladybird Deed requires additional work if the property is sold or mortgaged and additional work upon the death of the owner. Probate may be avoided, but legal work is still required.

Lady Bird Deed vs. Traditional Life Estate Deed

With both lady bird deeds and traditional life estate deeds, the owner of the property, the life estate holder, also called the grantor or life tenant, maintains possession of his / her home as long as he / she is alive. Upon the death of the homeowner, the life estate ends, and the home is automatically transferred to the beneficiary, also called the grantee, remainderman, or the remainder beneficiary. With a standard life estate deed, the life tenant (the homeowner) no longer has full control over his or her home. For example, the life tenant cannot sell or mortgage his / her home without beneficiary approval. Lady bird deeds differ from traditional life estate deeds in that the life tenant continues to have the right to sell or mortgage his / her home without beneficiary consent. In fact, the life tenant is even able to cancel the deed or change the beneficiary. Stated clearly, the beneficiary will receive the title of the home after the death of the homeowner, but he / she but has no right to the home (or decisions made in regards to the home) as long as the homeowner is alive.

Lady Bird Deed as an Estate Planning Tool

To better understand the relevancy of a lady bird deed for the purposes of using it as a Medicaid estate planning tool, it is important to discuss how assets, and in particular, the home, is viewed by Medicaid. In order to be financially eligible for long-term care Medicaid, assets are limited. While the limit varies by state, generally speaking, the asset limit is $2,000 for a single applicant. (See asset limits by state here). If a Medicaid applicant is over the asset limit, the excess assets must be "spent down" in order to meet the limit.

That said, there are several higher valued assets that are exempt (not counted) towards the asset limit. One of which is the Medicaid applicant's primary home, given the applicant's equity interest (the amount of the home's value that is owned by the applicant) in the home is under a certain amount, which is state-based. In most cases, in 2020, the limit is either $595,000 or $893,000. However, California is an exception in that there is no limit on equity interest. In addition to the equity interest limit, the Medicaid applicant must live in the home. If an applicant is unmarried and has to move into a nursing home, an "intent" to return to his / her home is sufficient to keep the home an exempt asset. If an applicant is married, and his / her spouse lives in the home, it is also exempt, regardless of any other circumstances.

It is important to mention that Medicaid has a look-back period, in which all asset transfers 60-months (30-months in California) immediately prior to one's Medicaid application date are reviewed. This rule is in place because, as mentioned above, Medicaid has an asset limit, and states do not want applicants to give away assets or sell them for less than they are worth in order to meet the asset limit. If an applicant is found to have violated the look-back rule, a period of Medicaid ineligibility will be established.

Traditional life estate deeds violate Medicaid's look-back rule because the beneficiary immediately has ownership rights, and therefore, it is considered a gift. On the other hand, lady bird deeds do not violate the look-back rule. This is because the Medicaid recipient maintains ownership of the home during his / her life and the beneficiary does not have ownership. Therefore, there is no penalty for establishing this type of life estate deed.

How Do Lady Bird Deeds Work?

Upon the death of a Medicaid recipient, the state will try to recover expenses spent on long-term care through the individual's estate. This is called estate recovery, and since a Medicaid recipient's home is generally the largest asset still owned, the state generally tries to recoup funds by making a claim against it. However, lady bird deeds protect one's home from estate recovery. This is because they allow persons to automatically transfer property (in the case of a Medicaid recipient, their home) upon their death without it going through probate. (Probate is a court process in which the property of a deceased person is transferred to his or her beneficiaries). If one's home does not go through probate, Medicaid cannot try to collect reimbursement from it.

On that note, it is important to mention expanded estate recovery, in which some states apply. In these states, estate recovery is not limited to property that goes through probate. Stated differently, a lady bird deed does not protect a home in a state that employs expanded estate recovery.

How Much Do They Cost?

Creating a lady bird deed is very inexpensive. In fact, the approximate "do it yourself" cost is only $30. Professional assistance is also very affordable, and on average, costs between $200 and $400. This includes drafting the deed and filing it with the local register of deeds.

Forms

Lady Bird Deed

This Deed is made on this day of ___________, 20__, between the

Grantor ________________________

Of address _____________________________ and the

Grantee Beneficiary ___________________________

Of address ____.

For good and valuable consideration paid by the Grantee Beneficiary, the receipt of which is hereby acknowledged, the Grantor does transfer and convey the following described property to the Grantee Beneficiary effective on the Grantor's death:

Property Address: ____

Legal Description: ____

____

____

The Grantor reserves a life estate for himself/herself during the Grantor's lifetime Coupled with an unrestricted power to convey during the Grantor's lifetime, which includes the power to sell, gift, mortgage, lease and otherwise dispose of the property, and to retain the proceeds from the conveyance.

Executed this day of ________________, 20__.

Grantor Name: ______________________

Grantor Signature: ___________________

STATE OF ____________________

COUNTY OF __________________

On this day, personally appeared before me, ____________________, to me known to be the person(s) described in and who executed the within instrument and acknowledged that he/she signed the same as his/her voluntary act and deed, for the uses and purposes therein mentioned.

Witness my hand and official hereto affixed on this day of ________________, 20__.

Notary's Public Signature: __________________________________

Vermont Transfer on Death Deed Revocation

Form Recording requested by (name):

____

When recorded mail to
and mail tax statements to:

____

____

____

____

Recorder's Use Only

REVOCATION OF REVOCABLE TRANSFER ON DEATH DEED

This document is exempt from documentary transfer tax under Rev. & Tax. Code § 11930. This document is exempt from preliminary change of ownership report under Rev. & Tax. Code § 480.3.

Assessor's Parcel No.:

____

Declaration of Exemption From Gov't Code § 27388.1 Fee

- ☐ Transfer is exempt from fee per GC § 27388.1(a)(2):
  - ☐ recorded concurrently "in connection with" transfer subject to Documentary Transfer Tax
  - ☐ recorded concurrently "in connection with" a transfer of residential dwelling to an owner-occupier
- ☐ Transfer is exempt from fee per GC 27388.1(a)(1):
  - ☐ Fee cap of $225.00 reached ☐ Not related to real property

IMPORTANT NOTICE: THIS FORM MUST BE RECORDED TO BE EFFECTIVE

This revocation form MUST be RECORDED before your death or it will not be effective. This revocation form only affects a transfer on death deed that YOU made. A transfer on death deed made by a co-owner of your property is not affected by this revocation form. A co-owner who wants to revoke a transfer on death deed that he/she made must complete and RECORD a SEPARATE revocation form.

PROPERTY DESCRIPTION

Print the legal description of the property affected by this revocation:

____

____

____

REVOCATION

I, ______________________________, am the transferor under the Revocable TOD deed dated ______________ and recorded on ______________ as Instrument No. ____________ in Book/Reel _______, Page/Image _______, of Official Records of ______________________________ County, Vermont, which named as beneficiary(ies) ______________________________

____.

I hereby revoke any TOD deed to transfer the described property that I executed before executing this form, including the TOD deed described above.

SIGNATURE AND DATE

Sign and print your name below (your name should exactly match the name shown on your title documents):

Date: ____________________

____
(Signature of declarant)

____
(Typed or written name of declarant)

ACKNOWLEDGMENT

A Notary Public or other officer completing this certificate verifies only the identity of the individual who signed the document to which this certificate is attached, and not the truthfulness, accuracy, or validity of that document.

State of Vermont)
County of ____________________)

On ________________________ before me, _________________________________
(insert name and title of the officer)

Personally appeared

____

who proved to me on the basis of satisfactory evidence to be the person(s) whose name(s) is/are subscribed to the within instrument and acknowledged to me that she/he/they executed the same in his/her/their authorized capacity(ies), and by his/her/their signature(s) on the instrument the person(s), or the entity upon behalf of which the person(s) acted, executed the instrument.

I certify under PENALTY OF PERJURY under the laws of the State of Vermont that the foregoing paragraph is true and correct.

Witness me hand and official seal. **(Seal)**

Signature _______________________________________

Washington

Table of Contents

Washington Transfer on Death Deed

The Washington transfer-on-death deed form allows property to be automatically transferred to a new owner when the current owner dies, without the need to go through probate. It also gives the current owner retained control over the property, including the right to change his or her mind about the transfer.

Does Washington State recognize a transfer on death deed?

There is incredible interest from clients and accountants about a relatively new form of deed recently allowed in Washington State, the transfer on death deed (a "TOD deed"), which is designed to allow property to pass outside of probate. Under the Washington Uniform Real Property Transfer on Death Act (RCW 64.80).

How do I file a transfer on death deed in Washington state?

You must sign the deed and get your signature notarized, and then record (file) the deed with the county recorder's office before your death. Otherwise, it won't be valid. The beneficiary's rights. The person you name in the TOD deed to inherit the property has no legal right to it until your death.

Is a transfer on death deed a good idea?

If you'd like to avoid having your property going through the probate process, it's a good idea to look into a transfer on death deed. A transfer on death deed allows you to select a beneficiary who will receive your property, but only when you've passed away.

Does a transfer on death deed supersede a will?

A Transfer of Death Deed trumps a will. Later, you make a will leaving the same property to your spouse. When you die, the property will pass to your child under the Transfer on Death Deed. If you want your spouse to inherit the property instead, you must change or cancel the old Transfer on Death Deed.

How is property transferred after death?

However, in the case of death of a spouse, the property can only be transferred in two ways. One is through partition deed or settlement deed in case no will or testament is created by the deceased spouse. And second is through the will deed executed by the person before his/her last death.

How does a TOD account work?

A TOD account automatically transfers the assets to a named beneficiary, when the account holder dies. Let's say you have a savings account with $100,000 in it. Your son is the beneficiary for the TOD account. When you die, the account's assets are transferred directly to him without having to go through probate.

How do I change the deed on my house after my spouse dies in Washington state?

To transfer title to real property from the name of the two spouses to the one surviving spouse, the agreement needs to be recorded with the county recorder's office, along with a certified copy of the death certificate.

How do I remove a deceased spouse from my deed in Washington state?

File an affidavit of survivorship with the recorder's office to remove the deceased person's name from the title.

Can I take money out of my TOD account?

This account is wholly owned by both spouses while they're both alive. As a result, a creditor of one spouse could make a claim against the entire account, without any approval or say from the other spouse. Either spouse could also withdraw all the money it the account and not tell the other.

How is property transferred after death?

However, in the case of death of a spouse, the property can only be transferred in two ways. One is through partition deed or settlement deed in case no will or testament is created by the deceased spouse. And second is through the will deed executed by the person before his/her last death.

What happens if a TOD beneficiary dies?

In the event that there are no living beneficiaries, life insurance policies, TOD and POD accounts will go to the decedent's estate. If the beneficiary outlives the person creating the estate plan, but dies before receiving the gift, the gift will go to the probate estate of the deceased beneficiary.

Can you put a TOD on a trust account?

A TOD beneficiary designation means "Transfer on Death". Some financial institutions also call this a POD designation (or "Pay on Death"). Usually, the people who name TOD beneficiaries on an account or transfer it to a Trust are trying to avoid probate.

Can a TOD be contested?

But whatever you do, a lawsuit to challenge a TOD Deed must be filed within three years of the property owner's death. The bottom line: you have the right to contest a TOD Deed, just as you can a Will or Trust, but in many cases that will be no easy task.

Can you put a TOD on a house?

Including California, TOD deeds are now permitted in 26 states and the District of Columbia. The TOD deed allows a person to leave his or her real property to a designated person or persons such as a family member, friend, life-long partner or other loved one without having to set up a living trust.

What is the benefit of a transfer on death account?

TOD becomes effective for joint accounts if both owners pass away simultaneously. Joint and TOD registration generally allows an account to pass outside the probate estate, enabling the surviving owner or beneficiaries to avoid the time and expense of that process for this account.

What is a transfer on death individual?

The transfer on death designation lets beneficiaries receive assets at the time of the person's death without going through probate. With TOD registration, the named beneficiaries have no access to or control over a person's assets as long as the person is alive.

Do transfer on death accounts get stepped up basis?

Do assets in a TOD account receive a "step up" (or "step down") in cost basis when the account owner dies? Yes. Securities held in TOD accounts receive a new cost basis as of the account owner's date of death using the same income tax rules that apply at the death of an individual.

Forms

Recording requested by:

When recorded mail to and mail tax statements to:

Space above this line for recorder's use

Washington Transfer on Death Deed

(Beneficiary Deed)

I, ______________________, with a mailing address of ______________________ ____ (hereinafter referred to as the "Owner") being of competent mind and having the legal capacity to execute this document, as owner transfer on death to ______________________ with a mailing address of ______ ____ (hereinafter referred to as the "Primary Beneficiary") as grantee beneficiary, the following described interest in real estate:

____

____

____

____

____

____

____

Legal description of the property (including square, suffix, and lot number)

If the Primary Beneficiary does not survive me, I designate ______________________ with a mailing address of ____ _________ (hereinafter referred to as the "Alternate Beneficiary") as grantee beneficiary.

This Transfer on Death Deed is revocable. It does not transfer any ownership until the death of the owner. It revokes all prior beneficiary designations by this owner for this

interest in real estate. The grantor has the right to withdraw or rescind this deed at any time. Any beneficiaries named in this deed are hereby advised that this deed may be withdrawn or rescinded whether or not money or any other consideration was paid or given.

Owner's Name	Primary Beneficiary's Name	Alternate Beneficiary's Name
Owner's Signature	Primary Beneficiary's Signature	Alternate Beneficiary's Signature
Date	Date	Date

Notary Acknowledgment

State of ____________________

County of ___________________

The foregoing was acknowledged before me this ____ day of _______________, by the undersigned, ________________, who is personally known to me or satisfactorily proven to me to be the person whose name is subscribed to the within instrument.

____

Printed Name of Notary Public

____

Signature of Notary Public

My commission expires: __________________ (seal)

Washington Transfer on Death Deed Revocation Form

Recording requested by (name):

____

When recorded mail to
and mail tax statements to:

____

____

____

____

Recorder's Use Only

REVOCATION OF REVOCABLE TRANSFER ON DEATH DEED

This document is exempt from documentary transfer tax under Rev. & Tax. Code § 11930. This document is exempt from preliminary change of ownership report under Rev. & Tax. Code § 480.3.

Assessor's Parcel No.:

____

Declaration of Exemption From Gov't Code § 27388.1 Fee

☐ Transfer is exempt from fee per GC § 27388.1(a)(2):
- ☐ recorded concurrently "in connection with" transfer subject to Documentary Transfer Tax
- ☐ recorded concurrently "in connection with" a transfer of residential dwelling to an owner-occupier

☐ Transfer is exempt from fee per GC 27388.1(a)(1):
- ☐ Fee cap of $225.00 reached ☐ Not related to real property

IMPORTANT NOTICE: THIS FORM MUST BE RECORDED TO BE EFFECTIVE

This revocation form MUST be RECORDED before your death or it will not be effective. This revocation form only affects a transfer on death deed that YOU made. A transfer on death deed made by a co-owner of your property is not affected by this revocation form. A co-owner who wants to revoke a transfer on death deed that he/she made must complete and RECORD a SEPARATE revocation form.

PROPERTY DESCRIPTION

Print the legal description of the property affected by this revocation:

____

____

____

REVOCATION

I, ________________________________, am the transferor under the Revocable TOD deed dated _______________ and recorded on _______________ as Instrument No. _____________ in Book/Reel ________, Page/Image ________, of Official Records of ______________________________________ County Washington, which named as beneficiary(ies) ____.

I hereby revoke any TOD deed to transfer the described property that I executed before executing this form, including the TOD deed described above.

SIGNATURE AND DATE

Sign and print your name below (your name should exactly match the name shown on your title documents):

Date: ____________________

____
(Signature of declarant)

____
(Typed or written name of declarant)

Notary Acknowledgment

State of ____________________

County of __________________

The foregoing was acknowledged before me this ____ day of ________________, by the undersigned, ________________, who is personally known to me or satisfactorily proven to me to be the person whose name is subscribed to the within instrument.

____
Printed Name of Notary Public

____
Signature of Notary Public

My commission expires: __________________ (seal)

West Virginia

Table of Contents

Does West Virginia have a transfer on death deed?

As of June 2014, West Virginia allows you to leave real estate with transfer-on-death deeds, also called beneficiary deeds.

Is a transfer on death deed a good idea?

If you'd like to avoid having your property going through the probate process, it's a good idea to look into a transfer on death deed. A transfer on death deed allows you to select a beneficiary who will receive your property, but only when you've passed away.

Does a transfer on death deed supersede a will?

A Transfer on Death Deed trumps a will.

Later, you make a will leaving the same property to your spouse. When you die the property will pass to your child under the Transfer on Death Deed. If you want your spouse to inherit the property instead, you must change or cancel the old Transfer on Death Deed.

Is transfer on death considered an inheritance?

Because TOD accounts are still part of the decedent's estate (although not the probate estate that the Last Will establishes), they may be subject to income, estate and/or inheritance tax. TOD accounts are also not out of reach for the decedent's creditors or other relatives.

Do you pay taxes on transfer on death?

The amount that's in a TOD account at the time of your death is not taxable under federal law to the person who receives the account, although it may be taxable to your estate. If your beneficiary or the account are in a state with an inheritance tax, he may have to pay that.

Is a trust better than a TOD?

With a trust, you can avoid unintended outcomes more easily than with a TOD asset. In addition, if you have multiple assets that you would have designated as "transfer on death," keeping them in a trust allows you to change beneficiary designations by changing the beneficiaries of the trust.

What is difference between POD and TOD?

A POD account is very similar to a transfer-on-death (TOD) arrangement but deals with a person's bank assets instead of their stocks, bonds, mutual funds, or other investment assets. Both POD and TOD agreements offer quick means of dispersing assets, as both avoid the probate process, which can take several months.

Does a TOD supersede a will?

A TOD designation supersedes a will. Once you're dead, your beneficiaries receive these assets by filling out forms provided by the financial institution and providing a certified copy of your death certificate.

Can you withdraw money from a dead person's account?

Once a Grant of Probate has been awarded, the executor or administrator will be able to take this document to any banks where the person who has died held an account. They will then be given permission to withdraw any money from the accounts and distribute it as per instructions in the Will.

Can you put a TOD on a trust account?

A TOD beneficiary designation means "Transfer on Death". Some financial institutions also call this a POD designation (or "Pay on Death"). Usually, the people who

Can a POA add a TOD?

The POA retains access to any of the decedent's assets that name them as a joint owner or payable-on-death (POD) or transfer-on-death (TOD) beneficiary. Assets that commonly carry POD/TOD designations or can be jointly titled include life insurance proceeds, bank accounts, retirement accounts and brokerage accounts.

Can I put a TOD on my house?

Including California, TOD deeds are now permitted in 26 states and the District of Columbia. The TOD deed allows a person to leave his or her real property to a designated person or persons such as a family member, friend, life-long partner or other loved one without having to set up a living trust.

Can a TOD be contested?

But whatever you do, a lawsuit to challenge a TOD Deed must be filed within three years of the property owner's death. The bottom line: you have the right to contest a TOD Deed, just as you can a Will or Trust, but in many cases that will be no easy task.

Forms

Recording requested by:

When recorded mail to and mail tax statements to:

Space above this line for recorder's use

West Virginia Transfer on Death Deed

(Beneficiary Deed)

I, ______________________, with a mailing address of ______________________ ______________________________________ (hereinafter referred to as the "Owner") being of competent mind and having the legal capacity to execute this document, as owner transfer on death to ______________________ with a mailing address of ______ ____ (hereinafter referred to as the "Primary Beneficiary") as grantee beneficiary, the following described interest in real estate:

____

____

____

____

____

____

____

Legal description of the property (including square, suffix, and lot number)

If the Primary Beneficiary does not survive me, I designate ______________________ with a mailing address of ____ _________ (hereinafter referred to as the "Alternate Beneficiary") as grantee beneficiary.

This Transfer on Death Deed is revocable. It does not transfer any ownership until the death of the owner. It revokes all prior beneficiary designations by this owner for this

interest in real estate. The grantor has the right to withdraw or rescind this deed at any time. Any beneficiaries named in this deed are hereby advised that this deed may be withdrawn or rescinded whether or not money or any other consideration was paid or given.

______________________	______________________	______________________
Owner's Name	Primary Beneficiary's Name	Alternate Beneficiary's Name
______________________	______________________	______________________
Owner's Signature	Primary Beneficiary's Signature	Alternate Beneficiary's Signature
______________________	______________________	______________________
Date	Date	Date

Notary Acknowledgment

State of ____________________

County of __________________

The foregoing was acknowledged before me this ____ day of ________________, by the undersigned, ________________, who is personally known to me or satisfactorily proven to me to be the person whose name is subscribed to the within instrument.

____
Printed Name of Notary Public

____
Signature of Notary Public

My commission expires: __________________ (seal)

West Virginia Transfer on Death Deed Revocation Form

Recording requested by (name): ______________________ When recorded mail to and mail tax statements to: ______________________ ______________________ ______________________ ______________________	Recorder's Use Only

REVOCATION OF REVOCABLE TRANSFER ON DEATH DEED

This document is exempt from documentary transfer tax under Rev. & Tax. Code § 11930. This document is exempt from preliminary change of ownership report under Rev. & Tax. Code § 480.3.

Assessor's Parcel No.:

____

Declaration of Exemption From Gov't Code § 27388.1 Fee

- ☐ Transfer is exempt from fee per GC § 27388.1(a)(2):
  - ☐ recorded concurrently "in connection with" transfer subject to Documentary Transfer Tax
  - ☐ recorded concurrently "in connection with" a transfer of residential dwelling to an owner-occupier
- ☐ Transfer is exempt from fee per GC 27388.1(a)(1):
  - ☐ Fee cap of $225.00 reached ☐ Not related to real property

IMPORTANT NOTICE: THIS FORM MUST BE RECORDED TO BE EFFECTIVE

This revocation form MUST be RECORDED before your death or it will not be effective. This revocation form only affects a transfer on death deed that YOU made. A transfer on death deed made by a co-owner of your property is not affected by this revocation form. A co-owner who wants to revoke a transfer on death deed that he/she made must complete and RECORD a SEPARATE revocation form.

PROPERTY DESCRIPTION

Print the legal description of the property affected by this revocation:

____

____

____

REVOCATION

I, ______________________, am the transferor under the Revocable TOD deed dated ______________ and recorded on ______________ as Instrument No. ______________ in Book/Reel ________, Page/Image ________, of Official Records of ______________________ County West Virginia, which named as beneficiary(ies) ______________________

____.

I hereby revoke any TOD deed to transfer the described property that I executed before executing this form, including the TOD deed described above.

SIGNATURE AND DATE

Sign and print your name below (your name should exactly match the name shown on your title documents):

Date: ______________________

____
(Signature of declarant)

____
(Typed or written name of declarant)

Notary Acknowledgment

State of ____________________

County of __________________

The foregoing was acknowledged before me this ____ day of ________________, by the undersigned, ________________, who is personally known to me or satisfactorily proven to me to be the person whose name is subscribed to the within instrument.

____

Printed Name of Notary Public

____

Signature of Notary Public

My commission expires: __________________ (seal)

Wisconsin

Table of Contents

What is a Transfer on Death Deed?

In Wisconsin, a Transfer on Death Deed allows an interest in real property that is solely owned, or owned by spouses as survivorship marital property, or owned by two or more persons as joint tenants, to transfer real estate to beneficiaries without probate.

Is a transfer on death deed a good idea?

If you'd like to avoid having your property going through the probate process, it's a good idea to look into a transfer on death deed. A transfer on death deed allows you to select a beneficiary who will receive your property, but only when you've passed away.

Does a transfer on death deed supersede a will?

If you'd like to avoid having your property going through the probate process, it's a good idea to look into a transfer on death deed. A transfer on death deed allows you to select a beneficiary who will receive your property, but only when you've passed away

A Transfer on Death Deed trumps a will?

Later, you make a will leaving the same property to your spouse. When you die the property will pass to your child under the Transfer on Death Deed. If you want your spouse to inherit the property instead, you must change or cancel the old Transfer on Death Deed

Does Wisconsin allow TOD account?

Wisconsin lets you register stocks and bonds in transfer-on-death (TOD) form. If you register an account in TOD (also called beneficiary) form, the beneficiary you name will inherit the account automatically at your death.

Because TOD accounts are still part of the decedent's estate (although not the probate estate that the Last Will establishes), they may be subject to income, estate and/or inheritance tax. TOD accounts are also not out of reach for the decedent's creditors or other relative.

Can a TOD account be contested?

Because transfer-on-death beneficiary deeds do not become effective until you pass away, someone can challenge the validity of the deed after you die. Or, beneficiaries and family members can sue each other to take the property entirely. In this case, a court proceeding may be required to resolve the issue.

Does a TOD supersede a will?

A TOD designation supersedes a will. Once you're dead, your beneficiaries receive these assets by filling out forms provided by the financial institution and providing a certified copy of your death certificate.

Is a TOD better than a will?

A will is more comprehensive than a TOD deed. It tells the authorities how to distribute your cash, investments and other types of belongings. This document can also provide instructions regarding the care of minors and pets. A transfer-on-death deed doesn't enable you to express all of your final wish.

What is difference between POD and TOD?

A POD account is very similar to a transfer-on-death (TOD) arrangement but deals with a person's bank assets instead of their stocks, bonds, mutual funds, or other investment assets. 2 Both POD and TOD agreements offer quick means of dispersing assets, as both avoid the probate process, which can take several months.

Does transfer on death avoid estate tax?

When someone dies and their property transfers to their beneficiaries, the federal government impose an estate tax on the value of all that property. Since the transfer on death account is not a trust, it does not help you avoid or minimize estate taxes.

Is a TOD a retirement account?

Understanding Transfer on Death (TOD)

Individual retirement accounts, 401(k)s, and other retirement accounts are TOD. The Uniform Transfer on Death Securities Registration Act lets owners name beneficiaries for their stocks, bonds, or brokerage accounts. The process is similar to a payable-on-death bank account.

What happens if a TOD beneficiary dies?

In the event that there are no living beneficiaries, life insurance policies, TOD and POD accounts will go to the decedent's estate. If the beneficiary outlives the person creating the estate plan, but dies before receiving the gift, the gift will go to the probate estate of the deceased beneficiary.

Can I put a TOD on my house?

Including California, TOD deeds are now permitted in 26 states and the District of Columbia. The TOD deed allows a person to leave his or her real property to a designated person or persons such as a family member, friend, life-long partner or other loved one without having to set up a living trust.

What Is a TOD Account?

A transfer on death (TOD) account automatically transfers its assets to a named beneficiary when the holder dies. For example, if you have a savings account with $100,000 in it and name your son as its beneficiary, that account would transfer to him upon your death.

Does a TOD expire?

Yes, your Transfer on Death deed will remain valid as long as it is executed before January 1, 2022. However, with the uncertainty of the status of this law, there is no guarantee that future changes to the TOD deed law may not affect you

Can a POA add a TOD?

The POA retains access to any of the decedent's assets that name them as a joint owner or payable-on-death (POD) or transfer-on-death (TOD) beneficiary. Assets that commonly carry POD/TOD designations or can be jointly titled include life insurance proceeds, bank accounts, retirement accounts and brokerage accounts.

How much does probate cost in Wisconsin?

How much does probate cost? The cost of probate is dependent on the complexity of the case. In Wisconsin, the average probate in Wisconsin is about 4-5%, with attorney fees being about half.

Can you put a TOD on a joint account?

TOD becomes effective for joint accounts if both owners pass away simultaneously. Joint and TOD registration generally allows an account to pass outside the probate estate, enabling the surviving owner or beneficiaries to avoid the time and expense of that process for this account.

How does a transfer on death account work?

So, how do Transfer on Death accounts work? A TOD account automatically transfers the assets to a named beneficiary, when the account holder dies. Your son is the beneficiary for the TOD account. When you die, the account's assets are transferred directly to him without having to go through probate.

Forms

Recording requested by:

When recorded mail to and mail tax statements to:

Space above this line for recorder's use

Wisconsin Transfer on Death Deed

(Beneficiary Deed)

I, ______________________, with a mailing address of ________________________ ______________________________________ (hereinafter referred to as the "Owner") being of competent mind and having the legal capacity to execute this document, as owner transfer on death to ______________________ with a mailing address of ______ ____ (hereinafter referred to as the "Primary Beneficiary") as grantee beneficiary, the following described interest in real estate:

____

____

____

____

____

____

____

Legal description of the property (including square, suffix, and lot number)

If the Primary Beneficiary does not survive me, I designate ______________________ with a mailing address of ____ _________ (hereinafter referred to as the "Alternate Beneficiary") as grantee beneficiary.

This Transfer on Death Deed is revocable. It does not transfer any ownership until the death of the owner. It revokes all prior beneficiary designations by this owner for this

interest in real estate. The grantor has the right to withdraw or rescind this deed at any time. Any beneficiaries named in this deed are hereby advised that this deed may be withdrawn or rescinded whether or not money or any other consideration was paid or given.

Owner's Name	Primary Beneficiary's Name	Alternate Beneficiary's Name
Owner's Signature	Primary Beneficiary's Signature	Alternate Beneficiary's Signature
Date	Date	Date

Notary Acknowledgment

State of ____________________

County of __________________

The foregoing was acknowledged before me this ____ day of ________________, by the undersigned, ________________, who is personally known to me or satisfactorily proven to me to be the person whose name is subscribed to the within instrument.

____
Printed Name of Notary Public

____
Signature of Notary Public

My commission expires: __________________ (seal)

State Bar of Wisconsin Form 9-2009

DESIGNATION OF TOD BENEFICIARY

Under Wis. Stat. § 705.15

Document Number

Document Name

THIS DESIGNATION is made by ______________________________

______________________________ (collectively, "Owner") of the following described real estate located in ______________ County, State of Wisconsin (the "Property") (attach Exhibit A if more space is needed):

Recording Area

Name and Return Address

____

Parcel Identification Number (PIN)

This is not homestead property.
(is) (is not)

Owner transfers the Property without probate upon death of the sole owner, or upon the last to die of multiple owners, to the following TOD beneficiary, without warranties:

Select A or B:

☐ A. ______________________________
Insert name of beneficiary, whether one or more. This revokes all previous TOD beneficiary designations.

☐ B. The sole purpose of this instrument is to revoke all previous TOD beneficiary designations.

This designation is effective only upon the recording of this instrument.

This transaction is Fee Exempt under Wis. Stat. § 77.25(10m), and exempt from the filing of a transfer return under Wis. Stat. § 77.21(1).

Dated ______________________________.

______________________________(SEAL) ______________________________(SEAL)
* ______________________________ * ______________________________

______________________________(SEAL) ______________________________(SEAL)
* ______________________________ * ______________________________

AUTHENTICATION

Signature(s) of ______________________________

____

authenticated on ______________________________.

____

* ______________________________

TITLE: MEMBER STATE BAR OF WISCONSIN
(If not, ______________________________
authorized by Wis. Stat. § 706.06)

THIS INSTRUMENT DRAFTED BY:

____

____

ACKNOWLEDGMENT

STATE OF WISCONSIN)
) ss.
______________ COUNTY)

Personally came before me on ______________,
the above-named ______________________________

____

to me known to be the person(s) who executed the foregoing instrument and acknowledged the same.

____

* ______________________________

Notary Public, State of Wisconsin
My Commission (is permanent) (expires: ______________)

(Signatures may be authenticated or acknowledged. Both are not necessary.)

NOTE: THIS IS A STANDARD FORM. ANY MODIFICATIONS TO THIS FORM SHOULD BE CLEARLY IDENTIFIED.

* Type name below signatures.

Wisconsin Transfer on Death Deed Revocation Form

Recording requested by (name):

____

When recorded mail to
and mail tax statements to:

____

____

____

____

Recorder's Use Only

REVOCATION OF REVOCABLE TRANSFER ON DEATH DEED

This document is exempt from documentary transfer tax under Rev. & Tax. Code § 11930. This document is exempt from preliminary change of ownership report under Rev. & Tax. Code § 480.3.

Assessor's Parcel No.:

____

Declaration of Exemption From Gov't Code § 27388.1 Fee

☐ Transfer is exempt from fee per GC § 27388.1(a)(2):
  ☐ recorded concurrently "in connection with" transfer subject to Documentary Transfer Tax
  ☐ recorded concurrently "in connection with" a transfer of residential dwelling to an owner-occupier
☐ Transfer is exempt from fee per GC 27388.1(a)(1):
  ☐ Fee cap of $225.00 reached ☐ Not related to real property

IMPORTANT NOTICE: THIS FORM MUST BE RECORDED TO BE EFFECTIVE

This revocation form MUST be RECORDED before your death or it will not be effective. This revocation form only affects a transfer on death deed that YOU made. A transfer on death deed made by a co-owner of your property is not affected by this revocation form. A co-owner who wants to revoke a transfer on death deed that he/she made must complete and RECORD a SEPARATE revocation form.

PROPERTY DESCRIPTION

Print the legal description of the property affected by this revocation:

____

____

____

REVOCATION

I, ______________________________, am the transferor under the Revocable TOD deed dated ________________ and recorded on ________________ as Instrument No. ______________ in Book/Reel ________, Page/Image ________, of Official Records of ______________________________ County Wisconsin, which named as beneficiary(ies) ______________________________
____.

I hereby revoke any TOD deed to transfer the described property that I executed before executing this form, including the TOD deed described above.

SIGNATURE AND DATE

Sign and print your name below (your name should exactly match the name shown on your title documents):

Date: ____________________

____
(Signature of declarant)

____
(Typed or written name of declarant)

Notary Acknowledgment

State of ____________________

County of __________________

The foregoing was acknowledged before me this ____ day of ________________, by the undersigned, ________________, who is personally known to me or satisfactorily proven to me to be the person whose name is subscribed to the within instrument.

____
Printed Name of Notary Public

____
Signature of Notary Public

My commission expires: __________________ (seal)

Wyoming

Table of Contents

Wyoming Transfer of Real Property on Death Act

Wyoming's No testamentary Transfer of Real Property on Death Act went into effect on July 1, 2013. As defined at 2-18-103, a TODD conveys the owner's interest in real property, subject to any debts or obligations in place during the owner's lifetime, to a designated grantee beneficiary.

Is a transfer on death deed a good idea?

If you'd like to avoid having your property going through the probate process, it's a good idea to look into a transfer on death deed. A transfer on death deed allows you to select a beneficiary who will receive your property, but only when you've passed away.

A Transfer on Death Deed trumps a will.

Later, you make a will leaving the same property to your spouse. When you die, the property will pass to your child under the Transfer on Death Deed. If you want your spouse to inherit the property instead, you must change or cancel the old Transfer on Death Deed.

How do you avoid probate in Wyoming?

In Wyoming, you can make a living trust to avoid probate for virtually any asset you own -- real estate, bank accounts, vehicles, and so on. You need to create a trust document (it's similar to a will), naming someone to take over as trustee after your death (called a successor trustee).

Do you pay taxes on transfer on death?

The amount that's in a TOD account at the time of your death is not taxable under federal law to the person who receives the account, although it may be taxable to your estate. If your beneficiary or the account are in a state with an inheritance tax, he may have to pay that.

Is transfer on death considered an inheritance?

Because TOD accounts are still part of the decedent's estate (although not the probate estate that the Last Will establishes), they may be subject to income, estate and/or inheritance tax. TOD accounts are also not out of reach for the decedent's creditors or other relatives.

What is difference between POD and TOD?

A POD account is very similar to a transfer-on-death (TOD) arrangement but deals with a person's bank assets instead of their stocks, bonds, mutual funds, or other investment assets. 2 Both POD and TOD agreements offer quick means of dispersing assets, as both avoid the probate process, which can take several months.

Does a will supersede a TOD?

A TOD designation supersedes a will. For bank accounts, you can set up a similar account known as payable-on-death, sometimes referred to as a Totten trust. Your beneficiaries can't touch the account while you're alive, and you're free to change beneficiaries or close the accounts at any time.

Is a TOD better than a will?

A will is more comprehensive than a TOD deed. It tells the authorities how to distribute your cash, investments and other types of belongings. This document can also provide instructions regarding the care of minors and pets. A transfer-on-death deed doesn't enable you to express all of your final wishes.

How much does probate cost in Wyoming?

Wyoming effectively sets the default executor fee as a percentage of probate estate assets: 10.0% for the first $1K. 5.0% for the next $4K. 3.0% for the next $15K.

How long does probate take in Wyoming?

The probate process can take up a large part of a year, although Wyoming law requires that probate be completed within one year of the PR's appointment unless there is good cause for delay.

Does Wyoming require probate?

The short answer to this question is “yes.” Probate is required in Wyoming unless the estate meets the exception. Most estates will need to follow this process for the assets to be distributed to the heirs.

Are proceeds from a POD bank account taxable to the beneficiary?

The value of a POD account generally will not be included in your taxable income because bequests aren't taxable as income. Any income earned by the POD account prior to the date the bequeathed died is reported on their final income tax return.

Can I withdraw money from my own TOD account?

This account is wholly owned by both spouses while they're both alive. As a result, a creditor of one spouse could make a claim against the entire account, without any approval or say from the other spouse. Either spouse could also withdraw all the money in the account and not tell the other.

Can a TOD be contested?

But whatever you do, a lawsuit to challenge a TOD Deed must be filed within three years of the property owner's death. The bottom line: you have the right to contest a TOD Deed, just as you can a Will or Trust, but in many cases that will be no easy task.

How does a transfer on death account work?

So, how do Transfer on Death accounts work? A TOD account automatically transfers the assets to a named beneficiary, when the account holder dies. Your son is the beneficiary for the TOD account. When you die, the account's assets are transferred directly to him without having to go through probate.

Does transfer on death avoid estate tax?

Estate Taxes

When someone dies and their property transfers to their beneficiaries, the federal government impose an estate tax on the value of all that property. Since the transfer on death account is not a trust, it does not help you avoid or minimize estate taxes.

Can a POA add a TOD?

The POA retains access to any of the decedent's assets that name them as a joint owner or payable-on-death (POD) or transfer-on-death (TOD) beneficiary. Assets that commonly carry POD/TOD designations or can be jointly titled include life insurance proceeds, bank accounts, retirement accounts and brokerage accounts.

What type of account is a TOD?

An investment account can transfer fairly easily, as long as you designate a beneficiary and consider his or her ability to manage the account. On a nonretirement account, designating a beneficiary or beneficiaries establishes a transfer on death (TOD) registration for the account.

Is a TOD a retirement account?

Understanding Transfer on Death (TOD)

Individual retirement accounts, 401(k)s, and other retirement accounts are TOD. The Uniform Transfer on Death Securities Registration Act lets owners name beneficiaries for their stocks, bonds, or brokerage accounts. The process is similar to a payable-on-death bank account.

What happens if TOD beneficiary dies?

In the event that there are no living beneficiaries, life insurance policies, TOD and POD accounts will go to the decedent's estate. If the beneficiary outlives the person creating the estate plan, but dies before receiving the gift, the gift will go to the probate estate of the deceased beneficiary.

Is Wyoming a probate state?

Wyoming, which is not a Uniform Probate Code state, offers a simplified probate process for smaller estates, as well as an affidavit process that allows heirs to completely skip probate.

How does probate work in Wyoming?

The process of probate includes:

- Filing the deceased person's will with District Court
- Identifying and inventorying the deceased person's property
- Having the property appraised
- Paying off debts and taxes
- Having the will proved valid by the court
- Distributing what is left of the estate as the will directs.

Is there inheritance tax in Wyoming?

Wyoming does not levy an inheritance tax or an estate tax. However, if you are inheriting property from another state, that state may have an estate or inheritance tax that applies.

Can I put a TOD on my house?

Including California, TOD deeds are now permitted in 26 states and the District of Columbia. The TOD deed allows a person to leave his or her real property to a designated person or persons such as a family member, friend, life-long partner or other loved one without having to set up a living trust.

Does a TOD expire?

Yes, your Transfer on Death deed will remain valid as long as it is executed before January 1, 2022. However, with the uncertainty of the status of this law, there is no guarantee that future changes to the TOD deed law may not affect you.

Forms

Recording requested by:

When recorded mail to and mail tax statements to:

Space above this line for recorder's use

Wyoming Transfer on Death Deed
(Beneficiary Deed)

I, _______________________, with a mailing address of _________________________ ____ (hereinafter referred to as the "Owner") being of competent mind and having the legal capacity to execute this document, as owner transfer on death to ________________________ with a mailing address of ______ ____ (hereinafter referred to as the "Primary Beneficiary") as grantee beneficiary, the following described interest in real estate:

____

____

____

____

____

____

Legal description of the property (including square, suffix, and lot number)

If the Primary Beneficiary does not survive me, I designate ______________________ with a mailing address of ____ _________ (hereinafter referred to as the "Alternate Beneficiary") as grantee beneficiary.

This Transfer on Death Deed is revocable. It does not transfer any ownership until the death of the owner. It revokes all prior beneficiary designations by this owner for this

interest in real estate. The grantor has the right to withdraw or rescind this deed at any time. Any beneficiaries named in this deed are hereby advised that this deed may be withdrawn or rescinded whether or not money or any other consideration was paid or given.

____________________	____________________	____________________
Owner's Name	Primary Beneficiary's Name	Alternate Beneficiary's Name
____________________	____________________	____________________
Owner's Signature	Primary Beneficiary's Signature	Alternate Beneficiary's Signature
____________________	____________________	____________________
Date	Date	Date

Notary Acknowledgment

State of ____________________

County of __________________

The foregoing was acknowledged before me this ____ day of ________________, by the undersigned, ________________, who is personally known to me or satisfactorily proven to me to be the person whose name is subscribed to the within instrument.

____
Printed Name of Notary Public

____
Signature of Notary Public

My commission expires: __________________ (seal)

Wyoming Transfer on Death Deed Revocation Form

Recording requested by (name):

____

When recorded mail to
and mail tax statements to:

____

____

____

____

Recorder's Use Only

REVOCATION OF REVOCABLE TRANSFER ON DEATH DEED

This document is exempt from documentary transfer tax under Rev. & Tax. Code § 11930. This document is exempt from preliminary change of ownership report under Rev. & Tax. Code § 480.3.

Assessor's Parcel No.:

____

Declaration of Exemption From Gov't Code § 27388.1 Fee

☐ Transfer is exempt from fee per GC § 27388.1(a)(2):
  ☐ recorded concurrently "in connection with" transfer subject to Documentary Transfer Tax
  ☐ recorded concurrently "in connection with" a transfer of residential dwelling to an owner-occupier
☐ Transfer is exempt from fee per GC 27388.1(a)(1):
  ☐ Fee cap of $225.00 reached ☐ Not related to real property

IMPORTANT NOTICE: THIS FORM MUST BE RECORDED TO BE EFFECTIVE

This revocation form MUST be RECORDED before your death or it will not be effective. This revocation form only affects a transfer on death deed that YOU made. A transfer on death deed made by a co-owner of your property is not affected by this revocation form. A co-owner who wants to revoke a transfer on death deed that he/she made must complete and RECORD a SEPARATE revocation form.

PROPERTY DESCRIPTION

Print the legal description of the property affected by this revocation:

____

____

____

REVOCATION

I, ______________________________, am the transferor under the Revocable TOD deed dated ______________ and recorded on ______________ as Instrument No. ______________ in Book/Reel ________, Page/Image ________, of Official Records of ______________________________ County Wyoming, which named as beneficiary(ies) ______________________________
____.

I hereby revoke any TOD deed to transfer the described property that I executed before executing this form, including the TOD deed described above.

SIGNATURE AND DATE

Sign and print your name below (your name should exactly match the name shown on your title documents):

Date: ____________________

____
(Signature of declarant)

____
(Typed or written name of declarant)

Notary Acknowledgment

State of ____________________

County of __________________

The foregoing was acknowledged before me this ____ day of ________________, by the undersigned, ________________, who is personally known to me or satisfactorily proven to me to be the person whose name is subscribed to the within instrument.

____
Printed Name of Notary Public

____
Signature of Notary Public

My commission expires: __________________ (seal)

Check out other books from Front Page Publishing

Don't be left out in the rain! Get that extra layer of protection.

To keep some type of privacy, learn more with this book!

There are different types of Wills, and they vary from state to state. Just in the know!

If you don't have a home safe, you may need this additional layer of protection from fire, flood or prying eyes.

Made in the USA
Monee, IL
08 November 2026

68136725R00326